My Side of Life

The Hank Thompson Biography

By Warren Kice

Front Cover: Hank holding his plaque on the evening he was
inducted into the Country Music Hall of Fame.

Library of Congress # 2004556088

ISBN 13: 978-0-615-17731-1

FIRST EDITION

Branch-Smith: Printing

Special credit to: Sandra Beddow and Norma Olmos at Branch-Smith
for their patience and guidance.

This book is
dedicated to
all of Hank's fans.

Preface

By Hank Thompson

Over the past several years people have asked me, "When is your biography coming out?" I never thought the time was ripe until about three years ago when Warren Kice told me he would be interested in doing it.

I readily accepted Warren's offer since he's been a fan and a friend of mine for over fifty years and knows my music as well as anyone. Although Warren made it clear that he had never before written a book, I had observed his writing ability first hand when, as a lawyer, he represented me in several legal matters. With this knowledge, I was confident that he could make the transition from lawyer to biographer.

One thing we agreed on at the outset was that we didn't want to simply do a "textbook" biography, replete with facts, but with little style or humor. One of the reasons for this was that several very humorous events transpired over the course of my career that I have enjoyed relating to fans and friends, and we both wanted to feature them in the book.

Warren and I met once or twice a month for over two years for taping sessions in which I outlined my entire career starting from age five. In each of the sessions I would sprinkle in one of the humorous events that left us both howling with laughter.

During this time, Warren also interviewed several people that were very important in my life and my career.

The results speak for themselves. When I read his first draft I realized that he had exceeded my highest expectations. The book is very reader-friendly, yet it accurately and completely captures the history of my career. In fact, when I read it, it brought back many pleasant memories-especially with respect to the music-that I had simply forgotten.

Just as important, Warren also captured the wit and frivolity of the humorous events mentioned above, including many colorful adventures of The Brazos Valley Boys. I should add that, in those days, most of The Brazos Valley Boys were good-looking, young, single and/or between steady girlfriends and marriages. Therefore it was natural for them to pursue friendships with the opposite sex, and vice versa. And it's a good thing that it was this way-otherwise our human race would fade into obscurity, like the age of the dinosaurs.

I hope you enjoy reading the book as much as Warren and I enjoyed putting it together.

Have a good time.

October 2007

Chapter One

The quiet serenity of a neighborhood in Waco, Texas was suddenly interrupted by the siren of a police car as it made its way towards the Whitaker home on 17th street. As the police officers knocked on the Whitakers' door, some of the neighbors appeared on their front porches to witness the scene. However, there was really nothing to get excited about. They knew what was going to happen and had grown used to it.

These were the days of Prohibition, and Mrs. Whitaker was the local bootlegger. The drill would consist of police officers going in the house, bringing out Mrs. Whitaker and her stash of liquor, and ushering her into the paddy wagon. But she did not go easily, and not without a dramatic display of anger laced with some select four letter words, which added to the onlookers' entertainment. Then the wagon would roar away to the police station, where she would pay the fine before returning home in time to make her evening deliveries.

Jule Thomas Thompson and his wife, Zexia Ida Wells Thompson, who lived five doors down from the Whitakers, were among the observers. But it was for an entirely different reason that their young son knew, and became friends with, Mrs. Whitaker. With a healthy income from her business and her husband's electrical contractor business, the Whitakers were able to afford a state-of-the-art, wind-up Victrola, a console with huge built-in speakers that played 78 rpm records. Just as important, Mrs. Whitaker enjoyed country music and was a fan of one of the premier country music artists of the time - Jimmie Rodgers. She wasn't shy about playing his recordings often and loud, so loud that the Thompsons could often hear the music from their house five doors down.

The music struck a nerve in the Thompson's young son, so much so that he garnered enough courage to knock on the Whitaker's front door and ask Mrs. Whitaker if he could come in and listen to the records. Although she had records of other recording artists, such as the Carter Family, Vernon Dalhart, and Carson Robinson, he usually asked for, and she played, the music of Jimmie Rodgers. When she noticed that the boy was completely enthralled, Mrs. Whitaker allowed him to come over and listen on his own and even gave him some extra needles to put in the tone arm of the player, since each needle had to be replaced after ten or fifteen plays.

Typically, after a listening session, the young man would walk and skip home, singing one of the Jimmie Rodgers songs at the top of his voice. One particular favorite was Jimmie's *Blue Yodel No. 1 (T for Texas)*:

> T for Texas, T for Tennessee
> T for Texas, T for Tennessee...
> T for Thelma,
> That gal done made a fool out of me

The young boy was Henry William Thompson. He was five years old.

"I became consumed with the music at that age," he states today, "and I was so for the rest of my life."

Soon Henry William started playing the harmonica, one of the most popular instruments for amateur musicians, especially among the younger set. It was easy to play and required a capital outlay of only twenty-five cents. He practiced often and became a regular at a loosely organized harmonica club in Waco where the kids would meet periodically to play.

As his knowledge and appreciation for country music in general, and Jimmie Rodgers's music in particular, increased because of his visits to the Whitakers, he would play the songs on the harmonica or sing the songs to himself or to anyone who would listen.

*

If there were Las Vegas odds on the annual talent contest at the Brook Avenue grade school in Waco in 1935, a ten-year-old harmonica player would have been a heavy favorite. He had already gained a reputation at the school with his skillful technique, usually dazzling the kids at recesses with his play. He was a very nice look-ing boy with a pleasing personality. His name was Bobby Taylor.

The talent contest, open to all students of the grade school, was held at the school auditorium before a live audience. Any type of performance, such as tap danc-ing, singing, magic acts, playing various musical instruments, etc., was permitted, and the winner was determined by the response of the audience to each contestant. That particular day, the other participants included a piano player, a tap dancer and anoth-er harmonica player.

On the big day, Bobby Taylor took the stage with his harmonica and started play-ing a popular instrumental tune. But very early on, it was apparent that something was wrong. In contrast to his informal performances at the harmonica club and on the school playground, the notes just weren't coming and many of the ones that that did were wrong. Flustered by a classic case of stage fright, he walked off the stage in tears before the song was finished.

A hush came over the audience as the dynamics of the event were dramatically altered, a fact that was not lost on the other harmonica player as he took the stage and launched into his rendition of "Old Susanna". If there was any nervousness involved, it wasn't apparent as he played the harmonica while kicking the floor to the beat and shaking his legs for effect.

The audience came to life.

First place belonged to Henry William Thompson, also ten years old.

"I knew that the other kid was a better harmonica player, and would very probably win first place," said Henry William, over seventy years later, "but I planned to play a tune I knew fairly well, ham it up a little bit to impress the kids in the audience, and possibly win second place. I developed a philosophy early on that its really not how good your are, but how good the audience thinks you are, and I was able to convince the kids in the audience that I was pretty good, even though I was not an exceptional harmonica player."

The first place prize was twenty-four bottles of a new soft drink, Pepsi Cola, donated to the school as a promotion. The bottles were housed in a heavy wooden carton, and the package was so heavy that Henry William could not lift it, much less carry it home. So he took off his belt, attached it to the carton and dragged it for about a mile to his house. But it seemed as if he were flying.

"You'll never guess what happened!" he said to his mother as he came running in the house. "I just won the contest, and I have a case of Pepsi-Cola outside."

"That's wonderful, son," his mother replied, "I am so proud of you! But what is Pepsi-Cola?"

Young Henry William also became a fan of the western movies that were shown at the Saturday afternoon matinees in Waco. They starred the likes of Tom Mix, Buck Jones, Charles Starrett, Johnny Mack Brown, Sunset Carson, and Hopalong Cassidy. In fact, a revelation occurred when he was watching his first Gene Autry movie and Gene pulled out his guitar and accompanied himself while he sang not just any song, but a Jimmie Rodgers song.

"I have never heard anybody sound so much like another singer as Gene Autry sounded like Jimmie Rodgers," said Henry William. "You could close your eyes, and you couldn't tell the difference. I never got to see Jimmie Rodgers[1], but I could see Gene Autry up there on that screen, and to say that it inspired me is putting it mildly. I said, 'By golly, I think I can do that.' But it wasn't as easy as it looked."

Soon, the harmonica was history and Henry William became the proud owner of a used Vernon acoustic guitar that his parents purchased for four dollars and gave to him as a present for his tenth Christmas in 1935. He learned to play the hard way - by teaching himself. (There were very few guitar players in Waco at the time and certainly no guitar *teachers*). But he did have help from various sources.

"One day a friend of my mother came to visit and saw my guitar in the house," he recalled. "She asked if she could play it, and I was amazed at how good she was, despite the fact that she had very long finger nails. She taught me several chords and came back several other times and gave me some more help."

Also, Henry William would often go by his dad's automobile repair shop with the guitar in hand and practice. Many times, the local Coca Cola delivery man would drop in, take a break from his deliveries, and help the young boy with the guitar.

"I tried to apply the basic chords that I learned with the songs that I had been singing without any accompaniment," Henry William said, "and pretty soon, things starting falling into place."

---

[1] Jimmie passed away in 1933 from tuberculosis.

Chapter Two

The influence of radio in the late nineteen-thirties in the United States cannot be overstated, since it was simply the only game in town. Country music, broadcast live from the studios of the radio stations, proliferated throughout the Southwest, and Texas' unique culture was spawning its own musical styles, with the Light Crust Doughboys and other early Western Swing bands broadcasting their brand of up-tempo swing music every day. Also, the million-watt Mexican border radio stations located just south of the Texas border were broadcasting a signal that easily penetrated the southwestern states and even further, as they advertised and sold a myriad of products between each country record they played. And *The Grand Ole Opry*, with its hill country music dominated by banjos and fiddles, was broadcast from Nashville every Saturday night.

Young Henry William was often glued to the radio as his interest in, and knowledge of, country music increased along with his proficiency in singing and playing the songs. He was also interested in sports and played a sandlot form of football and basketball, but he discovered early on that he was too slow to make any of the school teams. This freed up more time for guitar practice and he often took the guitar to school with him. He never passed up an opportunity to play and sing on the playground, in the halls, and even in the classroom.

An opportunity for a bigger audience presented itself when the Waco Theater, looking for a way to keep the kids coming for the Saturday westerns, started a weekly event that gave them more than movies for their five cents. A weekly *Kiddies Matinee* talent contest was held every Saturday morning and was broadcast live over the local radio station, WACO. Any youngster from age 10-15 could enter, and the winner would be decided by the amount of audience applause. The first prize was a dollar, second prize was fifty cents, third prize was a quarter, and all the contestants automatically received a pass to see the afternoon movie.

This did not go unnoticed by Henry William.

"The fact that each contestant got a free pass to the regular movie was a huge deal to me. This meant that we could see a movie when it initially came out, rather than wait until it played much later on at a lower price."

He replaced the Vernon guitar with a Sears Silvertone acoustic, stepped up his practice sessions, and entered the *Kiddie's Matinee* as often as he could, singing the hits of the day such as *The Wabash Cannonball, The Great Speckled Bird, It Makes No Difference Now, Walking the Floor Over You,* and *May I Sleep In Your Barn Tonight Mister?* Of course, the Jimmie Rodgers songbook was well represented with *Waitin' For A Train,* the above-mentioned *Blue Yodel No. 1 (T for Texas),* and *In the Jailhouse Now,* as well as some of Ernest Tubb's earlier songs including *I'll Get Along Somehow* and *When the World Has Turned You Down.*

It was during this time that the announcer of the talent show starting calling him "Hank" when announcing the winner of the contest, which was often. In fact, the wins started coming so frequently that Hank was asked to reduce his participation to only once every six weeks.

One of the sponsors of the *Kiddies' Matinee* was Jones Fine Bread, a local independent bakery. Mr. Jones, the owner of the bakery, was always at the matinee and became acquainted with Hank when he started winning the contests. This gave Hank an idea based on a popular song at the time – *When Pa Was Courting Ma* – that included the line:

There were no airplanes or streamlined trains, when Pa was courting Ma.

Hank came up with a change in this line to:

There was no Jones Fine Bread when Pa was courting Ma.

With the revised version of the song in mind, Hank walked to the bakery on the outskirts of town with his guitar and asked the receptionist for Mr. Jones. When told he was not in, Hank exited the front door, but as he passed by a window, he saw Mr. Jones in an office. A knock on the window got the attention of Mr. Jones, who recognized Hank and waved him in. Hank walked back into the building and went directly to Mr. Jones' office and gave Mr. Jones a quick pitch.

"Mr. Jones," said Hank, "I have a song to sing for you about Jones Fine Bread," and he began singing *When Pa Was Courting Ma* with the new line.

Mr. Jones was all ears and, after Hank finished, he offered to buy the song from Hank and wrote him a check for five dollars. Hank had never seen a check for so much money in his life.

"I was shocked when he offered me the five dollars," Hank said. "It might as well have been five thousand! Later I realized that since the song was already copyrighted, he didn't have to pay me anything, but he did so as a favor to me."

Hank knew that if he showed his newly-found riches to his parents they would have used it for clothes, school supplies, or other mundane items. So he cashed the check for five one dollar bills which he stored in a fruit jar in the family barn and used for more luxurious items such as popcorn and candy when he went to the movies. Later, Mr. Jones asked Hank to sing the revised song as a commercial for the Kiddies' matinee.

The Silvertone guitar was average at best, and as Hank got more proficient with it, he longed for a Martin, one of the best guitars on the market. However, even a used Martin was well beyond Hank's financial means. (In fact, he couldn't even afford the legendary Black Diamond guitar *strings*). But he painted "Martin" down the headstock of his Silvertone and continued with his music education.

Hank with "Martin" guitar

As the months went by, the number of songs in Hank's repertoire increased along with his desire to perform. The director of the *Kiddies' Matinee*, Mrs. Holiday, would often "book" him for various special events, such as school socials, PTA meetings and other similar functions in Waco.

He also continued to perform for his captive audience at school, and usually strapped the guitar to his back so that he could carry it and his books on his bicycle to and from school. One school year, Hank enrolled in a basic music class and, on one of the first days, he brought his guitar and performed on the spot. After witnessing this performance, his teacher called him aside and admitted that he was too advanced musically to obtain any real benefit from her class. She suggested that it would be more beneficial to him to just go in the hall and practice during that hour, which he did.

Another performance in junior high was not so successful. Hank took a Spanish class and was soon leading the class singing Spanish songs accompanied by his guitar, much to the delight of the teacher. One day, the assignment for the day ended a few minutes early, and the teacher asked Hank to sing a song. He had been working on the *Deep Ellum Blues*, a song that he heard on a record by the Delmore Brothers, and went though a version in front of the class. This was not a good choice.

The lyrics included the following lines:

Once I had a girlfriend, she meant the world to me,
She went down to Deep Ellum, now she ain't what she used to be.

Once I knew a preacher, preached the bible through and through,
Went down to Deep Ellum now his preaching days are through.

When you go down to Deep Ellum, put your money in your pants,
The women in Deep Ellum they don't give a man a chance.

When you go down to Deep Ellum, put your money in your socks,
The redheads in Deep Ellum, they'll put you on the rocks.

After the song ended, the teacher chewed Hank out, exclaiming, "What a waste! Here you are with a nice voice, and you play the guitar and sing the Spanish songs very well, yet you do trash like that."

"Heck," thought Hank, "I didn't write the song. I was only singing it."

Chapter Three

In 1942, during Hank's second year of high school, he was able to land a part-time job that had a profound effect on his future. As a result of the attack on Pearl Harbor, mass conscription into the armed services depleted the work force around the country. This reverberated in Waco, where the repairman at the local radio repair shop resigned to join the Army, creating an opening at the shop. Hank applied for the job with the understanding that he could only work in the afternoons after school. He got the job and was paid fifteen dollars a week.

It was a good job. The vacuum tube radios of those days were fairly easy to repair, and the owner of the shop was a good mentor. As he developed his skills in electronics repair, he also developed a keen interest in ham radio and, although he did not have a license, he was able to "bootleg" on a friend's frequency. He also built a few radios, transmitters, and audio amplifiers, and became well versed in the theory of each. Little did he know at the time how valuable this experience would prove to be.

He was also keeping up with his music. Much to his delight, he was able to dial in a live radio show broadcast over station KGKO in Fort Worth, hosted by one of the most popular country singers of the day – Ernest Tubb. It was clear to Hank that Jimmie Rodgers was a strong influence in Ernest's music, and Ernest became a role model. Peg Moreland, the king of the ditty singers, also got Hank's attention and Hank often practiced singing some of Moreland's over-the-top novelty tunes such as *When Father Hung The Paper On The Wall, Everybody Works At My House But My Old Man* and *Big Rock Candy Mountain*.

During this time he made friends with a schoolmate and budding steel guitarist, Jimmy Gilliland. Hank would often take the bus across town, guitar in hand, to Jimmy's house and play and sing with him until the last bus returned that night. He was also trying to learn as many songs as possible and became especially enamored with two other country music artists at the time, Jimmy Davis and Roy Acuff.

The steady salary from the radio repair shop enabled Hank to purchase a used twelve-string Stella acoustic guitar, which he found at a pawnshop for twelve dollars.

He loved the sound of the twelve-string and continued to seek out opportunities to pick and sing in front of any audience he could find. This led to a fortuitous event.

An officer of a big grocery store/flour company in Waco saw Hank perform at one of his informal appearances and agreed to sponsor him on a live radio show on local radio station WACO three days a week at 6:30 A.M., which gave Hank time to get to school on time after the show. The radio station suggested *Hank the Hired Hand* as the name of the show and Hank was paid five dollars per show.

Hank the Hired Hand debuted in early 1942. Each show consisted of three or four songs, all sung by Hank accompanying himself on the guitar, a little banter, and several commercials. Typical songs included *Wabash Cannonball, Walking the Floor Over You, The Great Speckled Bird, Makes No Difference Now, I'll Keep on Loving You, Milkcow Blues, Trouble in Mind, You are my Sunshine,* and other hits by Ernest Tubb, Bob Wills, Jimmy Davis, Jimmie Rodgers, Vernon Dalhart, and the like. Since the attack on Pearl Harbor had occurred only a few months earlier, Hank often sang *There's a Star-Spangled Banner Waving Somewhere,* which became his show's theme song.

Thus, three days a week, Hank would take off on his bicycle for the radio station, with his guitar and school books strapped on his back, do the 6:30 A.M. show, and still get to school on time at 8:00. He would get out of school around 1:00 P.M. and would then bicycle to the radio shop and work until 6:00.

On Saturday mornings, he would sing and play guitar on the square in Waco, sign publicity photos for his radio show, and talk to passers-by, a mix-and-mingle approach that became one of his trademarks later on.

With the income from *Hank the Hired Hand* and the radio shop, Hank was able to purchase one of the best acoustic guitars available at the time, a top-of-the-line Gibson J-200, with a sunburst finish, that turned up at the local music store where he

often hung out. He worked a deal with the store owner to purchase the guitar for sixty dollars, paying five dollars a week to the owner for twelve weeks. This guitar ended up having an amazing history.

Hank the Hired Hand stayed on the air until January 1943, with the last show airing on a Monday after Hank had graduated from high school on the previous Friday. After that last show, he walked around the corner to the Interurban depot, carrying only a small suitcase and his cased J-200, and boarded the Interurban, a giant electric streetcar that shuttled between Waco and Dallas. In Dallas, he enlisted in the U.S. Navy, for "the duration of the war plus six months". He was seventeen years old, and did not return to Waco for two and a half years.

*

Soon after his enlistment, Hank, with several other Navy recruits from the area, boarded a train in Dallas and were shipped out to San Diego, California.

"The trip took three days, and the train was not much more than a glorified cattle car. It was so bad that even Jesse James wouldn't have considered robbing it," remembered Hank.

After two months in boot camp in San Diego, Hank expressed an interest in communications and was transferred to the naval radio school held on the refurbished U.S. Boston docked in a harbor at Yerba Buena Islands in the San Francisco/Oakland bay area. The U.S. Boston had been a mainstay of the Spanish American war and provided a pleasant environment for the Navy's radio school.

With his background in radio repair and with the knowledge acquired as a ham radio operator, Hank quickly discovered that he was far ahead of most trainees at the school, and he excelled during the five-month course. During his off hours, the guitar became his best friend and he was not shy about picking and singing around a group of his fellow sailors, a practice that continued throughout his Navy career.

He also checked out the country music scene in the Bay area and discovered a club in Oakland that had a country band. One night he brought his guitar with him to the club, went up to the band leader, told him he was a singer, and asked if he could sing a couple of songs. This wasn't the first time that a sailor had asked to do this, and the band leader, in deference to the sailors, told him to come on up. Hank mounted the stage with the band, selected *Walking the Floor Over You*, a very popular song of the day that he knew the band could play, and made his California debut in front of a live band. The response was less than overwhelming, but Hank knew that a major factor in this was because the bandstand was located on a balcony far removed from the bar and the dance floor, and the band was largely just going through the motions ("Oh no, another sailor that wants to sing – well at least he's sober."). But it was a start.

Meanwhile, back at the barracks, Hank was practicing the guitar one night and singing a few Ernest Tubb songs when an idea popped into his head. One of Ernest's big songs at the time, and the first song he performed on *The Grand Ole Opry*, was entitled *You Nearly Lose Your Mind*. It had a melody not unlike a Jimmie Rodgers blues tune and lyrics that included the following line:

When your baby starts to stepping, Lawd, you nearly lose your mind.

Another thing that was at least at the back of Hank's mind at the time was the beautiful girls that he was encountering in California. He started playing a Jimmie Rodgers blues chord pattern while juxtaposing the thought of California women with the lyrics to *You Nearly Lose Your Mind*. A few minutes later he had written his first song, aptly titled *California Women*. The chorus goes like this:

Those California women, you can't trust 'em,
Those California women got to adjust 'em,
To be like your gal back home,
They'll lie and call you honey,
And squander all your money,
Lawd, Lawd, that's wrong.

Chapter Four

The U.S. Navy destroyers were large and fast, but they were not very maneuverable and were fairly easy pickings for enemy submarines. Therefore, the U.S. Navy developed a "destroyer escort", a smaller and more agile ship that would accompany each destroyer and, using a sonar detection system, would seek out and hopefully destroy any enemy submarines before they could get to the destroyer.

Training for the destroyer escorts, as well as for other small craft, took place at the Small Craft Training Center at Roosevelt Base at San Pedro, California, outside of Long Beach, near Los Angeles.

In 1943, after completing the five month course at the Yerba Buena Islands, Hank graduated from the school as a "Radioman Third Class" and was assigned to the Small Craft Training Center as a trainee in both sonar detection and radio transmission. He easily picked up the intricacies of each, and was soon switched from trainee to trainer.

One of Hank's assignments included teaching others how to tune transmitters and how to install and use the sonar detection system. But Hank noticed early on that his trainees had a very difficult time learning these techniques.

"I don't want to give the impression that I was a genius or anything," said Hank, "but I soon discovered that, in the Navy, for the most part I was surrounded by people that were incompetent, including my warrant officer and my chief petty officer. Although they were nice guys, they couldn't pour piss out of a boot, work-wise; and I, in effect, ended up doing their jobs."

The training at Roosevelt Base was only a day job, and Hank kept up his own self-training in music after hours and on weekends. In addition to improving his guitar-playing skills, he was adding the top country songs of the day to his repertoire so that he could play and sing for his buddies in the barracks. Also, he was always searching out other musicians to play with. He was pleasantly surprised to meet another sailor in his barracks who played the guitar, the only sailor that Hank met who was better than he was. They played together often and became fast friends.

One day the new friend spoke up, "Hank, I know this girl, Marianne, who is very cute and more in your age bracket than mine. She loves country music and very probably would go out with you." Hank took her telephone number and promised to call her. Inspired by this possibility, in December of 1943, he wrote his second song, *Swing Wide Your Gate of Love*, to impress the young lady. A verse went like this:

Swing wide your gate of love; open up your heart,
I knew from the first time that you'd be my sweetheart,
Make up your mind to love me and to be my turtledove,
I love you, so swing wide your gate of love.

This was a very important song in many respects, not the least significant of which was that he made a very positive impression with Marianne when he sang her the song.

"I went out with her several times," recalled Hank, "and we had a lot of fun. She also knew all of the country music clubs around that area and went with me to see a lot of real good live country music."

For example, during that time, Ernest Tubb was on the west coast to make his first movie and was to appear at the Venice Pier, a famous club near Los Angeles, which also hosted notables from Bob Wills to Lawrence Welk. The Venice Pier featured a huge ballroom with a bar adjacent the ballroom.

That night Ernest played to a packed house that included Hank and Marianne. After Ernest's first set, Hank noticed that he exited from the rear of the stage, went through the bar area and to a dressing room. Hank decided to follow.

He worked his way through the crowded bar and to the dressing room area where he encountered another artist, Jimmy Short, whom Hank had seen perform in Waco the previous year, and who had opened for Earnest that night.

Hank went up to Jimmy, stuck out his hand, and said, "I'm Hank Thompson, I'm from Waco, Texas, and I'm a country singer. I had a radio show in Waco, Texas when I joined the Navy and I remember seeing you and your brother perform in Waco last year."

Jimmy was impressed.

Hank went on. "I'm a big fan of Ernest. In fact, I sing a lot of his songs. Is he around?"

"Yes, he's in that room over there," said Jimmy. "Would you like to meet him?"

"Yes I would," replied Hank, trying to act casual. When they got in the room, Ernest was there by himself, sipping on a beer. Jimmy introduced them and left.

Ernest offered Hank a beer and they visited for several minutes. Hank was in seventh heaven.

"He was gracious, humble and could not have been nicer," remembered Hank.

One of the subjects of the conversation was Ernest's guitar, which was lying on a table next to them. Hank was especially interested because it had JIMMIE engraved on the neck. Ernest explained that Jimmie Rodgers' wife had given him the guitar and it was the actual guitar that Jimmie had used before he died. Ernest had been using it for the past several years.

Hank was astonished.

A few minutes later, Ernest looked at his watch and told Hank that he had to get back to work. He then asked Hank a favor.

"I'm fixing to go back on," said Ernest. "Would you mind carrying my guitar for me. It's quite a ways to the stage. We have to go through the bar, and sometimes it gets a little tight in there."

"Sure, I'd be glad to," said Hank. A gross understatement.

So there was eighteen-year-old Hank Thompson, holding the guitar of his first idol and walking by the side of another.

"It was a month before I came out of the clouds," remembered Hank.

But the Venice Pier was just the tip of the iceberg when it came to country music venues in the southern California area. There were many clubs that served liquor by the drink, had a large bandstand and decent sound, and featured live music, usually of the country variety. Notable among these clubs were the *Four Aces*, *Murphy's*, and the *Main Street Club*. Unlike the club in Oakland, these clubs featured a bandstand right in the center of things, and Hank has an apt description of a typical floor plan.

"In most places, the bandstand was next to the bar; and, if a gal was at the bar, you could almost lean over from the bandstand and pinch her on the butt."

With this backdrop, Hank began a methodical campaign to obtain some experience performing in front of an audience. His plan was to hang out at the clubs and, when the opportunity arose, approach the bandleader with something like "Hey, my name is Hank Thompson, I am a country singer, and had a radio show back in Waco Texas. I would love to come up and sing a couple of songs." This worked more often than not and, as the appearances increased, so did the crowd response.

At one of the clubs, Hank met Doris Ricky, an attractive young lady who captured his fancy. Marianne soon became history, and Doris became a steady girl friend and Hank's eager companion at the country music clubs and dances. Although Doris lived at Redondo Beach, several miles southwest of Los Angeles, transportation to and from her house was not difficult.

"During this time, the civilians would do anything in the world for the service men," Hank remembered. "Traveling around the area was the simplest thing in the world. All I had to do was step out on the highway in my uniform and raise my thumb, and people didn't hesitate to pick me up. Often they would detour from their destination just to take me to mine. It didn't make any difference what time it was, since, with all the swing shifts going in California, there was traffic everywhere at all hours of the day and night."

Typically, Hank would hitchhike from the base to Doris' house to pick her up, and her parents would let them use their car. The parents also saved stamps for gas and used rationed sugar to bake cakes for Hank to share with the other sailors. Hank became close with Doris and her parents.

"Her parents were two of the most delightful people I have ever met in my life," Hank said. "I'll never forget how great they were to me."

One night Hank and Doris were at the *Four Aces* when Hank noticed that the keyboard/accordion player in the band looked familiar. He went up to the bandstand for a closer look and was amazed to discover that the band member was a neighbor from Waco, Buddy Woodie, whose family had lived about a half a block from Hank's family when they were growing up. Hank remembered hearing Buddy practicing the piano at his house.

Hank looked at Buddy and said "Hey Buddy, how are you doing?" Buddy instantly recognized Hank, and when the band took a break, they caught up on old times.

Then, Hank popped the question.

"Buddy, I love to sing country music and in fact I had a radio show in Waco after you left. I would love to come up and sing a couple of songs with your band. Would this be possible?"

"Hell yes," Buddy replied. "Come on up at the start of the next set."

Just before the second set, Buddy introduced Hank to the other band members, and Hank suggested a song that was popular at the time and joined the band on stage.

"Back then," remembered Hank, "every good band in the area knew all the popular country songs at the time, because there just weren't that many." The song went over well and Hank returned several times to perform.

The importance of the fact that he was now performing on stage with a band behind him was not lost on Hank.

"I had been on a stage before back in Waco at some fairs and other venues, and it wasn't that being on stage was a new thing. But, before, it was always just my guitar and me, which was a lot different from singing with a band, and I was grateful for the opportunity to do so in California."

*

Hank with Doris Ricky.

Back at the training base, one of the exercises in the sonar training that Hank supervised included the dropping of sonar-guided depth charges. Several depth charges were dropped each day; and after about five months of constant explosions, Hank's nerves started to fray. Also, he was getting restless.

"I joined the Navy to be on a ship," he said to himself. "There's a war going on in the South Pacific, and I want to be a part of it. The way it's going now, I'm going to have to tell my grandchildren that I fought the war of San Pedro."

Finally, he went to his chief petty officer and asked to be transferred.

"Hell", said the officer, "you've got a good deal here and you shouldn't leave. Besides you are the only one here who really understands this stuff."

After he got the same result with the chief warrant officer, Hank decided to take a fairly drastic step – he went over their heads.

A few days later, Radioman Third Class Thompson was standing in front of the commanding officer of his unit who happened to be Robert Montgomery, the movie star. (The Navy men called him "Fighting Bob" because he never got near any action.)

"Sir," Hank stated to Montgomery, "I didn't join the Navy to be here at San Pedro; I joined it to be on a ship. I hope this request is not unreasonable, but there's a war going on in the South Pacific, and I want to be a part of it."

"We probably can take care of that," was the reply.

"I sure would appreciate it."

In about two weeks, Hank got his orders. He received a promotion to Radioman Second Class and was assigned to be the chief radio officer for a brand new auxiliary tug and rescue ship, designated the ATR 33. It was an all-purpose ship that did everything from salvaging sunken craft and towing other ships, to delivering mail between the various U.S. controlled islands.

In March 1944, Radioman Second Class Thompson reported to a receiving ship at the Puget Sound Naval Shipyard at Bremerton, Washington, just across the Puget Sound from Seattle. He then traveled by ground to Bellingham, Washington, about ninety miles north of Seattle/Bremerton, where the ATR 33 was built, and served on the ship for about two weeks during its "shake-down" cruise to make sure that it was ship-shape.

At the conclusion of the cruise, the ATR 33 docked in Seattle and Hank was on watch late one night when one of his shipmates came in somewhat impaired from several rounds of drinks at a local bar. He started ranting about his adventures and misadventures.

"I had just cashed my pay check and was drinking at this bar," the sailor said. "I zeroed in on this pretty girl and was trying everything I could think of to get her attention. But, she wouldn't give me the time of day and kept saying 'Whoa Sailor!' to every one of my advances. But when I pulled out my cash, her attitude changed completely, and I made out pretty well after that."

Hank was intrigued by this story and, after he got off duty later that night, he went down to his bunk, pulled out the J-200, and wrote the song *Whoa Sailor*, which well captured the sailor's exploits.

A few days later, the ATR 33 took off from Bremerton with Hank proudly manning his new post. He stayed on the ship for most of the remainder of his Navy career.

Chapter Five

By 1944, as the war in the Pacific moved from Pearl Harbor to and through the islands in the South Pacific, one of the toughest assignments of the ATR 33 was to salvage sunken Navy ships.

"The rub was that we had to recover any ammunition from the sunken ships," remembered Hank. "We had three or four divers who had to go down and recover the ammo. Then we had to haul it back to shore, not knowing whether the water had ruined it or whether it was still live. That certainly got our attention."

The ATR 33 would also go to recently vacated islands and dock for several days in order to carry out duties that were presumably consistent with the war effort but weren't exactly clear to the enlisted men. Never mind. What *was* clear was that there were a plethora of beautiful beaches on each island, and the men made the most of it. On most days, after performing their military functions, the men would meet on the beach, break out some beer, and Hank would tune up the J-200 and perform for his fellow shipmates.

One day, as the ATR 33 was headed to another island, Hank was on duty sitting by the transmitter in the radio shack of the ship. Since it was late afternoon with very little radio traffic, he put on the headphones to monitor the traffic, picked up the J-200, and started playing. Suddenly a "general quarters" sounded, meaning a possible emergency. Hank jerked off the headphones, put the guitar down between the transmitter and the bulkhead, and headed to his proper position for the maneuver. After learning that it was a false alarm, he returned to the radio shack and discovered that a large wave had rocked the ship causing the transmitter to slip towards the bulkhead. The guitar was sandwiched between the two, and the force of the sliding transmitter had cracked the neck of the guitar.

On the next island, some of Hank's shipmates related this story to a crew member of a Navy tender ship that was also docked at the island to help maintain and service the larger craft. The crew member immediately replied, "Boys, don't worry, this is what we do. Hell, we can fix anything! Let us take the guitar and meet us back here in a couple of hours."

The "surgery" on the J-200 took place about thirty minutes later in the operating room of the tender ship. Three skilled surgeons participated in the procedure, which consisted of grooving out the neck, putting in a brass reinforcement, installing a brass plate on the neck and gluing everything back together. The patient went off the critical list and the convalescence period was fairly short – about one hour. Soon, on the beach the beer was flowing, Hank was picking and singing, and the crews from both ships were celebrating the news that the J-200 would live a normal life.

During this time, Doris Ricky, of Redondo Beach fame, drove with her parents to Ft. Hood in Killeen, Texas to visit a family member. Their route took them through Waco, and Doris persuaded her dad to stop so that she could visit Hank's parents. He did, and she did. Hank's parents were delighted to hear about Hank, his Navy career, and all the country music clubs and dances they attended. Doris also mentioned that Hank had written a few songs, one of which was about a sailor in the Navy, entitled *Whoa Sailor*.

*

Back in the South Pacific, Hank was picking the J-200 one day while sitting on the fantail of the ATR 33, which was docked at a small island. A native of the island came rowing over in an outrigger canoe filled with seashells and other trinkets.

"Can I see your guitar?" he asked in broken English.

"Sure," said Hank, and handed the J-200 down to him. The native grabbed the guitar, hit an opening chord, and started singing *The San Antonio Rose*.

"He was no Tommy Duncan[2]," said Hank, "but I've heard worse."

After the song ended, the native offered all of the trinkets in the boat for the guitar; but Hank, without hesitation, refused his offer and took the guitar back.

Undaunted, the native informed Hank that he would soon be back with another offer, and took off in the canoe. Sure enough, about an hour later, the native came rowing back with an added supply of trinkets and an attractive woman sitting with him in the canoe.

"I will give you all of these trinkets *and the girl* for your guitar," offered the native.

This time, there was hesitation, as Hank mulled over the possibility of the ATR 33 having a new, very special, crew member. However, common sense prevailed.

"The offer was certainly intriguing, but I realized that the Navy would take a dim view of the transaction," said Hank. "So I refused the offer, and the guy shook his head in disappointment and rowed away."

The ATR 33 would also deliver mail to the service men stationed at the various U.S.-occupied islands throughout the South Pacific. On these islands, the Army Corps of Engineers had built some rudimentary recreational areas along many of the beaches. The facilities included picnic tables, benches, latrines, etc., so that the service men could go to the beach, have a swim and a beer or two, and enjoy themselves. Hank remembered a sign posted in some of the latrines that said:

IN CASE OF AN AIR RAID, GET UNDER ONE OF THE URINALS. NO ONE HAS HIT ONE OF THEM YET.

*

---

2 Tommy Duncan was one of the lead vocalists for Bob Wills and the Texas Playboys and was one of Hank's favorite singers.

With their duty in the South Pacific drawing to a close, most of the crew of the ATR 33 was sent to the U.S. naval base at Guadalcanal, a processing station for returning the troops back to the States to be discharged or to finish their enlistment. Hank was sent there for a processing-out period of about three weeks. Since his tour of duty had not expired, he was very pleased when he learned that he was selected for the Naval Officer's Training Program. The U.S. Naval Academy couldn't handle the number of officer candidates at the time, so the training had been farmed out to several universities and Hank was selected to report to Princeton University in Princeton, New Jersey.

In the meantime, he had to bide his time at Guadalcanal until he was shipped back to the States. During this time, he hung out with three or four sailors who were also waiting to be sent home, and an immediate bond developed between the men based on their mutual appreciation of the synergy between the scenic beaches around the area and malt-flavored beverages. Included in the group was a cook from Mississippi who had been injured on the deck of a previous ship after an encounter with an enemy submarine. One night, the subject of food at the base came up and, not surprisingly, all of the reviews were negative.

"Boys", said the cook, "I have an idea. We're going to have a gourmet dinner tonight. Thompson, you come with me and the rest of you go to the beach, ice the beer, and start a fire. Thompson and I are going to get some chickens, and I have access to everything we need to cook them."

The cook then led Hank to a chicken coop that happened to be located behind an officer's club and laid out the plan to Hank.

"I can't jump that fence due to my leg injury, so you will have to go in and get the chickens. Jump over the fence, grab a chicken, kill it by wringing its neck and then throw it over the fence to me. We need four or five, and you need to do it quietly and quickly."

The visions of a roasted chicken feast unencumbered by the limitations of standard navy cooking overcame any negatives that Hank could think of at the time, so over the fence he went. The first three chickens were easy prey and Hank nailed them without any disturbance. However, the fourth victim slipped from Hank's hand, raised a ruckus, and the coop was suddenly a beehive of noisy activity. Hank had the presence of mind to grab another chicken and twist its neck as he was running for the fence. He threw the chicken to the cook, jumped the fence, and they took off into the cover of the jungle between the officer's club and the beach. The noise died down before any general alarm sounded.

Two hours and many beers later at the beach, everybody was enjoying naturally roasted chicken and marveling at how much better it was than standard Navy fare.

"That was one of the best meals I had while in the Navy," said Hank. "After being subjected to all the prefab dishes the Navy fed us, this simple roasted chicken was like a gourmet meal at a five-star restaurant."

During his processing-out period, Hank wanted to meet Cactus Jack, a disc jockey who had a very popular country music radio show that was broadcast by the Armed Forces Network from a studio at Guadalcanal. Hank had been able to receive the show on the ATR 33 and, after connecting and rerouting a few cables in the radio shack of the ship, had piped the show throughout the ship as it toured the Pacific islands, much to the delight of Hank's fellow sailors. The show was termed *The Adabat Cocktail Hour* on the *Mosquito Network* (Adabat was a pill that all armed service personal had to take to combat malaria from mosquito bites). If this was not enough to confirm Cactus Jack's warped sense of humor, one need not look any further than the following verse that opened the radio show:

The canteen cups are clinking,
The conversation is intimidating,
Seven thousand miles from the sunny shores of California,
Its time to relax and put that pellet down the pallet,
And listen to the Adabat Cocktail Hour.

One day, Hank went, guitar in hand, to the studio, knocked on the door, and introduced himself to Cactus Jack.

"I love your show," said Hank. "I was a radio operator on an ATR 33 and I piped your show throughout the ship. I'm a country singer and had a radio show back in Waco, Texas, before I joined the Navy. I would love to come on and sing a song on the Adabat Cocktail Hour."

"Come on in," replied Cactus Jack, "and let me hear a song or two."

After the audition, Cactus Jack said, "The show starts in twenty minutes, and you are on it."

"Great," said Hank, "how many songs shall I do?"

"You're going to do the whole show."

Hank the Hired Hand comes to Guadalcanal.

Chapter Six

After about three weeks at Guadalcanal, the big event finally came to pass – Hank was put on a ship and sent to San Diego. The first person he called when he got off the ship was Doris Ricky, who drove down from Redondo Beach and picked him up. After several months on the ATR 33, Hank was anxious to renew their acquaintance.

"Have you called your parents yet to tell them you are back?" was the first thing Doris said after she picked Hank up.

"Gosh, no I haven't," replied Hank, trying to make it clear that he had something else on his mind. "I wanted to see you first."

Doris immediately pulled the car over at a gas station, pointed to the phone, and said "Go call them now. They are anxious to hear from you."

Hank's parents were thrilled to hear from him, but not as thrilled as Hank was later when he renewed his acquaintance with Doris.

After a few days in San Diego, he boarded a train with about forty others and headed for Grand Central Station in New York. From there, he was to travel to Princeton and enroll in the spring term at the university.

"The four-day train ride from California to New York was a blast", said Hank. "We were on a Pullman car, complete with a porter, which was a far cry from the cattle train that transported us to San Diego. Even better, we discovered early on that no one was in charge. Here we were, a group of kids between the ages of eighteen and twenty, who had just returned to the good ole USA. To say that it was a party atmosphere on the train is putting it mildly. By noon each day, all of us were about half-drunk, and we kept the porter in the same condition. I remember him saying 'You kids are impossible!' as he took another swig on a fifth of whisky. I don't think he even made a bed during the whole trip."

Hank reached Princeton in early 1945 to begin his new phase with the Navy. For all practical purposes, officer's training at that time consisted simply of enrolling in several regular college courses at the university.

"There was still some military life involved," recalled Hank, "but not much. For example, we would still have to get up in the morning at the same time, and do a few calisthenics. Also, we would march on some Saturday afternoons and have to undergo a few inspections. But the rest of the day, we were, in fact, no different than regular college students attending regular classes at the university." He chose electrical engineering and took courses that any first-year engineering student would take, such as basic math and calculus, along with some physics lectures by Albert Einstein[3].

Being near New York City had its advantages, and Hank made the most of them. On some weekends, he and a fellow Texan and officer's training candidate, Jim Newton, took the train from Princeton to Penn Station, where they met Jim's brother, who arrived on a train from Long Island, to begin a weekend of frivolity. The train schedules were such that Hank and Jim had a fairly long wait before the brother's train arrived. Undaunted, they headed to the bar at Penn Station, Hank uncased the J-200, and they entertained and shared strong drink with the patrons in the bar. This happened so often that Hank and Jim became "regulars" at the bar and, over sixty years later, Jim remembered the scene.

"Those Yankees really got a kick out of the two boys from Texas singing country songs in that bar. I remember singing *Whoa Sailor* and *California Women* with Hank many times."

Since Hank was a big boxing fan and had enjoyed watching films of old championship boxing matches in the Navy, one place he had to visit in New York City was Jack Dempsey's restaurant in Manhattan. Hank was thrilled when he went to the restaurant and shook hanks with Jack.

"He couldn't have been nicer," said Hank. "He was also a Navy man, and I had a nice talk with him and got his autograph. When I went back to Waco later, my dad and his friends were very impressed with the autograph and it elevated me to a higher status in their circle. Unfortunately I lost the autograph later on, and I certainly wish I had it now."

After a semester at Princeton, Hank was sent to Dallas in early 1945 to continue his officer's training as a student at Southern Methodist University (SMU) for a semester. A few days after settling in a dorm on the campus and starting classes, he made friends with a co-ed at SMU. She soon became a very close friend.

Soon after they met, she volunteered to give him a tour of the finer sites of Dallas. Since the university prohibited the consumption of alcohol within a one-mile radius of the campus, the first stop on the tour was a campus beer joint on Knox Street, just outside the one-mile limit.

"I can't remember the name of the place," said Hank. "I'm not even sure it had a name other than 'The Beer Joint'."

Hank was pleased to discover that the crowd at The Beer Joint was definitely country and that the jukebox was teeming with the latest country songs. After surveying the scene on the first night he was there, Hank had an idea and approached the owner with a proposal.

"I'm a student at SMU and a country singer," said Hank. I would like to come here, bring my guitar and sing. For free. Hopefully I'll get a few tips and you will have some real live music."

---

[3] For about twenty years, Albert Einstein did his research at the "Institute for Advanced Study" at Princeton and often lectured at the University.

"Why not?" was the reply.

It worked. The Beer Joint was jam-packed every night and Hank, in his sailor suit, performed as a "roving minstrel" as he went from table to table with his guitar and sang a country favorite.

"I didn't get paid," said Hank, "but people would come up and put money in the hole of my J-200 when I was singing – anything from a quarter to a twenty dollar bill. I would generally get around ten to twenty dollars a night, which was damn good money back then; and I remember one night I made over a hundred dollars. In any case, it was a lot more money than my sixty-five dollars per month pay from the Navy!"

His new girl friend also lived in the dorm but had a friend with an apartment near the campus. So, on a typical day Hank would attend classes, work on his studies, then grab his guitar, walk across the campus to Hillcrest Avenue, and jump on a trolley that would take him to Knox Street and to The Beer Joint. Often, after closing time, he and the girl friend would hightail it to the friend's apartment and get to know each other even better, an activity that often lasted to the wee hours. Then he would jump on the streetcar, go back to his dorm, and try to get enough sleep to stay awake in class the next day.

Thus, in the context of preparing for class every day, his time management was suffering.

"I was supposed be going to class, but I was spending most of my time at The Beer Joint," said Hank. "Of course, it was what I liked to do, but it was playing havoc with my education."

He tried to slow down the pace and concentrate on his studies and even thought about quitting his new night job, but then he would get a call from the girl friend live from The Beer Joint, and she would speak in a soft, sexy voice. "Hank, everybody is asking for you down here and we would sure like to see you. Please come on down."

"Can't do it," replied Hank with a firm voice. "I've got to study."

Hank at SMU Dorm. "Shall I study or shall I go to The Beer Joint"

"We can go over to my friend's place later," as her voice got even sexier.

Later that evening, as Hank boarded the trolley headed to The Beer Joint, he said to himself, "One of these days I'm going to tell that girl no!"

Later, one day in August, Hank was visiting another girl friend in her apartment near the campus when they heard her roommate crying in the next room. They rushed in her room and found out that she was crying for joy as she told them the good news. The war was over!

Chapter Seven

After the semester at SMU, the Navy required Hank to select a school with a permanent ROTC program, and Hank chose the University of Texas in Austin, where he attended the fall semester beginning in September 1945.

Naturally, he sought out the live country music scene in Austin and found a band in Austin that he liked – The Jesse James Band. Of particular note was their steel guitar player, a young man by the name of Lefty Nason. Hank marveled at his technique and struck up an acquaintance. Little did either man know at the time that they were to play an important role in each other's careers.

The stay in Austin enabled him to go to Waco on weekends and visit his folks. One cold night in Waco, he borrowed his dad's 1942 Chevrolet and went to a dance club for some R&R. He made quick friends with a young lady at the club, who later on in the evening bought in to Hank's plan to vacate the club together and go somewhere where they could get better acquainted. Hank headed for the nearest deserted country road and parked the car. After a few minutes it became obvious that additional room was sorely needed to better pursue their newly-found friendship. In order to avoid opening the door and letting in the cold, Hank suggested that they crawl to the back seat. He made it back fine, but when the girl tried, she kicked out the interior dome light on the ceiling of the car with one of her high heels. This was only a temporary distraction; business was resumed in the back seat, and the evening ended on a high note.

The next day Hank went down to his dad's shop and told his dad, "Pa, I owe you for the dome light in your car."

"What are you talking about?" queried his Dad.

"The dome light in you car was broken last night."

"*What* light?"

"The one on the interior of the ceiling of the car."

"Why don't you show me?"

They went out to the car, and Hank showed him the broken dome light.

"Now, one more time, how did this happen?" asked his Dad.

"Well I was with this girl last night and she kicked it."

There was a long pause before his dad replied.

"If you will explain the position she was in when she kicked it, I'll pay for the damned thing myself."

Meanwhile, back in Austin, Hank completed the fall semester at the University of Texas, and with his discharge date on the immediate horizon, he was given the option of re-upping in the Navy, joining the reserve, or taking a discharge. He chose the last and was sent to Houston to be processed out of the Navy. He became a civilian in February 1946, hitchhiked to Waco, and settled in with his parents. He also began planning his future.

*

The GI Bill of Rights, signed by President Roosevelt on June 22, 1944, was designed to provide greater opportunities to returning war veterans. The bill, among other things, provided tuition, subsistence, books, supplies, and counseling services for veterans who wanted to continue their education in high school or college. Since the veterans were free to attend the educational institution of their choice, Hank decided to stay in Waco until the fall and then enroll in SMU's electrical engineering school.

During this time, he remembered that the manager of the radio station WACO had told him when he left for the Navy that his old job would be waiting when he returned. He made an appointment with Lee Glasgow, the new general manager of the station, took his guitar in the event he had to audition, and inquired about the possibility of resuming his radio career until the fall term at SMU started.

In effect, "Don't call us; we'll call you," was the very disappointing reply.

After leaving the studio, Hank was heading back to his car in downtown Waco and ran into an old friend on the street.

"Hank, are you going to do your radio show again?" asked the friend, hitting a nerve dead-center.

"I guess not. I went to see them and they didn't seem to be too enthusiastic."

"Did you know they have a new radio station in Waco? It comes on the air in a few days. In fact, their studio is just around the corner. You should give them a try."

Hank went around the corner, still carrying his guitar, to the soon-to-be radio station KWTX, which was about a block and a half from the WACO studio. The general manager and the program director were there, busily putting the finishing touches on the studio. Hank introduced himself.

"I'm Hank Thompson. I don't know if you remember my name, but I had a radio show called *Hank the Hired Hand* at WACO before I went in the Navy. Since then I've had the opportunity to play and sing quite a bit in the Navy, and I am much better now. I would like to do a show on your station."

"I remember you," said the general manager, looking at his guitar case, "let's hear something."

Hank uncased the J-200 and sang *Swing Wide Your Gate of Love, California Women,* and another song he had written in the Navy – *The Brazos Valley Rancho.* Afterwards, the general manager and the program director huddled for a minute and came back.

"You're hired," said the general manager. "We'll pay you fifteen dollars a week and put you on in the 12:15 P.M. – 12:30 P.M. slot between our two top national network shows –*Cedric Foster's Mutual News* and *Queen for a Day*. Also, we want you to use the *Brazos Valley Rancho* as your theme song."

The *Hank Thompson Show* opened on KWTX in April 1946. The format was essentially the same as *Hank the Hired Hand*, with Hank doing most of the heavy lifting while sharing the mike with any guest artists who were in town. Since the station did not have a phone system suitable to take in a volume of outside calls, Hank asked the listeners to mail in their requests and, as the show gathered momentum, the requests poured in.

He also was able to parlay his newly acquired notoriety from the radio show into some personal appearances through the listening area. Since he wanted to enlist some local musicians to back him up, the question of transportation came up.

Not a problem. Hank had made pretty good money in the Navy, especially after he was promoted to Radioman Second Class, and there was very little in the Navy to spend it on. In fact, the essentials were very inexpensive – a beer cost ten cents and cigarettes were fifty cents a carton. As a result, he had been able to save enough to purchase a car. Since no new cars had been manufactured in the U.S. since 1942 because of the war, he became the proud owner of a second-hand, 1939 Oldsmobile.

Hank enlisted several musicians in the area, including the above-mentioned Jimmy Gilliland on steel, Charlie Adams on bass, and guitarist Bobby Murrell. He also purchased a small P.A. amplifier and a trailer for the instruments, and the Hank Thompson Road Show was born.

The most common venues were various schoolhouses throughout the county, since they usually had a decent auditorium. A typical show would last around an hour and fifteen minutes in front of a sit-down, family audience, with no alcohol or dancing. The charge was usually fifty cents for adults and twenty-five cents for children. Hank's aunt was enlisted as business manager and would usually go with them and handle the "door". After each show she would give the "house" around twenty-five percent of the door, pay the band members a fair fee, and have a little left over for gasoline.

The shows revolved around Hank singing the popular hits of the day, as well as the songs that he had written in the Navy. As the shows evolved, they began to take on a vaudeville flavor, with "guest artists" such as a harmonica player, a girl singer, and even a rope trick artist. Comedy, usually of the slapstick variety, was an integral part of each show, and Hank would often bring along a guest comedian to do some cornball jokes. If no comic was available, Hank would do the jokes himself, alone or with members of the band. No attempt was made to establish a new frontier for leading-edge comedy. Rather, they would simply rehash all of the tried-and-true comedy skits and jokes.

"Minnie Pearl used to say that it's better to stick with the old jokes," said Hank. "That way, the audience knows when to laugh."

Hank felt that the band needed a name even though it was a "pick-up" band by nature. He looked no further than his immediate surroundings and, in particular, the history of his hometown.

*

Waco had its beginning when the Huaco Indians lived along a crossing at the Brazos River, where the Texas Rangers built Fort Fisher in 1837. Their tribal name was anglicized to "Waco" and the town grew up around the river and the surrounding valley. By 1857 it was a full-blown city, albeit small in size. Then, in 1870, a suspension bridge, one of the longest such bridges in the world, was built across the Brazos. When the railroad arrived a year later and Baylor University was established, the city's future was secure.

Hank decided to name his new band The Brazos Valley Boys – an easy choice, especially since precedent for this type of name had been established with Bob Wills and the Texas Playboys, Roy Acuff and the Smokey Mountain Boys, and Bill Monroe and the Bluegrass Boys.

"There had been a small group that played on occasion around Waco called The Brazos Valley Boys," recalled Hank, "but as far as I could tell, they had disbanded. Since the Brazos Valley was an important part of the landscape in that part of the country, it seemed like a natural."

With Hank being able to promote his personal appearances on the radio show, the demand grew steadily to the extent that he gave the bass player, Charlie Adams, the added responsibility of booking agent. Charlie would call on the various schools throughout the county and try to book Hank Thompson and The Brazos Valley Boys in advance. However, this wasn't the easiest thing to do, since the schools were often located on secluded country roads that were unmarked and hard to find, especially at night.

One of Charlie's bookings was at a school at Ben Hur, Texas, a fairly large consolidated school district in the center of a large surrounding community. On the evening of the scheduled performance, the group packed up the trailer, piled in the Oldsmobile, and headed out, but it soon became obvious that Charlie was rapidly losing his confidence as to the exact location of the school. They finally came upon a farmhouse set back from the road, and Hank suggested that Charlie go up to the house and ask for directions. Charlie got out of the car and starting walking up to the house, but when he was about halfway there, he turned around and came back.

"What's wrong?" asked Hank.

"I can't go up there," said Charlie. "When I came out here to book the job last month I also got lost, and went to this very house for instructions. If I knock on their door again tonight, they will think I am still lost!"

*

As the mail poured in to KWTX about Hank's radio show, Hank learned something. A large majority of the letters simply stated how they enjoyed the show and/or requested a song or two, but several, in an attempt to be complimentary, stated that Hank sounded just like Ernest Tubb. It was true that Hank sang a lot of Ernest's songs on the show, but it concerned Hank that people thought that he sounded so much like Ernest

"I knew I would never get anywhere sounding like Ernest, just like Ernest would not get anywhere sounding like Jimmie Rodgers," said Hank. A plan went into effect.

Hank asked the engineer at the radio station to record a few of his shows on some fifteen-inch acetate discs used by the station at the time. Then Hank carefully listened to the discs, which was the first time he had actually heard himself on a recording, and he said to himself, "Boy I sure *do* sound like Ernest Tubb."

After a few more replays, Hank knew the reasons. He sang in the same register as Ernest and his inflections were the same; i.e., they both hit the low notes very strongly and backed off some on the high notes. Without hesitation, he decided to do just the opposite and sing the high notes with authority and soften the low notes. He then started practicing.

"From then on it was a softening of the low notes and an emphasis on the high notes," remembered Hank. "I worked and worked at it until it became second nature."

From then on he sounded like Hank Thompson.

*

Hank was asked to make a personal appearance at a fund-raiser for a friend of his Dad's who was running for constable of Waco. The location was *The Syrian Club* in Waco, and Hank played a few songs accompanied only by his guitar. Afterwards, he was mingling in the crowd and trying to play a little politics when he spotted a very striking brunette dressed in fashionable western clothes. Hank made it over to her, introduced himself, and a conversation ensued. Her name was Dorothy Jean Ray, she lived in Waco, and she worked at the local glass plant. Knowing that she, like most people at that time, probably did not have a telephone, Hank asked if she would give him her address, and if he could come by and visit her the next day. She did and he did, and a courtship began.

With the fall, 1946, term at SMU on the horizon, Hank had a conversation with Ray Lewis, the program director at KWTX.

"How long are you going to do this show?" asked Ray.

"I'll stay on until this fall; then I plan to go back to SMU and finish my electrical engineering studies."

"What do you want to go back to college for? You have got a lot of talent in music and you should stay with it."

"I've been interested in electrical engineering all my life, and I want to get my college degree."

"Let me tell you something. I have a college degree and it really didn't help me a damn bit in this job. I know a lot of other people who went to college and were not able to use their degree when they got out. You're in the same boat – you don't need a college degree for what you are doing now."

"But I can use the music as a hobby or something to fall back on after I get my degree."

"What you should do is pursue your music career and use the electrical engineering as something to fall back on."

"Let me think about that," said Hank, knowing that he had a few weeks to make his decision.

Chapter Eight

One of Hank's biggest fans was his mother, who marveled at his musical talents and didn't miss any of his radio shows. But she was puzzled over the fact that there was nobody who was musically inclined on her side of the family. She realized that Hank may have inherited his musical DNA from his dad's oldest brother, who played accordion, guitar, mandolin, and organ, and tried to sing a little bit.

"Of course, we thought he was pretty good," said Hank, "but I was very young at the time and, since he was the only one around doing it, we had nothing to compare it to."

Hank and his mother were discussing this one morning over breakfast, and she brought up a related subject.

"Hank," said his mother, "I listen to your radio show every day but I never hear you play that song about the sailor."

"You must mean *Whoa Sailor*," replied Hank, who had almost forgotten about the song. "How do you know about that song?"

"Do you remember your friend from California, Doris Ricky who visited us? She told us about it and said it was a good song. I want to hear it."

Hank picked up his guitar and sang it for her.

"That's very good! You should play it on your show."

"I don't know. It's about the war, and people are tired of that."

"No it's not, it's just about a sailor who meets a girl. Try it on your show and see what happens."

The next day Hank introduced *Whoa Sailor* to his listening audience and the response was amazing.

"I always got a pretty good sized stack of mail requesting songs," remembered Hank, "but after I sang *Whoa Sailor*, the stack turned into several stacks, nearly all requesting that song. And what's remarkable is that, if it weren't for Doris Ricky visiting my parents and telling them about the song, and my mother insisting that I play it, I probably would have forgotten about it. And it turned out to be the song that launched my career!"

*

A series of events occurred in the summer of 1946 that cost SMU an engineering student.

A friend of Hank's, Garland DeLamar, worked in the record business in Waco, primarily as a jukebox operator for the Waco area and as a record buyer for his father's retail record store. The record store was about a half a block from the radio station, and Hank would often go in the store after his show, and Garland would play him the latest country music releases. Gordon's father also owned a "one-stop" record distributorship in Dallas where all the retail stores in the area could purchase records, and Garland would often travel to Dallas to pick up some records. On one such trip, Garland had a conversation with Herb Rippa, the manager of the one-stop.

Herb told Garland that Globe Records, a small label in California, was looking for some talent in the Southwest to record, and Garland told Herb about Hank. When Garland returned to Waco, he passed the news to Hank and suggested that he get in touch with Herb. Hank did, and Herb was able to convince Globe to send Hank a recording contract. Although Globe was a "regional" label with distribution only in the Southwest and California, Hank jumped at the opportunity. Since he was a month away from turning 21, his mother signed the contract on his behalf, and Hank was a recording artist.

This was a huge factor in Hank's decision to forego, or at least postpone, his electrical engineering studies at SMU. But his dad was not pleased, largely because he had a hard time believing that Hank could earn a living singing country music.

"My dad certainly was disappointed that I wasn't going to get a 'real job,'" remembered Hank.

Globe quickly set up a recording session that took place at Pappy Seller's studio in Dallas in August 1946. Hank brought a pick-up band consisting of four Waco musicians who had been backing him on some of his personal appearances – including Jimmy Gilliland on steel, Bobby Murrell on guitar, Tommy Williams on bass, and Carlisle Mills on fiddle.

"As far as I knew, Pappy had the only recording studio in the Southwest at the time," Hank recalled. "I wasn't that familiar with everything that was done in the recording process, but the basic set-up was not unlike the setup for my radio show. Pappy was kind of a fussy guy, which was good. After the set-up, we just gathered around a microphone and started cutting songs. We'd been playing the songs quite a bit on the road, so it wasn't like everybody was learning for the first time."

The songs were recorded on acetate discs. If they were acceptable, the recording engineer would cut a master lacquer disc from the acetate disc and send it to a pressing plant for mass-producing 78 rpm records. The final product was a relatively heavy, double-sided disc, ten inches in diameter and manufactured from a shellac resin.[4]

However, if an error were made during the recording, the acetate disc being used would have to be discarded and the song recorded from the beginning on a new disc. Thus, the pressure on the artists and the recording engineer to get it right the first time was high.

---

[4] All of Hank's single (two-sided) releases from 1946 through 1949 were on 78 rpm records.

The first song recorded was *Swing Wide Your Gate of Love*, followed by *Whoa Sailor*. These two songs would be on Hank's first two-sided "single" release for Globe. He also recorded *California Women* and *What Are We Going To Do About the Moonlight*, another song he had written while in the Navy. The sessions went down without a hitch, and that night Hank and the four musicians packed up and drove back to Waco, not realizing at the time that they had been on the premier voyage of a recording career that was to span seven decades.

Globe released "*Whoa Sailor*" backed with "*Swing Wide Your Gate of Love*", in September 1946, the month that Hank turned twenty-one. Garland DeLamar saw to it that the record was put on all the jukeboxes that he serviced, and Hank took copies of the record to the various radio stations in the area. This wasn't easy, since there were virtually no full-time country music stations in the Southwest. Instead, a large number of stations had a thirty-minute or one-hour country music show interspersed with their regular programming. Therefore, there were many stations to cover, and Hank put a lot of mileage on the Oldsmobile.

One of the stations Hank targeted was KRLD, a 50,000-watt station in Dallas. On an unannounced cold-call one day, Hank was able to meet Hal Horton, one of the Southwest's most prominent and influential country music disc jockeys at the time. Hal hosted a top-ten country song hit parade each week that was beamed out over a huge coverage area across the country. The influence of Hal's top-ten country show at that time cannot be overstated. It was really the only way anyone could get a fairly quick read on the sales potential of a record in the Southwest.

The meeting went well, and Hal agreed to play the record. It also led to a business relationship and friendship between Hal and Hank that lasted several years.

Chapter Nine

The inability of the Oldsmobile to start began occurring with increasing regularity and led to a routine between Hank and his mother. Hank would park on the street in front of the Thompson residence, facing downhill. When the car didn't start, he would call his mother out, and they would push the car down the street. When sufficient momentum was reached, Hank would jump in, engage the clutch, and the engine would usually kick in. Since all of the houses on the street often had their windows open, this frequent scene did not go unnoticed by many of the neighbors, which, in turn, did not go unnoticed by Hank's mother.

The crowning blow occurred one day when Hank was driving in downtown Waco and he suddenly heard a loud noise coming from beneath the car. The engine was still running but nothing else was happening. Hank looked in his rear view mirror and saw the driveshaft bouncing on the street towards the curb, a result of a broken U-joint. His dad came and picked Hank up, hauled the car in to his shop and replaced the U-joint.

This apparently led to a conversation between Mr. and Mrs. Thompson, followed by a conversation that Hank had with his dad that Hank will never forget.

"Son, you need a car that you can depend on for what you are doing," said Hank's dad. "They haven't made new cars since 1942, but they are resuming production as we speak. I'm going to take you down to the local Chevrolet dealer, who is a friend, and we are going to order you a new car."

The next day they were in the dealer's showroom talking to the dealer about the car and the price, which turned out to be non-negotiable. Mr. Thompson pulled out a roll of one hundred dollar bills and handed fifteen of them to the dealer. Hank was aghast, since he had never seen a hundred dollar bill in his life, much less fifteen.

"I want the first new 1946 car that comes in," said Mr. Thompson to the dealer, as he handed over the cash.

On the way out, Hank said, "Pa, I appreciate this very much and I'll pay you back."

The car, a brand new 1946 two-door Chevrolet, arrived a few weeks later and was the first new Chevrolet to hit Waco since 1942. Hank had "The Hank Thompson show, 12:15 P.M, KWTX" painted on the sides of the car in gold lettering. He could have not been prouder.

*

In addition to Hank Thompson and The Brazos Valley Boys, there were two other first-rate country music bands in Waco at the time – Chuck Harding and his band, which also had a daily show on KWTX; and The Lone Star Playboys, which did the same on WACO. Both groups played a role in Hank's future.

One day, Hank was called into the office of Buddy Bosic, the general manager of KWTX, who informed Hank that one of the station's large sponsors, Cooper Grocery, wanted to do a live music show as a promotion. Buddy wanted Hank to perform and sing with Chuck Harding and his band, for a fee of five dollars. Not only was Hank underwelmed by the offer, he wasn't interested in playing with Chuck Harding's band, since he now had a band of his own. He reminded Buddy of this.

"Well, let me put it this way," said Buddy, "You are an employee of this station, and we are not asking you to do this; we are telling you."

"Let me think about it, and I'll get back to you," said Hank.

Hank walked out of the office, out of the building, around the corner, and into the offices of WACO. He met with the station manager, Lee Glasgow, the same person who turned him down for a radio show on WACO when he returned from the Navy.

"You know," said Hank, "I'm reaching a lot of people on KWTX and my show is very popular. But your station is more powerful, and I could reach a lot more if I came over here. What do you think about my moving my show to WACO?"

"Your timing is good," was the reply. "There just happens to be an open slot between the noon news and The Lone Star Playboys Show at 12:30, and we could put you in there." He offered Hank thirty dollars a week on the spot, which was twice the amount that he was getting on KWTX. Hank had trouble containing himself as he accepted.

"When can you start?" asked Lee.

"Not before tomorrow," said Hank

The next day, an employee of KWTX called Bosic at his office and spoke in an excited voice.

"Are you listening to the Hank Thompson show?" he asked.

"No", said Bosic, who thought it was a stupid question, since the studio in which Hank did the show was only a few doors down from Bosic's office.

"You better do so. By the way, its on WACO."

*

As the new Chevrolet transported Hank, The Brazos Valley Boys, and their equipment to their personal appearances throughout central Texas, Hank kept a keen ear on KRLD in Dallas, especially to Hal Horton's top ten shows. One Saturday night, a few weeks after his initial meeting with Hal, Hank tuned in and was very pleasantly surprised to discover that Swing Wide Your Gate of Love was number two on Hal's Hit Parade, and Whoa Sailor was number one.

This did not go unnoticed by Herb Rippa, the manager of the one-stop record outlet in Dallas, who had referred Hank to Globe Records. He decided to go to a higher level in the record business and founded Bluebonnet Records. One of his first moves was to buy the unreleased masters of *California Women* and *What Are We Going To Do About the Moonlight* from Globe. He also asked Hank about doing a recording session for Bluebonnet, which was possible since the Globe contract was open-ended and didn't preclude a defection to another label.

Hank agreed, went to work with the J-200, and wrote two songs – *A Lonely Heart Knows* and *My Starry-Eyed Texas Gal*.

The Bluebonnet session was also held at Pappy Sellers studio in Dallas. Hank brought Jimmy Gilliland on steel, Charlie Adams on bass, accordionist Bill Dukas and two members of the Lone Star Playboys that Hank knew from WACO – electric mandolinist Morris Booker and fiddler Cotton Collins. *A Lonely Heart Knows* and *My Starry-Eyed Texas Gal* were recorded, and Rippa released them immediately while holding the two songs he purchased from Globe in the can.

A Lonely Heart Knows is still one of Hank's favorite songs and was especially important back then. It became a hit for Hank in the usual manner – No. 1 on Hal Horton's hit parade – and it opened a line of communication between Hank and Ernest Tubb, who also recorded the song, leading to some nice royalty checks to Hank as the writer. It also helped define the Thompson sound and set the standard for what he could do with a ballad. This song is representative of Hank's ability to interweave catchy heartfelt lyrics lamenting the effects of lost love on broken and lonely hearts:

A lonely heart knows,
A lonely sorrow,
A lonely heart knows,
A troubled mind.

Down in a heart grows,
A sad tomorrow,
When in a heart flows,
A love that's blind.

When the shadow is descending,
And your tears fall like rain,
A lonely heart knows the fate that's pending,
A lonely heart knows only pain.

And when those bonds you resolve to sever,
To reweld them with someone new,
I hope then, dear, that you would never,
Know the pain that I've gone through.

Then you were cheated by your new love,
And your tears fell like rain,
And now you know, dear, that your true love,
With a lonely heart knows only pain.

*

Later, Hank had an idea for another song.

"I was writing a song entitled *Rock in the Ocean* and trying to get some kind of a feel for the thing," remembered Hank, "but I was having a difficult time getting the lyrics to jive with the melody. My mind started drifting, and for some reason the expression "Humpty Dumpty" came to mind. I turned the paper over and wrote *Humpty Dumpty Heart* in about fifteen minutes. That song was one of the easiest songs that I ever wrote. Then I turned the paper back over and started working on *Rock in the Ocean* again.

After his daily radio show on WACO, Hank often would stay in the studio to watch the following show by The Lone Star Playboys. He was pleasantly surprised to notice that Lefty Nason, the steel guitar player who had impressed Hank in Austin, had moved to Waco and was a regular member of the Playboys. One day, with *Humpty Dumpty Heart* fresh on his mind, Hank hung around the studio and waited until the Lone Star Playboys finished their show. He then asked if they would back him while he recorded an acetate demo of *Humpty Dumpty Heart,* fully aware that he would use Lefty on the instrumental break. The engineer at the station came on board, and the song came out surprisingly well on the one and only take. Hank was very pleased and marveled at Lefty's performance. He then piled in the Chevrolet and took the demo to Hal Horton in Dallas. Hal put it on heavy rotation on KRLD to a terrific response, and it shot its way to number one on Hal's hit parade in a few weeks.

In the meantime, Hank received a royalty check from Globe records for *Whoa Sailor* and *Swing Wide Your Gate of Love.* The check was for $171 dollars, based on sales of 8709 records.

STATEMENT

GLOBE
RECORD CO.
DISTRIBUTORS
4716 South Hoover Street, Los Angeles 37, California

5/23/47

Statement of royalty due Mr. Hank Thompson
for the first quarter of 1947 on
Whoa Sailor
Swing Wide Your Gate of Love.

Number of records sold 8709

Royalty rate 1¢ ea. (2¢) per record

Am't due	174.18
less two collect wires	3.14
Net Am't	171.04

Chapter Ten

Capitol Records was the first major record label on the West Coast and successfully competed with RCA-Victor, Columbia and Decca, all based in New York. Included in Capitol's roster of artists in the nineteen-forties were Les Baxter, Bing Crosby, Les Paul, Peggy Lee, Stan Kenton, Les Brown, Nat King Cole, and Tex Ritter. Tex had established his reputation as a "singing cowboy" in the early thirties and went on to make eighty-five movies, seventy-eight of which were westerns. He skillfully intertwined his movie career with a singing career and, by 1947, had several hit songs on Capitol – *Rye Whiskey* (1931), *Boll Weevil* (1945), *Wayward Wind* (1946), *Hillbilly Heaven* (1946), and *You Are My Sunshine* (1946).

Tex was also a friend of Hal Horton and, in early 1947, he was in Dallas on a theater tour that included Waco. Hal knew that Capitol Record's country A&R head, Lee Gillette, had asked Tex to scout for potential talent for Capitol when on tour. With this in mind, Hal played *Whoa Sailor*, *Swing Wide Your Gate of Love*, and the demo of *Humpty Dumpty Heart* to Tex and suggested that Tex look Hank up when he got to Waco.

Hal passed the word to Hank, who met Tex when he arrived in Waco and took him to dinner. The evening was filled with good food and cheer, and Tex agreed to appear on Hank's radio show the next day to sing one of his songs and promote his live show in Waco that night. The radio show went smoothly, and Tex also sang a duet with Hank; but, more importantly, Tex got to hear Hank sing *Humpty Dumpty Heart*. Tex was convinced; the next day he placed a call to Gillette, who, in turn, called Hank and offered him a record deal on the spot. Since Capitol was a major label, it was a no-brainer for Hank; and a contract, which Hank readily signed, followed in the mail.

In the meantime, playing on the success of *Humpty Dumpty Heart* and *A Lonely Heart Knows*, Bluebonnet Records released *California Women* and *What Are We Going to do About the Moonlight* This increased Hank's arsenal of self-written songs that he could sing, and therefore promote, during his personal appearances. And it also enabled him to at least partially ameliorate a difficulty that had been bothering him for some time in connection with his personal appearances, which was his reliance on the popular songs of the days recorded by other artists.

"Back in those days, there were very few people who just wrote songs for others, like Harland Howard and Cindy Walker, who came on later," said Hank. "Therefore, everybody that was recording, such as Jimmie Rodgers, Ernest Tubb, Gene Autry, Roy Acuff, and Hank Williams, wrote their own songs, mostly out of necessity. At that time I had no choice but to sing songs written and recorded by others, and I didn't like it, since people already had those songs available to them. I realized early on that, in order to survive in this business, I needed songs that people could identify with *me*, and the only way to do that was to write them myself.

"The art of songwriting is very difficult to define. Most of the time I would write with an idea of the song, the lyrics and the melody in mind. But first I would develop the mood, and then the melody would often flow along with the mood. Merle Travis told me that the secret to songwriting is to write the first line, then the last line, and then fill in between. This makes sense, since you've got to know where you're going with a song. Also, I always try to write a song in cadence, much like a march or a dance. You can almost feel the beat as you write.

"Of course, it always helps to start with an idea. For example, Tex Williams did a song called *The Leaf of Love*. It didn't do much as far as sales go, but I really liked it. It had a verse that included the expression 'The leaf of love is slowly falling'. I thought that was a nice thing and I wanted to write a song with a similar mood. I set down with my guitar and, using *The Leaf of Love* as a starting point, I came up with

'Today, I'm like a leaf in autumn,
Never again to know the spring...'

The song, *Today*, just fell into place after that."

*

Since, under the GI Bill of Rights, veterans were free to attend the educational institution of their choice, Hank wanted to dovetail this opportunity with a desire that he had been nurturing for several years. He wanted to learn how to fly.

In 1947, after making a few inquires in Waco and filling out the proper paperwork with the government, he was able to commission a flying school in Waco to give him lessons that were paid for under the GI Bill. Not only did the Government front for the lessons, Hank received an additional $65 a month. Upon completing the necessary class work and forty hours of supervised flying, he received his private pilot's license. But, since the GI Bill covered even more, and since he wanted to go to the next level, he also completed another 180 hours of training in Waco and got his commercial license. Although he had no designs on being a commercial pilot, he improved his skills with the extra training in the hope of someday owning and flying his own plane.

Around that time, Capitol's Lee Gillette and his assistant, Cliffie Stone, agreed to fly to Dallas, meet Hank, and produce Hank's first songs for Capitol. The studio at radio station WFAA in Dallas was selected as the recording venue for the simple reason that it was the best facility in the Southwest at the time.

Fully realizing the importance of the event, Hank put together an A-team of musicians, including Lefty Nason who came up with Hank from Waco, KRLD's bass fiddler Rip Giersdorf, and none other than Buddy Woodie on accordion, the same Buddy Woodie whom second class radioman Thompson had met and played with in California. The two fiddlers were local – Georgia Slim Rutland and future Roy Acuff fiddler Howdy Forrester, then working at the State Fair of Texas. Hank thought so much of Forrester that the afternoon recording session was scheduled from 3 to 6 p.m. so that Forrester would be available to record in between his shows at the fair. Gillette recommended California guitarist Jack Rivers, who happened to be in town on a theater tour with Jimmy Wakely.

Hank was immediately impressed with Gillette and Stone.

"Lee certainly listened to everybody," said Hank. "He didn't come in and try to tell you how to run the show. He would get everybody's opinion, and he was very open and very easy to work with."

Cliffie Stone already had an impressive resume, the details of which will be discussed later.

On the afternoon of October 10, 1947, Gillette and Stone met Hank and the musicians at the studio along with a Capitol engineer who'd driven in from Los Angeles with a new device that nobody in the studio had seen before, but one that would end up revolutionizing the recording industry – a magnetic tape recorder.

"Take a look at this," Gillette told the assembled group in the studio, "it's a Magnecord tape recorder. We can now record directly to the tape and transfer it to a master and cut records from the master. The beauty of it is that if something goes wrong during the recording session, we can simply rewind the tape and record over it again. The procedure will be a lot easier since you don't have to worry about messing up these expensive 'one shot only' acetate discs."

They plugged WFAA's microphones into a sound board and connected the output of the board to the input of the tape recorder, and one of the first (if not the first) country music recording sessions using magnetic tape began.

Since Hank had not worked with most of the musicians, he ran through each song and the proposed arrangement very quickly, using only his guitar. Then he did a couple of run-throughs with the band, and the engineer started the recorder. Each song took only two or three takes, and the recording process went without a hitch.

One of the first recordings was a new version of *Humpty Dumpty Heart* that Capitol wanted to rush to market. It was easy to improve on the fairly rudimentary acetate demo that Hal Horton was playing on the radio. Also recorded were *Rock In The Ocean* and *Today*, along with another song that Hank had written entitled *Don't Flirt with Me*.

These recordings hinted at the Thompson sound to come, due, in no small measure, to the steel guitar work contributed by Lefty Nason. Although Hank did not fully realize it at the time, bringing Lefty on board was one of his most sagacious business decisions.

"I never heard anybody play like that," said Hank, "but I knew immediately that he was the man that I wanted for my recordings and, if possible, for my personal appearances. Later, when Lefty became a member of The Brazos Valley Boys, he came up with all the steel guitar "licks" or "fills" that I started using early on and kept using throughout my career. Initially, when I'd hear him do one for the first time, I'd say, 'Hey, Lefty, remember that thing, right there that you do, use that lick more often.'

The little chime thing, and crunching the bar, hitting the bar on the strings, and the 'Dut-Dut Do-Wha'. By adding these licks that were so unique, my songs had an identification that distinguished our sound from everybody else. You could hear the intro and know who it was. Those things that he did on that particular recording session, and later on when he worked as a regular member of The Brazos Valley Boys, became identifiable as the Hank Thompson sound, and we still use them today."

Hank's tenure as a Capitol recording artist was thus launched. It continued for the next eighteen years, during which approximately three hundred and twenty additional songs were recorded.

Chapter Eleven

Hank's paternal grandparents' name was Tomacek, which they changed for the more conventional Anglo-Saxon name of Thompson when they came to Texas from Czechoslovakia. Hank's dad, Jule, was raised on a farm before he got interested in the mechanical end of things, which led to a stint as a railroad engineer. When he realized the impact that the automobile was going to have on society, he opened his automobile repair shop in downtown Waco in the nineteen twenties and maintained it as an active business until a few years before his death in 1978.

Jule and young Hank would often go fishing or squirrel hunting on a Sunday, and Jule would turn the car radio to The Czech Melody Hour on KTEM in Temple, Texas, where a lot of Czech and German people lived. The show featured a lot of old polkas and waltzes, which had special appeal to his dad's Bohemian roots.

One song that particularly caught Hank's attention was *The Bartender's Polka*.

"This song was a favorite of mine because of its beautiful melody," remembered Hank. What he did not know at the time was that he would record the song approximately ten years later for a national record label with the number one Country and Western band in the nation.

*

Capitol Records' version of *Humpty Dumpty Heart*, backed with *Rock in the Ocean*, was released around December 1, 1947. Hal Horton simply replaced the demo of *Humpty Dumpty Heart* which he was playing on the radio with the new Capitol version, and it stayed at No. 1 for several additional weeks. More importantly, due to Capitol's national distribution, the record was available throughout the country and spent thirty-eight weeks on the Billboard magazine charts in 1948, peaking at No. 2.[5]

---

[5] All references to chart positions in this book are based on the Billboard Magazine charts as compiled by Joel Whitburn in the various editions of his book entitled "Joel Whitburn's Top Country Singles 1944-1988".

Unfortunately, there was an aberration in connection with the charting of several of Hank's songs, including *Humpty Dumpty Heart,* which should be addressed. Due to the limited lines of communication between the various sections of the country at that time (no television, very little national radio and no national publications of record sales), a song that charted in one region of the country often would not make it to the charts in other regions until later. In the meantime, the song would fall down in the first region. This seesaw effect prevented many songs – Hank's included – from attaining their peak position at the same time and this was reflected in a lower rank in the Billboard chart.

"In the early days, Billboard never listed a lot of my songs as number one," recalled Hank, "because on some of the regional charts, such as in the Southwest and the West Coast, my songs would go to number one, but the East Coast was slow picking up on the song. Then two months later it would get to number one in Philadelphia, but, by that time, it was already off the charts in Dallas-Fort Worth. Thus, on several occasions my song would be number one in all those regions, but since it was not at the same time, the song would never hit number one on the Billboard charts."

But *Humpty Dumpty's* ascension to number two was not bad. In the first quarter of 1948, Hank received a royalty check based on 155,000 units, and the record went on to sell approximately 400,000 units before it dropped off the charts. But that's not all.

"With all of the re-recordings of the song for release on "greatest hits" albums and other compilations for the U.S. and foreign markets," Hank said, "I wouldn't be surprised if the total sales of *Humpty Dumpty Heart* is in excess of a million." And counting.

In the meantime, another hit song was on the horizon. In late 1947, while driving home from a personal appearance, Hank had his car radio tuned to one of the Mexican border stations and heard a song recorded by T. Texas Tyler called *Red Light.* His first reaction to the song was that it was a great idea but a very poor execution of the mes-

sage. His second reaction was an idea to change the basic premise to *Green Light* and do a completely different song. It was late at night, but as soon as he arrived at his house, he got out the J-200 and started composing and writing down the first things that came to mind with the thought that he would come back later and polish it up.

But later, during polish-up time, he got discouraged.

"I thought the lyrics weren't too bad, but it was the dullest melody I had ever heard," remembered Hank. "I knew I needed to spice it up and got the idea of using this little delay in the chorus, 'I turned your whole card [delay] upside down', to give it a bit of boost. Doing that split bar really put zest to the song, and I finished it very quickly after that."

*

In late 1947, The American Federation of Musicians, a very strong union at the time, announced that all of its members were going on strike against the U.S. record companies over royalties, starting in early 1948. This caused a rush to the studios in 1947 so that the record labels could record everything they could get from their artists before the strike date. Capitol Records sent Hank a plane ticket to Los Angeles in mid-December to record as many songs as possible, and they informed him that Cliffie Stone (the Capitol Records executive who assisted in Hank's recording in Dallas) and his band would back Hank at the sessions.

When Hank arrived in Los Angeles, every studio in town was going twenty-four hours a day, to build up a backlog of material. Capitol didn't yet have their own studio, so they had to book time with other studios. When this proved inadequate to meet the recording needs of its artists, a makeshift studio was put together in the lounge of the company's building at Sunset and Vine. Microphones were installed in the lounge, recording gear in the basement, and a talkback speaker system between the two. The music was piped from the mikes in the lounge downstairs to the control board in the basement.

Cliffie Stone checked in as bassist with his band, and the group made a very favorable impression on Hank.

"I learned early on that these guys were such great musicians that all I had to do was just run through each song very quickly with my guitar. We then decided on the arrangement and went ahead and cut it,"

Hank had written several songs for the occasion including *My Heart Is A Jigsaw Puzzle, Yesterday's Mail, I Find You Cheatin' On Me, Second Hand Gal, You Broke My Heart (In Little Bitty Pieces), You Remembered Me,* and *The Green Light.*

He also re-recorded the two earlier Bluebonnet numbers: *California Women* and *What Are We Going To Do About The Moonlight.*

"Both of these songs had gotten pretty good play," said Hank. "*California Women* in particular was quite a popular number for me. Being on a small label, it just never did get exposure, and I wanted to give it its just due with Capitol."

During the sessions, Eddie Kirk, the rhythm guitarist, told Hank that he had just acquired an airplane that he got for a good price at a war surplus sale. It was a PT-19, which was a low-wing Navy trainer, and Kirk asked Hank if he wanted to fly with him. Hank, who still had visions of owning a plane some day, readily accepted. One day after a session, they drove to a hangar in San Fernando, which, at that time was in the middle of an empty desert.

After the flight, they drove back to Los Angeles. On the way Eddie passed a motorcycle with a guy driving and a girl on the back. "That looks like Merle Travis," Eddie said.

"Merle Travis!" said Hank. "I am a big fan of his and would love to meet him."

Eddie flagged down Merle, and Hank jumped out of the car and went over to meet him.

"Merle, I'm Hank Thompson."

Merle smiled, shook Hank's hand, and replied, "Nice to meet you Hank."

After a short conversation, Hank came to an unusual realization.

"It was like seeing an old friend that I hadn't seen in a long time. We had an instant bonding, and he turned out to be the best friend I had in the music business."

*

One of the most unique and difficult styles of guitar playing is referred to in guitar player's parlance as "thumb picking". The intricacies of the thumb picking guitar style are very difficult to decode and, in fact, are even hard to describe, but you know it when you hear it. It features a strong rhythmic pattern achieved by using the thumb (and, under most circumstances, a thumb pick) to pick out a syncopated, alternating bass line while the right-hand index finger, and often the middle finger, pick out the melody on the treble strings. The net result is a self-contained, rich, varied sound that gives the illusion of a lead and rhythm guitar being played simultaneously. The reason the style isn't that popular is simple – not many guitarists can play it.

But not only was Merle Travis an accomplished thumb picker, he developed his own individual variation of the basic style to create a personal sound. For example, he also brushed the fourth, third, and second strings with the thumb on the upstroke while muting the strings with the heel of the right hand, which created a percussive bass-chord accompaniment to the lead. On occasion, he would add even more variety by interjecting banjo-type "rolls" to give a sparkling, almost rippling, effect.

When he met Hank, Merle was a heralded studio musician and recording artist for Capitol Records and one of the nation's preeminent country guitarists.

Chapter Twelve

In addition to his job with Capitol Records and his work as a musician and band-leader, Cliffie Stone wore still another (cowboy) hat. He practically owned the country music radio market in California in the late 1940s. He had a daily radio show entitled the *Dinner Bell Roundup* that, when it debuted in 1944, was broadcast by as many as twenty-eight stations to a huge audience throughout the state. Cliffie hosted the show and also performed as a singer and comedian. Tennessee Ernie Ford joined the cast in 1947 as a comic and vocalist, and the many guests that made periodic appearances on the show included Molly Bee, Merle Travis, Speedy West, Ferlin Huskey, Lefty Frizzell, Eddy Arnold, Jim Reeves, Johnny Horton, Tex Ritter, Johnny Bond, Tex Williams, Freddie Hart and Elvis Presley. It wasn't a coincidence that many of the artists recorded for Capitol.

His band members, who were also quickly becoming Capitol Records' de facto house band, were regulars on the show, along with Miss Coleen Summers, a beautiful and rather demure young lady who could sing like a bird.

The *Dinner Bell Roundup* was broadcast live daily from the studios of KXLA in Pasadena and followed a fairly tight format that usually consisted of the opening theme song followed by the band doing a song or two before Coleen would be introduced to do her song for the day. Cliffie kept things alive and spontaneous with a little cornball humor sandwiched in between the songs.

Cliffie asked Hank to drop by for a guest appearance on the show during Hank's stay in Los Angeles for the Capitol recording sessions. Hank got there about thirty minutes before air time to get tuned up and ready for the show. A few minutes before airtime, Cliffie and all the band members were ready and in place, with the exception of Coleen who had not made an appearance. Hank thought this was unusual and asked Cliffie if she was scheduled to be on that day.

"Yes, but she's always late," replied Cliffie. "She usually shows up about five minutes after the show starts, since she knows she won't be introduced until we do one or two songs. You can set your watch to it."

On this day, at about ten minutes before airtime, the engineer rushed into the studio and informed everyone that the show had just been cancelled for the day. Mutual News was going to preempt the regularly scheduled programming with a special on a breaking news matter. It was not an emergency, but it was significant enough to merit the cancellation. The band members started putting their instruments up when Cliffie's comedian brain lobe kicked in.

"Hold it guys. I've got an idea. I'll have the engineer turn on the red ON THE AIR light indicating that we are on the air, and let's go through a song or two until Coleen gets here. Then we'll introduce her and have some fun."

After Cliffie outlined more of the details, the band snapped to it, and, sure enough, Coleen walked in about five minutes after "air time" unaware of the cancellation. The red light was on and Cliffie and the band were just finishing their second song. When it ended, Cliffie stepped up to the mike, nodded towards Coleen and said, "Now we're going to bring sweet little Coleen up to the mike to do one for us. What will it be today, Coleen?"

"Thanks Cliffie, I think I'll do one of my favorites, *Have I Told You Lately That I Love You.*"

Very quickly, Cliffie replied in a disgusted tone of voice, "Oh no, not that fucking song again!"

"Same old shit!" from a band member.

Coleen's eyes widened as she looked at the red light and confirmed that it was still on.

"Goddamnit, why in the hell don't you learn something new?" from another band member.

A slight delay as everyone watched Colleen's face turn as red as the light.

"Fuck it. Let's skip the damn song. I've had enough of this shit," said Cliffie, capping his academy award performance.

The band members continued to play it straight, but the laughter from the engineer's room and the people in the rest of the studio became so raucous that Coleen finally caught on.

She apparently recovered fairly well. In 1949, she changed her name to Mary Ford after she married Les Paul and went on to their recording successes with the hit songs *How High the Moon, Mockingbird Hill, Vaya Con Dios*, and *The World is Waiting for the Sunrise*, among others.

*

The popularity of *Humpty Dumpty Heart* dramatically affected the demand for, and the dynamics of, Hank's personal appearances. Although most of his previous jobs had been largely confined to the schoolhouse circuit around the Waco area, he realized that this was the time to go to the next level, which involved two components. One, he wanted to graduate to the honky-tonks, clubs, and dance halls, a much more profitable scenario; and, two, he wanted to extend his horizons throughout Texas and the Southwest.

"You could do a schoolhouse and charge something like fifty cents for adults, and a quarter for kids; but even if the place was full, there wasn't a lot of money involved. Also, you couldn't go back in there for another year or so. However, in dance halls and clubs, you could charge something like a dollar, four to five hundred people would come, and we would get sixty to seventy percent of the door. Plus, you could play the dance halls and clubs as often as once a month and build up a following, and you would come out with pretty good money."

With this in mind, Hank established a "regular" version of The Brazos Valley Boys by adding a drummer and one or two other musicians to the existing group and committing to using them on a regular basis. He paid them on a job-by-job basis using the cash he received from the door. The famous 1946 Chevrolet and trailer were replaced by two station wagons; and the honky-tonks, clubs, and dance halls were in Hank's sights.

*

The Cornbread Matinee was a country music show broadcast by KRLD every weekday afternoon from their studios in Dallas. Hal Horton hosted the show in front of a live audience that was given cornbread to munch on during the show (yes, this really happened). A country "house band" held forth and was led by vocalist Dewey Groom, who later made a name as the owner of the famous Longhorn Ballroom in Dallas. The show became so popular that KRLD moved it to a larger theater in the Oak Cliff section of Dallas, and then to the Arcadia Theater on Greenville Avenue.

In February 1948, Hank was scheduled to appear on the Cornbread Matinee and sing *What Are We Gonna Do About The Moonlight*, which, in the meantime, had ascended to number 10 on the Billboard chart. During this time, Hank and Dorothy Jean Ray were seeing more and more of each other and neither were dating anyone else on any kind of a regular basis. Hank would often take her with him when he drove to Dallas to be interviewed on Hal's evening Hit Parade or to perform on *The Cornbread Matinee*. Hank and Dorothy were in the KRLD studios prior to the February 1948, show and Hal, ever the promoter, had a proposal.

"As far as I can tell, you guys have been dating now for at least two years," he said, "and it looks pretty serious to me. I have an offer you may not be able to refuse. Why don't you get married on *The Cornbread Matinee*? We'll furnish the preacher, the ring, broadcast the ceremony live and even host a reception after the ceremony. It won't cost you a cent, and with the right promotion you can be assured of a boatload of wedding gifts. In fact I can assure you that you will get all the cooking utensils that you will ever need."

Hank looked at Dorothy with a grin and said, "Well, what do you think?"

Hank and Dorothy

"Sounds OK to me," replied Dorothy. "What do you think?"

Hank nodded his approval.

With this proposal for marriage and acceptance completed, the wedding date was set for Wednesday April 13th.

A few days later, Hank got a call from James Denny, the manager of *The Grand Ole Opry*, who offered Hank a one-time guest appearance on the *Opry* in April. Hank accepted and was delighted that he was able to dovetail this job with his honeymoon.

After weeks of planning and promotion, the April 13th edition of *The Cornbread Matinee* opened in the usual manner, with Hal holding forth. Dewey Groom and the band did a song, and Hank followed with *What Are We Going To Do About the Moonlight*.

Then the ceremony began, the vows were exchanged, and Dewey Groom closed things off with a rendition of *I Love You Truly*. Afterwards, KRLD hosted a reception in the honor of Mr. and Mrs. Henry William Thompson at the Adolphus Hotel in Dallas, the location of KRLD's studios.

The honeymoon tour began that night in a motel in Jollyville, Oklahoma, in the heart of the Davis Mountains, about 50 miles north of Ardmore. This was a convenient stopping place since the plans were to drive on to Tulsa the next day and then to Nashville for *The Grand Ole Opry* job the next Saturday night.

In Tulsa, Hank planned to take Dorothy to the Cain's Academy, a large dance studio, to hear Bob Wills' brother, Johnnie Lee Wills, who had a very good Western Swing band and hosted a weekly country music show at the Academy. Johnny had not yet met Hank, but had certainly heard of him; and, when Hank came by that afternoon, arrangements were quickly made to have him appear on the show that night. Hank performed *Humpty Dumpty Heart* and *Whoa Sailor* to a very enthusiastic response, and then it was on to Nashville.

What really excited Hank about the invitation to perform on *The Grand Ole Opry* was the fact that he was to be on a segment of the show that was to be broadcast nationally by NBC (in addition to the regular broadcast on affiliated radio station WSM). *The Grand Old Opry* people couldn't have been nicer, and Hank went to a rehearsal in the afternoon where he met several artists for the first time, including Bill Monroe, Uncle Dave Macon, and the announcer George D. Hay, one of America's pioneer radio showmen, who proclaimed himself "The Solemn Old Judge" (even though he was only thirty years old).

Hank recalled his feelings as he later stood in the wings of Ryman Auditorium on April 16, 1948, waiting to be introduced by Red Foley, the host during Hank's segment.

"Although I was fairly well seasoned as a performer by then," remembered Hank, "I couldn't help being nervous as I waited for the introduction. I had been listening to this show nearly all my life and was well aware of the magnitude of the prestige that an appearance on this stage brought. All of this, plus the knowledge that a national radio audience from across the country was also listening, was almost overwhelming."

The introduction came. Hank went on stage with the J-200 and, with the *Opry* house band behind him, performed "*Whoa Sailor*" and "*Humpty Dumpty Heart*" without a hitch.

Forty-one years later, Hank again was standing on the stage of The Grand Ole Opry, this time for another reason. It was the nationally televised Country Music Association awards show and it had just been announced that he was selected for membership into the Country Music Hall of Fame, the highest honor that a country music artist can receive.

Chapter Thirteen

The marathon late-1947 recording sessions in Los Angeles started paying dividends. *Yesterday's Mail* was released by Capitol in September of 1948, and was a respectable success before *Green Light* made it to number seven later that year. These releases were the first for Hank on a new record format – the 45 rpm record – that had narrower grooves than the 78 and were playable with a smaller stylus. Like the 78s, the 45s came with one song on each side but were lighter and smaller than the 78s (seven inches in diameter vs. ten) and soon became the dominant format. From then on, all of Hank's single records were released on the 45 rpm format.

In the meantime, Hank got a call from a representative of the Brown Brothers, who had one of the leading talent agencies in Nashville, and who had put together a country music show entitled *The Smoky Mountain Hayride*. Since WSM in Nashville had Saturday nights tied up with *The Grand Ole Opry*, the *Hayride* was broadcast on rival station WLAC and the Mutual network on Saturday afternoons. The show featured thirty minutes with Eddy Arnold followed by thirty minutes with Ernest Tubb.

The people at WSM were not exactly overjoyed by the competition, and they countered by prohibiting any of their artists from appearing on the *Hayride*. That took care of Ernest Tubb. When Eddy Arnold decided to go on his own and was hired by CBS, the Brown Brothers needed someone to carry on with the *Hayride*, and Hank got the call. The offer was for one of the thirty-minute slots for ninety dollars a week. Hank was making about thirty dollars a week for his radio show in Waco and, despite the fact that Waco and the surrounding communities had been good to him, he had high hopes that this Nashville opportunity would help broaden his horizons. He accepted.

He resigned from his radio show; and he and Dorothy drove to Nashville, rented an apartment, and started the process of integrating into the Nashville scene.

The Smoky Mountain Hayride debuted on September 11, 1948. Hank had the "country" slot for thirty minutes and was assisted by Annie Lou and Danny Dill, who would later join Ernest Tubb's band. Other thirty-minute slots on the Hayride were filled with an eclectic cast including Snooky Lanson, a pop guy, who later made it big when he hosted "Your Hit Parade" on television, a black gospel group – the Fairfield Four, and a Dixieland band.

Despite Hank's best efforts, *The Smokey Mountain Hayride* could not stand up to the competition of *The Grand Ole Opry*, and it cratered in about two months. The Brown Brothers then decided to take it on the road, which also met with a less than enthusiastic response. When the show finally died, they tried to keep Hank in town by putting him on an early morning radio station six days a week.

"They put me over on WLAC in Nashville at some ungodly time like 5:45 in the morning," Hank recalls. "Just me and the guitar with a female singer named Donna Jean." They were billed as "The Boy from Texas and the Girl from Tennessee", the title of a pop song that Nat King Cole had recorded in 1947.

*

In May of 1949, Hank was booked at Cook's Hoedown, a large country and western dance hall in Houston. The owner, John Cook was no dummy. He had a huge investment in the dance hall and covered his overhead with astute bookings. For example, he booked Hank Thompson, Hank Williams, and Houston-based Floyd Tillman on the same night.

The format was unusual. Each performer rotated through three fairly short sets using Tillman's band. Williams was riding high with *Lovesick Blues*, his first number one song, and *Green Light* had ascended to the top ten for Thompson. The place was packed with over three thousand revelers.

Thompson and Williams had met before, probably sometime after Hank and Dorothy moved to Nashville.

"I had met Hank Williams before, but, as best as I can remember, the job at Cook's Hoedown was the first time I worked with him," said Thompson. "We established an instant rapport and became close friends."

Their respective backgrounds reveal a close parallel. Both started out doing a radio show in a small town – Williams in Montgomery, Alabama, and Thompson in Waco. They both did the schoolhouse circuit with a small pickup band in and around their respective hometowns. Both secured a record contract and placed songs on the charts for the first time in the late forties; and, of course, both were prolific songwriters. At the time Williams was living in Shreveport and was a regular on *The Louisiana Hayride*, and Thompson had been a regular on *The Smokey Mountain Hayride*. Williams was two years older.

"I had nothing but respect for Hank Williams," said Thompson, "even though he was not that well liked by people in the music business. He came off as being boastful, and sometimes a little arrogant. But that didn't bother me, since I knew of his very humble beginnings, including shining shoes on the streets of Montgomery Alabama. So, to me, it was understandable that he was very proud of the popularity and financial success that he enjoyed. There's an old saying that 'If you can do it, it's not bragging', and that was the case with Hank Williams, because he was a great performer."

At Cook's hoedown that night, Williams did *Lovesick Blues* in each of his first two sets, much to the delight of the crowd, and ditto for Thompson with *Green Light*. Backstage, during the break between the second and third sets, Williams came up to Thompson with a sly grin on his face.

"I'm tired of singing *Lovesick Blues* and I bet you're tired of singing *Green Light*. I've got an idea."

"What?" asked Thompson.

"Next set, I'll sing *Green Light* and you sing *Lovesick Blues*," said Williams. "It'll surprise the hell out of everybody."

"I can't sing *Lovesick Blues* as good as you can, but I'll give it a shot," replied Thompson.

Sure enough, during Williams' third and final set he performed a good rendition of *Green Light* and, in his set, Thompson did *Lovesick Blues*.

The switch-a-roo brought a positive response from those in the crowd that were sober enough to realize what was happening.

After the show and the usual autograph sessions, the Hanks were invited to an after-party at a motel near Cook's Hoedown. Drinks, food, stories, companionship, and general frivolity were in order. Thompson accepted, but Williams declined.

"Naw, I can't," said Williams. "I've got to get back to Shreveport. Audrey is going to have another brat."[6]

A few minutes later, as Williams was preparing to leave, he came up to Thompson.

"Why don't you come to Shreveport and meet the people on *The Louisiana Hayride*," said Williams. "I'll introduce you to the people at the radio station and the program director for the Hayride. They are really good folks, and, if you get the job, you and I will enjoy working together."

"I'd like to do that," said Thompson. "In a few days, I'm going to Waco to visit my parents and take care of a few things, and I'll drive from there to Shreveport and look you up."

A few days later, on May 24, 1949, Hank placed a phone call from Waco.

"Charlie, this is Hank. How are you doing?

"Great, Hank, good to hear from you," was the reply. Charlie lived in Overton, Texas, and was Hank's uncle. He had just graduated from Baylor's law school and was a big country music fan.

Hank went on. "I'm in Waco but I'm driving to Shreveport tomorrow to see Hank Williams and talk to the people at *The Louisiana Hayride*. I'll be passing through Overton on the way and thought you might want to ride with me."

There was no discernable hesitation from Charlie before he accepted.

Around midday the next day, Hank and Charlie knocked on the door of the Williams residence in Shreveport and was greeted by Williams, who invited them in.

Thompson introduced Charlie to Williams and they exchanged pleasantries as Williams ushered them into the living room.

Then Audrey walked in with a roiled look and negative vibes that were immediately palpable.

"Hank was very friendly," said Thompson, "but Audrey was anything but friendly. She looked at us with a sneer that seemed to say 'What the hell are you doing here?' Of course, she was in a late stage of pregnancy and was obviously quite uncomfortable, but she made it clear to us that we were not welcome."

---

[6] This was the first child for Hank Williams and his wife, Audrey, although Audrey had another child by a previous marriage.

Audrey disappeared into the back of the house, and Williams offered Thompson and Charlie a seat in the living room, pulled out his guitar, and started singing.

Oh the blues comes around, Oh the blues comes around,
Oh the blues comes around every evening when the sun goes down.

When the song was finished, he handed the guitar to Thompson and asked him to sing *Swing Wide Your Gate of Love*, one of Williams' favorites. Thompson obliged and handed the guitar back to Williams with a request. The afternoon turned in to a songfest with Williams and Thompson taking turns with the songs between conversations about music in general and the songs in particular.

One can only hope that Uncle Charlie – either then or later in his life – appreciated the significance of what he witnessed.

In the late afternoon, Williams took Thompson to meet the station manager at KWKH and the program director of *The Louisiana Hayride*, but Hank wasn't all that thrilled.

"They made me an offer to join, but I wasn't too thrilled with it, so I turned them down," said Hank.

After the meetings, Thompson and Charlie said goodbye to Williams and headed back to Texas. The next day, Randall Williams was born, otherwise known as Hank Williams, Junior.

Soon thereafter, Hank Williams, Senior accepted an offer to join *The Grand Ole Opry*, moved to Nashville and, on June 11, 1949 he made his debut and sang *Lovesick Blues* and became the first *Opry* performer to receive six encores.

*

In the late forties, Hank Thompson and Ernest Tubb worked some jobs together and Hank was able to watch Ernest in action and came away very impressed by Ernest's attitude towards his fans.

"He got out in the audience, mingled with the fans, shook hands and signed autographs," said Hank. "And he told me something I didn't forget and have tried to practice throughout the years, 'Don't ever forget your fans, they are the ones that made it possible for you to be here.'"

During this time Hank also frequented The Ernest Tubb record store in downtown Nashville, where he knew he could often find Ernest. Ernest stepped into the role of mentor, and urged Hank to alter his career path.

"Hank, forget WLAC," said Ernest. "You need to get on WSM and *The Grand Ole Opry*. You've got a good start and some hit records and you can stay with them two or three years, build up your exposure, and then do what you want." Ernest then took Hank to meet Jim Denny, the manager of the *Opry*, and pleaded Hank's case.

"Jim, you need to put this young man on the *Opry*," said Ernest. "We need people like him." Jim agreed, the deal was done, and Hank agreed to resign from the WLAC show, become a regular member of *The Grand Ole Opry*, and make his first appearance as a member the next Saturday night.

However, Hank was not completely overjoyed over the deal since he and Dorothy, over the course of the past several months, had sensed a vibe about Nashville that just wasn't right. And, unfortunately, it had to do with the music.

In those days, the so-called "Nashville sound" revolved around unamplified acoustic stringed instruments – the guitar, banjo, dobro, mandolin, and bass fiddle – playing music from the hills of Tennessee and surrounding states. Called "rural" or "hillbilly music" by some, it eschewed drums and electrically amplified instruments, which flew in the face of Hank's vision for his type of music.

"I very much enjoyed listening to hillbilly and bluegrass music, and very much enjoyed and respected the work of Roy Acuff, Bill Monroe, and others," said Hank, "but I was not interested in playing it. I wanted to play Western Swing and modify its principles somewhat as a foundation for my vocals. This entailed amplified guitars and steel guitars, and even piano, and certainly we wanted drums. The *Opry* prohibited drums and didn't even have an amplifier on the stage before Ernest Tubb came along with his electric-guitar-driven songs, and then they put just one small amplifier on stage for his guitarist."

This incompatibility with the Nashville music was never more apparent than when Hank tried to put together a band in Nashville that he could take on the road and had a hard time finding any musicians who could play his music. Although there were plenty of banjo and mandolin players in Nashville, there were only a few accomplished steel guitar players, and even the thought of using a drummer and a piano player in a Nashville band was a rare occurrence.

Thus, even before his successful debut as a regular member of *The Grand Ole Opry*, Hank had made some phone calls to friends in Dallas, including Hal Horton. He came away confident that there was plenty of work in Texas for his kind of music. He discussed it with Dorothy and the unanimous decision was that Hank should resign from *The Grand Ole Opry*, and he and Dorothy should head for Dallas.

The Monday following Hank's one and only appearance as a regular member of the *Opry*, he, as well as the rest of the artists and musicians that also appeared that night, went to the offices of WSM to receive their checks. Hank was not expecting a large amount, but he was certainly surprised when the check was for only a little over nine dollars. As he was leaving, he ran into Hank Williams in the parking lot outside the offices. Williams had already heard the rumors that Thompson might be leaving the *Opry*.

"What's this I hear about you leaving the *Opry*?" said Williams. "You can't do that. Hell, you and I both have been dreaming about this since we were kids. Now I'm hearing that you're going to leave. Why are you leaving?"

Thompson showed Williams the check and replied, "I know I'm going to be asked that question a lot. So I'm going to frame this check and show it to anyone that asks."

Williams got a big kick out of this reply and wished him luck.

The truth of the matter was that Thompson had to cash the check to pay for gas to get back to Texas.

Hank with Ernest Tubb

Hank with Ernest Tubb

Chapter Fourteen

In the late forties, after the strike by the American Federation of Musicians ended, Capitol Records started using a popular recording studio on Melrose Avenue in Los Angeles. Hank was scheduled to record there in June 1949, and arrived in Los Angeles a few days before the scheduled sessions. When he heard that Lee Gillette was producing some sides for Tennessee Ernie Ford, and that Merle Travis was sitting in as lead guitarist, he decided to drop by the studio and look in.

When Hank came in, the session was underway and a song called *Smokey Mountain Boogie* was being recorded. Merle had tuned his guitar down to get a boogie-woogie sound and also had pocketed a pint of whiskey, which he pulled on between takes. Hank watched with interest as a take was completed; he didn't feel Merle was up to his usual high standards, probably due to the alcohol.

Neither did Lee Gillette. At the conclusion of the take, Gillette played the tape back as he commented to each musician.

"Harold, that was a great fiddle break. John, good job on the drums. Speedy, the rhythm guitar was fantastic."

He then looked at Merle, who was wearing an alcohol-induced sheepish grin and said to one of the greatest guitar players on the planet, "Travis, that was the worst God-dammed guitar chorus I ever heard in my life."

But you could say that Merle got the last laugh. In 1955, the crossover megahit *Sixteen Tons* was sung by Tennessee Ernie, produced by Gillette, recorded in the same studio, and released by Capitol. And it was written by Merle.

The next day it was Hank's turn to record. Lefty Nason had come with him to Los Angeles to man the steel, Cliffie Stone played bass, and most of the other musicians were from Cliffie's band. In addition to *Soft Lips*, a beautiful ballad written by a friend of Hank's, Walt McCoy, Hank re-recorded *Swing Wide Your Gate of Love* and *Whoa Sailor* for distribution by Capitol.

Soft Lips is especially notable since Hank suggested that Nason do the entire instrumental break, or turn-around, rather than split it with the fiddles. Nason, using

B-flat seventh tuning, rose to the occasion and turned in a performance that is still talked about by steel guitar aficionados.

"It was a masterpiece," Hank reflects, "I was amazed at the performance. I've had countless people come up to me throughout the years and say it was the greatest steel guitar piece they have ever heard."

Also recorded was *The Grass Looks Greener Over Yonder*, a song Hank wrote for an obscure female singer in Dallas. His inspiration for the song was the Red Foley song *Rockin' Chair Money*, and Hank wrote it in sevenths.

"Every chord in *The Grass Looks Greener* is a seventh with the exception of the tonic chord, said Hank. "Thus, Lefty could bring out all those pretty seventh sounds on his steel all the way through the song. It turned out to be such a good song that I decided I'd do it myself rather than give it to that girl."

Hank urged Capitol to pair *Whoa Sailor* and *Soft Lips* on a single and make it the first release from the new inventory. Capitol obliged, and it became Hank's first double-sided Top Ten single.

*

Hank and Dorothy purchased a two-bedroom home on Redondo Avenue in East Dallas and settled in. Hal Horton welcomed them back with a suggestion that Hank check out radio station KSKY in Dallas, a country music station with good coverage and a lot of live country music. A deal was made quickly and Hank was assigned the 7:05 to 7:30 A.M. slot for *The Hank Thompson Show*, broadcast live from the studio. It would essentially replicate the radio shows he had done in Waco. Hank also started scouting the Dallas area for backup musicians and began booking some personal appearances.

Soon after the move, Hank received a call from Marty Landau, the owner of the Riverside Rancho in Los Angeles, a very popular and prestigious country music club that often hosted such California artists as Spade Cooley, Tex Williams, and the Maddox Brothers and Rose. At the time, Tex Williams was appearing with a band that Spade Cooley had just fired, but Tex had to take a few weeks off to go to a recording session, and Hank got the call.

"Why don't you come out here for a few weeks, and play in front of Spade Cooley's old band," asked Marty.

"You mean the old Spade Cooley band that now works with Tex Williams?" asked Hank.

"No," was the reply. "Tex is taking that one with him. Spade just fired another band, and it will be the one backing you."

Hank accepted and flew to Los Angeles a few days before his opening so that he could rehearse with Spade Cooley's fired band number two.

"Boy, were they good!" said Hank, referring to the musicians. "Vic Davis was playing piano and later joined The Brazos Valley Boys. Speedy West had just taken up the steel, and they had two good fiddlers and a terrific drummer. Speedy and I were about the same age and became fast friends. It was a very enjoyable time, and the pay was great."

Hank also got to watch Tex Williams and his band at the Riverside Rancho before they left for their recording session, and Hank noticed that they were decked out in snazzy uniforms that looked different from any thing he had ever seen. He asked Tex where they got them.

"Well, there's a new tailor in town," replied Tex, "and his name is Nudie."

*

Nudie Cohn had emigrated from the Ukraine before opening a shop in Times Square in New York City called *Nudies for Ladies* where he had made and sold costumes and G-strings for the fan-dancers, strippers, and chorus girls in New York. A five-foot, seven- inch bundle of personality with oversize ambition and a love of the limelight, he had moved to Los Angeles with his eye on the glamour of Hollywood. He hung out at the Riverside Rancho, quickly made friends with Tex Williams, and persuaded Tex to sell a horse and saddle and use the money to purchase him a sewing machine. Nudie set up shop in his garage and made western suits for Tex on a ping-pong table. But they were not ordinary western suits. They were adorned with forests of fringe, and embroidered with symphonies of sparkling oversize G clefs, among other designs, in colors that made pink look conservative. And they were absolutely stunning.

Tex was ecstatic with the results and made a point of giving Nudie a plug with all of his colleagues in the music business. Nudie then opened a store in North Hollywood in 1947 and became a pioneer in making country seem cool from a fashion standpoint.

Tex continued with his pitch to Hank.

"He's a little Jewish fellow out in the valley. He moved to Los Angeles recently and is a big country music fan. He came up to me after one of my shows and asked me where I got my western suit and how much it cost. I told him that a guy named Turk made it for me and it cost $125. He said that was too much money and offered to make me a better one for less money. You're looking at it and it cost about $40. You should give him a call."

Even though Turk, a well-known tailor in the industry, made Hank's wedding suit, Hank was intrigued by the new tailor in town. Before he left California, Hank went by the store, was impressed with Nudie and his effusive personality, ordered his first suit, and became his second customer. A friendship and business relation began that had a far-reaching effect.

"I bought a lot of clothes from Nudie," recalled Hank. At one time I was probably his second best customer behind Roy Rogers. Later, the fans not only appreciated a variety of the colorful wardrobes, they started *expecting* it."

Later, Nudie added galaxies of rhinestones to his suits, and, in addition to outfitting a great number of music and movie stars, he graduated to customizing cars in the same style. The Nudiemobiles would give the modern-day Department of Homeland Security apoplexy, since they included six-shooters for door handles and rifles affixed to the trunk and fenders. Also, steer horns were on the hood, hand-tooled leather saddles were placed between the front seats for young cowpokes, and rare silver dollars adorned nearly every surface of the interior. Needless to say, the customer profile for this type of garishness had to be a special type of egomaniac. Webb Pierce became a proud owner.

Chapter Fifteen

As Hank was trying to gain traction in Dallas, he made friends with, and received some career advice from, Rex Allen. Rex had started his career as a singer with *The WLS Barn Dance* in Chicago, one of the most popular and longest running shows on radio, and was in Dallas to promote his first movie. He suggested that Hank consider joining the *Barn Dance* and arranged an interview with George Biggars, the head honcho. Hank went to Chicago and spent an afternoon at the station talking to George and was offered a spot on the *Barn Dance*, and he told George he would consider it.

With this offer, it was time for Hank to make an assessment of his career to date. The past several months had drastically changed the landscape. With the success of *Humpty Dumpty Heart*, the recording of several new songs with a national label, and the completion of a successful engagement at a prestigious club in California, Hank knew he had reached a new plateau which opened up many opportunities. He just wasn't sure which one to take.

He could move to California where he had already enjoyed considerable success and be near the Capitol recording studios. He could join *The WLS Barn Dance* and establish a base in Chicago. He was confident that *The Louisiana Hayride* would renew their offer if he agreed to move to Shreveport. He was intrigued by the east coast, and especially its large population density, and felt he could establish a base there. Or, of course, he could stay in the Southwest, in Texas or Oklahoma, which was more centered between the west coast and the east coast, and where he had already established a growing fan base. The bottom line was that it was critical that he go in the right direction. In the meantime, he decided to continue to operate out of Dallas with his radio show and personal appearances until he was sure which way to go. One comforting factor was that his recent successes gave him confidence that he could earn a living as a country music singer.

His confidence was boosted at the end of the decade when Billboard announced its third annual Disc Jockey Poll in 1949, covering 414 disc jockeys nationally. Hank came in number 5 in the country music singer category, following Eddy Arnold, Red Foley, Hank Williams and Jimmy Wakely.

*

The KSKY studios were located at the fifth floor of the Stoneleigh Hotel in Dallas and were not exactly a beehive of activity during Hank's 7:00 A.M. live radio shows. In fact, Hank and John Hitt, the engineer, were the only ones in the studio. When Hank was not on the air, John would handle the station breaks and announcements and play the taped commercials.

One day when he was on the air, Hank noticed that John would pass the time by looking intently out the window with a pair of binoculars trained at a building next door. Hank asked what was going on.

"This building is full of young career women that work in the downtown area, most of whom are very good looking," replied John. "At this time of day they are showering and getting dressed."

When Hank broke for the next commercial, John started the first taped commercial, handed Hank the binoculars, and said, "Check out the fourth floor, third window from the left". As Hank took the binoculars, John went back to the engineer board and started cueing commercials. A few minutes later, after he cued the last commercial, he looked over at Hank.

Hank handed the binoculars to John and, with a big grin, said, "Fifth floor, second window from the right."

A routine developed.

*

During this time, Tennessee Ernie Ford was riding high with two recent hit records, *Shotgun Boogie* and *Mule Train*. His manager got in touch with Hank and suggested a tour through the Southwest, with Ernie and Hank headlining. At the time, on some jobs at larger venues, Hank had been using a Dallas-based Western Swing band, *Bob Manning and The Riders of the Silver Sage*. The band was a natural to back Hank and Ernie on the tour, which covered several states in the Southwest and was a big success. Bob Manning was more a figurehead than a musician, and Billy Gray, a young vocalist who played rhythm guitar, headed the band.

Gray, born in 1924 in Paris, Texas, had origins similar to Hank's. He had worked to buy himself a guitar, and, by age fifteen, was good enough to be doing some part-time performing on his hometown radio station. By the time he was nineteen, he had a full-blown radio show over KPLT in Paris. He had organized his own band and worked around Dallas before joining *The Riders of the Silver Sage*. During the tour with Tennessee Ernie, Hank quickly became aware of Billy's considerable talents.

This led to a conversation that turned out to be very important to both men.

"You know," Billy said to Hank, "we've really been doing good business on this tour, which demonstrates that there are many great opportunities throughout the

72

entire Southwest for Western Swing. Your style is well suited to Western Swing, and what you need is a band behind you that plays it well."

Hank was on the same wavelength. "I've been giving this some thought, too," he replied, "and that's exactly what I want to do. But, if I'm going to do it, I want to get great musicians, I want to rehearse the hell out of them, and I want to be the best."

Gray nodded with approval since he also believed in a tight, highly disciplined band. And he loved to rehearse.

Chapter Sixteen

With the radio show going well, Hank was concentrating on his public appearances and decided to hire two musicians on a permanent basis to back him up on the road and on the radio show. The first call he made was to Lefty Nason in Waco, who agreed to move to Dallas and join Hank. Hank also hired bassist Pee Wee Reed away from The Riders of the Silver Sage. He gave them fifty dollars a week for the radio show and extra for weekend duty. With this nucleus, it was fairly easy to complete a band by adding other musicians on a job-by-job basis. For example, Hank hired Billy Walker, a very good vocalist, rhythm guitarist and front man. Billy was also from Waco but was in Dallas at the time, and Hank used him quite often. Also hired on an as-needed basis was a female musician, Ludy Harris, who sang, played drums, guitar, and even did comedy – whatever was needed for a given show.

In June of 1950, Hank was at the studio at radio station WBAP in Fort Worth for two days of recording sessions, with Capitol's Lee Gillette at the helm. Since Lee was about to discontinue producing country sessions (except for Tennessee Ernie Ford) in favor of Nat King Cole and other Capitol pop artists, this was to be his last session with Hank.

Gillette obviously wanted to shove Hank into the country boogie craze growing in popularity on both coasts.

"The boogie things had gotten pretty popular," Hank said, referring to the success of such hits as Tennessee Ernie Ford's *Shot Gun Boogie*, "so I decided to do one called *The Humpty Dumpty Boogie*, just a little novelty song. It didn't particularly succeed commercially, but the twin fiddles on the chorus were excellent."

How Do You Feel, a typically sentimental number of the period, was recorded and stands up today as one of Hank's best ballads. Another track was *Daddy Blues*, Hank's version of a Jimmie Rodgers-style blue yodel, with a melody that was different than a typical Rodgers' melody, but one that possessed much of the same spirit. Hank was delighted to record a song in this style.

"Back in the earlier days, I didn't know anybody who didn't like Jimmie Rodgers," recalled Hank. "He was an idol of everybody I knew in the music business. And many of them liked to think that they alone should be the one who carried on the Rodgers legacy.

"For example, I remember Ernest Tubb did a lot of Jimmie Rodgers' stuff and was proud that he could emulate him. But Ernest did not like the fact that Gene Autry sounded like Jimmy. Also, when Merle Travis recorded Jimmy's *Blue Yodel No 1*, *(T for Texas)*, and had a huge hit on it in South Africa, of all places, Ernest commented that Merle should stick to picking, not singing Jimmie Rodgers. Then Bob Wills told me he resented Ernest's claim to the Rodgers' legacy. He even made the comment that 'Nobody can sing like Jimmie Rodgers. That man could *sing*. In comparison, Ernest Tubb sounds like a bull braying in a pasture.' *Daddy Blues* was, in effect, my tribute to Jimmie although I never was much of a yodeler. And that was my only attempt at some kind of a blue yodel."

Soon after the recording session, a personal appearance found Hank playing at a park just outside San Antonio. Cary Rodgers, Jimmie Rodgers wife, came to see Hank, and Hank told her what a big fan he was of Jimmy, a fact she already knew.

"Would you like to have his records?" asked Cary.

"What do you mean?" asked Hank.

"I had all of his recordings transferred to acetate," explained Cary, "and I would like to give them to you."

"I'd give the world for those records," was Hank's reply.

A few days later, Hank received a big package from San Antonio. It contained an acetate version of every recording Jimmy Rodgers ever made, a remarkable collection that Hank treasures to this day.

"I never saw Jimmie Rodgers in person," said Hank, "but I knew all of his songs by heart. His guitar was always in perfect tune, and his voice was right on. He was, without a doubt, my favorite singer of all time."

*

As Hank ramped up his personal appearance schedule, he asked John Hitt (of binoculars fame) to assist him in the bookings. John went over to Hank's house and Hank started mentoring him in the art of booking jobs, with the understanding that the goal was to graduate to the much more lucrative honky-tonks, clubs and dance halls as soon as possible.

In the meantime, Hank and Billy Gray continued their discussions regarding forming a full-time, expanded Western Swing band. Despite being aware that this type of music was not the most popular in many areas of the country, they were confident that the market demand was more than sufficient in the Southwest, Rocky Mountains and Pacific Northwest. They also felt that they could put together a group that was not only good, but great; and Hank soon committed to put a full complement of musicians, including Gray, on a salary.

Western Swing has been defined as "jazz played by musicians dressed in white hats and cowboy boots, and using steel guitars and fiddles." And these were exactly the type of musicians that Hank and Billy were looking for in their selection and hiring of musicians. Lefty Nason and Pee Wee Reed were no-brainers at steel guitar and stand-up bass, respectively, since they were already on the payroll. Gray, of course, would be the band-leader and play rhythm guitar, which eliminated Billy

Walker who went his separate way.[7] Wade Wood, one of the better fiddle players in Dallas at the time, accepted an offer to play fiddle. Then, they solidified their rejection of the Nashville sound in favor of Western Swing and hired a drummer. Wayne Foster got the nod, and the first full, formal, rendition of The Brazos Valley Boys was born. Hank was now the owner of a business.

Billy Gray started rehearsing the band with the much-anticipated goal of carving out a distinctive Western Swing-based sound of their own.

"In one respect, we wanted to sound like Leon McAuliffe[8], who had a highly disciplined band," said Hank, "and not like Bob Wills, who had a highly undisciplined band. Although Bob had a few songs, such as *Faded Love* and *San Antonio Rose* that were rehearsed and followed a set arrangement, a great majority of Bob's arrangements, especially during live shows, were simply determined by Bob pointing his fiddle bow at one of the musicians during the song, meaning that he would take the next chorus. This was not what we wanted to do."

Hank and Billy also agreed that they wanted to get a sound out of the fiddles that was different than Wills' – something between the sophistication of Spade Cooley's sound and the raw stuff that some bands were playing.

There was another change that Hank and Billy wanted to make, and it had to do with the vocals. All of the major country and popular bands at the time, including Glenn Miller, Tommy Dorsey, Charlie Spivak, Benny Goodman, Bob Wills, Spade Cooley, and Leon McAuliffe, were using a "lead" singer who simply blended in with the instruments, and, as such, became just another instrument.

"Another thing I didn't like about the Bob Wills' sound," said Hank, "was that the vocalist sang with a heavy background of instruments, especially the lead guitar, not unlike a popular-music, big-band approach. The trouble with that was that the background instrumentation would often drown out the vocals. When I'd listen to Tommy Duncan sing a song live with the Wills band, there would be all of this 'butterfly' guitar and other instruments in the background, and with Bob's hollering on top of it, I often couldn't hear Tommy's words.

"I wanted to change that concept to where it was Hank Thompson, the singer," said Hank, "with a good band behind me that had a Western Swing flavor."

One of the first projects for the new version of The Brazos Valley Boys was to commission Nudie to make western outfits for every band member. Although not as elaborate as Hank's suits, the band uniforms consisted of tasteful and highly colorful western pants and shirts.

*

Red Novac, a fan and friend of Hank, owned a music store in Houston and became the go-to guy for instruments and accessories for Hank and the band. At one of Hank's appearances in Houston, Red approached him with a suggestion.

"Hank, looks like you need a new guitar," said Red, as he looked at the battle worn J-200. "I can get you a new one through Gibson, and they will probably let you have it at a very good price."

---

[7] Billy Walker went on to become a star in his own right and scored several hit songs.

[8] Leon, a former steel guitarist for Bob Wills, became a very popular bandleader out of Tulsa and a purveyor of Western Swing.

"OK," said Hank. "See what you can do."

A few weeks later, Hank became the proud owner of a new J-200 with a sunburst finish and paid a reduced price, courtesy of Gibson. This guitar became his regular performing and recording guitar. He retired the original J-200 and kept it at home for back-up duty.

*

Two recording sessions were held in late 1950 and early 1951 at the WBAP studio, and in Pappy Sellers' Dallas studio, respectively. Capitol had established a Nashville office headed by Dee Kilpatrick, who was picked to produce the sessions. Notable songs that were recorded included the low-keyed weeper *If I Cry* along with two other strong ballads – *Where Is Your Heart Tonight*, and *Those Things Money Can't Buy*. *Hangover Heart* brought the tempo up slightly and *I Ain't Cryin' Over You*, completed the job, its bouncy arrangement a nod to the Thompson sound.

Kilpatrick brought a song entitled *Playin' Possum* to the session and told Hank that Lee Gillette wanted Hank to record it. Hank didn't like it and suspected that the fact that Gillette's buddy, Cliffie Stone, was a co-writer undoubtedly had much to do with Gillette's suggestion. At any rate, it was recorded.

Hank had written a ballad called *The Devil In My Angel's Eyes* that was recorded but never released by Capitol, one of only two unreleased numbers.

"I always liked that song, and they never released it," said Hank, "and so we had Sue Thompson record it. She did a real good job. That song was better than a lot of those others and a hell of a lot better than *Playin Possum!*"

In this time period, there were some changes to The Brazos Valley Boys. Billy Briggs Stewart took over the standup bass fiddle. Better known as "Round Boy", he had first played with Hank on the June 1950, recording session at WBAP, was very personable and likeable, and contributed significantly to the band chemistry for his next nine years as a Brazos Valley Boy. Also, Gil Baca was hired who was an excellent pianist and had a physical attribute that distinguished him in another category (more on this later). But the most far-reaching change of all was the graduation to twin fiddles. Big Red Hayes and Johnny Manson did the honors, replacing Wade Wood. For the next decade, Hank was never without at least two fiddles, and sometimes used three.

Chapter Seventeen

In the mid-forties, a Texas musician by the name of Jimmy Heap formed a country band with some of his buddies in Taylor, Texas, and started playing dances throughout Texas. They released a couple of records on a small label before joining Imperial records in 1948 as one of the first country artists on that label.

In 1950, their piano player teamed up with a friend to write a song which met an enthusiastic response on their road jobs, and it became their first A-side release for Imperial in 1950. However, Imperial's distribution was limited to the Southwest, and the sound quality of the recording was very poor. Despite this, the song was getting some air and jukebox play in the Southwest and, according to Heap, about 10,000 records were sold, "real fast."

During this time Dorothy heard the song several times on the Dallas country radio stations and talked to Hank about it.

"Hank, you've got to hear this song," said Dorothy. "It's by Jimmy Heap and the Melody Masters from Taylor, Texas, and it is being played around Dallas. It has a great line that goes like this: 'I didn't know God made honky-tonk angels'. You should record it."

"O.K, I'll listen for it," replied Hank.

*

In June of 1951, Hank brought The Brazos Valley Boys to Pappy Sellers' studio in Dallas to record four songs under the guidance of Dee Kilpatrick: *You Were The Cause Of It All*, *I'll Be Your Sweetheart For A Day*, *Love Thief*, and *Teardrops On The Tea Leaves*. Hank was the writer or co-writer on each.

Unfortunately, after the session, Lefty Nason quit the band and moved back to Waco after selling his pedal steel guitar to his replacement, Dusty Stewart. Lefty certainly left his mark with his trademarked style and creative fills that were mimicked, at Hank's request, by each and every steel guitar player who played for Hank for the next fifty years.

During this time, Dorothy heard that Jimmy Heap was in Dallas recording some new songs at a studio in Dallas. She went to the studio and asked Jimmy for a copy of the record of the song about the "honky-tonk angels". She took it home and played it for Hank.

After the song finished playing, Hank said, "It's OK. This guy has taken the same melody that has already been used in two songs – *Great Speckled Bird* and *I'm Dreaming Tonight of My Blue Eyes* and put in completely new lyrics. I do like that line in the chorus, 'I didn't know God made honky-tonk angels'. But what a terrible-quality recording!"

*

In the meantime, Hank and Billy Gray had the new version of The Brazos Valley Boys in high gear. Dressed in their new uniforms and well rehearsed with precise and creative arrangements, Hank and the band started cutting a swath through the dance-halls and clubs in Texas and Oklahoma with their version of Western Swing.

Usually, the arrangement with the club owners was that Hank would get a percentage of the door, with no guarantee. This worked out well for both parties, especially when they drew good crowds, which was often. Houston, Amarillo, Lubbock, San Antonio, Austin and many other Texas cities and towns were very receptive; but Hank was surprised and disappointed that this was not the case in Dallas/Ft. Worth, largely because he was perceived as just another local artist. However, there were exceptions to the exception.

Beginning in 1948, radio KRLD in Dallas (Hal Horton's old stomping grounds) started broadcasting its *Big D Jamboree*, a Dallas-based barn dance and radio program that built on the success of *The Grand Ole Opry* and Chicago's *National Barn Dance*. The *Jamboree* aired from The Sportatorium, a converted wrestling arena at the corner of Cadiz and Industrial boulevards, a center of country music nightclubs in Dallas at the time. The original metal building of The Sportatorium was noted for its octagonal design and also for its huge seating capacity, with the stage in the center. In addition to the *Big D Jamboree* on Saturday nights and wrestling on Tuesday nights, other special events were booked. One such event was a special country music show in 1951. The show's promoter should be enshrined in the promoter's hall of fame, based solely on this show. Hank Williams, Hank Thompson, Hank Snow, and Ernest Tubb all appeared on the same night. It was the only appearance by the three Hanks on the same show, and Ernest was icing on the cake. The show was a huge success despite a sound system that Hank still hasn't forgotten.

"It was a terrible place to play," said Hank. "The sound reflected off the metal roof and walls back to the stage in the center. It was so bad it was almost unbearable."

That evening, Hank and Ernest Tubb were having a sip or two between shows, and talking shop.

"Boy, Hank Williams hit it big with *Cold Cold Heart*," said Ernest.

"He sure did," said Hank.

"But that's the same damn melody as *You'll Still Be in My Heart* that my friend

80

T. Texas Tyler recorded a while back," said Ernest. "I asked Williams about that not long ago, and he said 'I wrote the lyrics and Fred Rose[9] helped me with the melody'".

*

In late 1951, all the planets aligned to create a career-defining opportunity for Hank. During the year, Hank had received a tremendous response from the clubs and dance halls in Oklahoma, especially from the Trianon Ballroom, a landmark dance hall in downtown Oklahoma City.

At the time, Bob Wills was based out of The Trianon but was in the process of moving to Dallas to work at his own ballroom, The Bob Wills Ranch House, and start a radio show on the Texas Quality Network. Thus, Lucky Moeller, who ran the Trianon, needed a steady headliner. He approached Hank, confirmed that Wills was leaving, and asked Hank to consider making his base in Oklahoma City and playing out of the Trianon. The prospect was attractive to Hank for several reasons:

- There was a cornucopia of opportunities for bookings in several cities and towns in Oklahoma within a short drive from Oklahoma City.
- They would be closer to Kansas and other states north of Oklahoma as well as California and the east coast.
- They would not be too far from Texas.

However, Bob Wills had set a high standard; and formidable competition was waiting in Oklahoma City with Leon McAuliffe and Johnny Lee Wills in Tulsa, and Merle Lindsey in Oklahoma City, each of which led a very popular Western Swing band.

Three Hanks

---

[9] Fred Rose was a co-owner of Acuff-Rose Music, a highly-successful Nashville-based music publishing company that had Hank Williams for a client. Rose was also a successful songwriter and served as a mentor and record producer to Williams and, at the very least, "helped" Williams with the melodies to many of his songs.

But Hank and Billy Gray were ready to do battle.

"The Brazos Valley Boys were fairly well seasoned at the time, and I felt we could do well despite the competition," said Hank.

Since Bob Wills was leaving at the end of 1951, Hank and Dorothy decided to move to Oklahoma City in early 1952 and make the Trianon his base.

*

Hank and the Capitol people agreed that Hank's future recording sessions should be at Capitol's studio in Los Angeles, and Hank made a point to schedule the sessions in December each year. This decision made sense since there was not a lot happening that time of the year in the Southwest, and, with the good weather in California, some jobs could be scheduled around the recording sessions. With a session coming up in December 1951, Hank started thinking about songs to record. He had written an up-tempo number, *Crying in the Deep Blue Sea*, earlier in the year and was looking forward to recording it since he felt that it had hit potential. Also, Billy Gray brought an idea for a song to Hank and they ended up co-writing *Waiting in the Lobby of Your Heart*. A ballad entitled *Don't Make Me Cry Again* was also in the works.

In November, Hank booked Pappy Sellers' studio in Dallas to record some audition, or demo, discs of these songs prior to the session in Los Angeles. In this manner, all concerned could listen to the playbacks and hopefully improve on the arrangements before the Capitol session in Los Angeles.

"I felt it was very important to work out the exact arrangements to be used on the record in advance of the final recording session," said Hank. "Often the playback would reveal that the arrangement was not as good as we thought, and sometimes it would turn out better than we thought. We ended up doing this before nearly every Capitol recording session in the early years."

A day or two before the scheduled session at Pappy's, Dorothy again reminded Hank of the Jimmy Heap song about the honky-tonk angels.

"This song is getting more and more popular in this area," said Dorothy, "and it suits you very much with the honky-tonk flavor. Plus, the Heap recording sounds scratchy and distorted. If you came out with a well-recorded Capitol version, it could really sell."

Hank wasn't convinced, but he agreed to record it, at least at the demo session. But there was another problem with the song in addition to the borrowed melody. The song had three verses plus a chorus, which made it too long to be radio-friendly. Since he didn't particularly like the second and third verses, he sat down with pen, paper and guitar and went to work.

"What I did," said Hank, "was to rewrite the second and third verses into just one single verse. The first verse and chorus were not changed."

The rewritten second verse went like this:

The glamour of the gay nightlife has lured you,
To the places where the wine and liquor flow,
Where you wait to be anybody's baby,
And forget the truest love you'll ever know.

The song, entitled *The Wild Side of Life*, was one of the demos that were recorded.

A few weeks later, Ken Nelson, Hank's new producer, greeted Hank and the band at the Capitol Studio in Los Angeles. Ken, a former Chicago singer, musician and radio announcer, had moved from Capitol's transcription division to handling country (and some pop) A&R.

The Brazos Valley Boys were all there, and Hank and Billy Gray were moving quickly toward a definable, distinctive sound. One of the band's additional strengths was a new steel guitarist, Harold Lee "Curly" Chalker, who replaced Dusty Stewart and who had worked with Blackie Crawford's band, The Western Cherokees, both before and after the Cherokees became Lefty Frizzell's backup unit.

Three songs were initially cut – Crying in the Deep Blue Sea, Waiting in the Lobby of Your Heart, and Don't Make Me Cry Again. Everyone agreed that Crying in the Deep Blue Sea had strong hit possibilities, and should be the A side of Hank's next release. Afterwards, a few minutes were left on the session, and Hank had an idea.

"Ken asked if there was anything else I could do in the few remaining minutes of the session, and I decided to play him the demo that we did of The Wild Side of Life. I told him that the Jimmy Heap recording was very popular in Texas but that, although I liked the 'honky-tonk angel' reference in the chorus, I was concerned about the borrowed melody."

Ken listened and said that he agreed with Hank on both counts. And then he said, "Oh hell, we've got about ten minutes, let's try to do it. Besides, we need something to put on the B side of Crying in the Deep Blue Sea."

About five minutes later, after they listened to the playback of the first take, Hank looked at Ken and said, "We can do it again but I don't think we can do it any better than that."

"I agree," said Ken. "Let's go with it."

In 1996, Bear Family Records issued a box set of all of the original recordings of the 324 songs that Hank made for Capitol. On the recording of The Wild Side of Life they included Ken Nelson's studio remarks announcing the song.

"The Wild Side of Life, take one," Ken is heard saying.

He could have rephrased this to say, "The Wild Side of Life, the one and only take."

*

Hank played several jobs at Danceland in Ft. Worth owned by Jimmy Blevins, who had a well-earned reputation of trying to short-change (literally) every person he dealt with. Hank was to get the entire door; and he asked John Hitt, who was still serving as Hank's booking agent/manager, to go with him to the job and monitor the door to make sure Blevins didn't try any fast ones. John had already dealt with Blevins and was well aware of his reputation.

After the show, Hank and John went to Blevins office to collect the money. As expected, Blevins started hemming and hawing.

John noticed a gun on Blevins desk, picked it up and said, "Blevins, you should file the site down on this barrel."

"What for?" was the reply.

"That way it won't hurt so bad when someone shoves it up your ass."

Full payment was received immediately.

Chapter Eighteen

As The Brazos Valley Boys were settling in with the Western Swing sound on the road, Hank was not happy with some of the arrangements, so he arranged a short meeting with Gray and the rest of the band.

"You guys are sounding too much like Bob Wills," said Hank. "I noticed the other night that when I was not on stage, a great majority of songs that you did were Bob Wills songs played the same way they play them. Hell, there's a Bob Wills type band in a honky-tonk in every town in Texas, Oklahoma, California, and all the states in between. And I'm not hiring The Brazos Valley Boys to be another Bob Wills band. We want to make The Brazos Valley Boys distinctive, with the arrangements that we talked about and have been rehearsing. There are plenty of songs by many others that you can play. As a matter of fact, you should not emulate anyone. Rather, each band member should just be himself, yet follow the arrangements that you rehearsed. From now on, lose all the Bob Wills arrangements except *Steel Guitar Rag* and *San Antonio Rose*."

End of meeting.

*

Hank and The Brazos Valley Boys had worked the *Big D Jamboree* in Dallas on a Saturday night, and had the next few days off. Hank, Gray and Round Boy decided to meet at Hank's house on Sunday and take their wives fishing for a few days. On Sunday, as they were loading Hank's station wagon at Hank's house, Gray made a suggestion.

"Ace, go grab your old guitar. We may get an idea for a song at the lake."

Hank went in and got his original J-200, brought it out in its case, and set it on the ground while the others finished packing. Several minutes later, when the packing was finished, everybody jumped into the car, Hank put it in reverse, starting backing out of the driveway, and ran over the case containing the guitar. Unlike the time when it was injured and brought back to life by the skilled surgeons on an island in the South Pacific, this time the old guitar suffered an instant death.

If there had been an obituary for the guitar, it would have read something like this:

This fine guitar was born in the Gibson Guitar factory in Kalamazoo, Michigan in early 1941 and shipped to a music store in Waco, Texas, later that year. It was purchased by Hank Thompson, an aspiring young country singer at the time, and it appeared with Mr. Thompson on his daily radio show in Waco before traveling overseas and contributing to the United States war effort by helping to entertain the troops in the islands of the South Pacific. After the war, it also accompanied Mr. Thompson on two other radio shows in Waco, at many personal appearances, and on numerous recordings by Mr. Thompson, including two number-one songs. This grand guitar met an untimely death in 1951 at the hands of a large rear wheel of a moving vehicle. It is survived by Mr. Thompson and several family members known as The Brazos Valley Boys.

*

As Hank and Dorothy were preparing to move to Oklahoma City, John Hitt informed them that he was not interested in moving. Hank and Billy Gray approached the Capitol record distributor in Oklahoma City, and offered him the job of manager/booking agent.

"He considered it," said Hank, "but he said 'I just don't know that part of the business – I'd be overstepping my bounds.' Gray and I were disappointed because we felt sure he'd take the job."

Gray then suggested a young man in Kansas by the name of Jim Halsey who had promoted Hank in various towns throughout Kansas, Missouri, Oklahoma and Arkansas, and who often went along with The Brazos Valley Boys to the jobs. Billy reminded Hank of the good job that Jim did. Hank agreed, picked up the phone, and called him.

"We're playing the Trianon Ballroom Saturday night," Hank told Jim after laying out the job opening. "Come on down Saturday afternoon and we'll get together and talk about it."

When he got the call from Hank, Jim was twenty years old and attending Independence (Kansas) Junior College. In addition to booking music acts, he was booking plays and other acts at the local Memorial Hall and had worked a little with a wrestling promoter.

On the Saturday in question, they met at the Biltmore Hotel in downtown Oklahoma City, and Hank outlined his vision for himself and The Brazos Valley Boys. He then asked Jim if he would be interested in serving as Hank's booking agent and manager. Jim answered with a question.

"When do I start?"

"January 1."

Although neither Hank nor Jim could appreciate it at the time, this began a personal and business relationship between the two men that was one of the most important in each of their respective careers and one that lasted for the next fifty years.

*

In early 1952, Hank and Dorothy packed up and moved to Oklahoma City, taking residence on North May Avenue. Hank was very pleased when all of The Brazos Valley Boys also made the move.

One of Hank's first projects in the new home was to set up a recording studio so that he and the band could rehearse and make demo recordings of songs prior to the recording sessions in Los Angeles. He set up six mikes in his living room and the adjacent dining room, and ran cables from the mikes through a closet, up to the attic and down to the den and into a mixing board. He purchased a state-of-the-art Ampex tape recorder and connected it to the output of the mixing board. The band set up in the living room and the dining room and the doors leading to the den were closed. During the recordings, Dorothy monitored the tape recorder and kept the proper levels during the recordings. Nearly every song that Hank released on Capitol records in that era was prerecorded at Hank's house in this manner.

Soon after Hank and Dorothy made their move, Jim Halsey also moved to Oklahoma City, although he kept his previous home and office in Independence. One of his first projects was to buy a large map and systematically plot the areas, states, and cities that he wanted to cover during his first year with Hank. His goal was to book Hank in as many states as practicable. "I read the trade journals (at that time, *Billboard*, *Down Beat*, and *Metronome* magazines), and, whenever I saw a band or attraction playing, I would write the name of the venue in a notebook I carried," said Jim. "This became the beginning of my database of prospective buyers for Hank. Then I sought out the venues, made the phone calls, put together a press kit, and sent it to each buyer. When I booked a job, I prepared the contracts that were usually typed on my Smith-Corona portable typewriter."

His efforts were aided by the history – albeit short – that Hank had with many of the honky-tonk, club and dance hall owners in the Southwest and California.

"One important thing was that Hank handed me a list of club owners and other buyers that he had already played for, and they turned out to be satisfied customers," Jim recalls

Jim also accompanied Hank and The Brazos Valley Boys on most of their road trips, and it didn't take long for him to make a very positive impression. Hank was delighted with the energy, vision and aptitude that Jim displayed, and the number and quality of the bookings increased significantly.

*

One evening, the two Hanks – Williams and Thompson – worked a job together and were chatting backstage between sets. By that time Thompson, and everybody else associated with country music, was well aware of Williams' drinking problem. Williams wasn't the least bit shy about detailing his difficulties to his friend, including the many binges, arrests, and visits to rehab centers, as well as the efforts of his mother, Lillian, and his wife, Audrey, to keep him sober. For, example, he told an interesting story to Thompson about the time Lillian literally dragged him, in a drunken state, into a hospital in Montgomery, and checked him in to dry out.

"By a stroke of luck, an old girl friend and fan of mine worked the night shift as a nurse at the hospital," Williams told Thompson. "She supplied me with all the liquor I needed. Then, later on each night she would also provide all the companionship I needed between the sheets. Best rehab I ever had. Three days later, Lillian came to pick me up at the hospital and was shocked at my condition. She went up to the nurse's station and shouted, 'What the hell's going on? He's been here three days and he's drunker now than when I brought him in!'"

"I was well aware of Hank Williams' drinking problems," recalled Thompson. "But during the four years that I knew him, including several jobs that we worked together and the times that I visited him in his home and his bachelor apartment, he was as sober as a judge. In fact, I never saw him take a drink. He fought it about as hard as any alcoholic could; but when he did relent, he apparently went way, way off the deep end.

"Also, I never saw him *eat* anything either, although there were many occasions when we were together when he had the opportunity to do so. He would go to restaurants and cafes with others and me, but I never saw him order anything to eat. He was very thin to begin with, and I don't know what kept him alive during that period."

Chapter Nineteen

Despite the increased influx of money from the record royalties and the expanded personal appearance schedule, Hank was concerned about the other side of the ledger, including travel expenses and the costs of the Nudie suits and the bus.

" I was making good money," said Hank, "but I was spending a hell of lot trying to build a reputation. I worried that I was trying to be big-time before I arrived. But I kept investing in the business, knowing, or at least hoping, that it would pay off in the future."

And indeed it did – in the *near* future. The first record from the previous December sessions was released in February 1952, with *Crying in the Deep Blue Sea* promoted as the A side. The song took off well on the radio and got a lot of jukebox play. Although it was impossible to distinguish between the A and B sides as far as jukebox play was concerned, the radio play was much in favor of *Crying in the Deep Blue Sea* over the B side, *The Wild Side of Life*.

The other two songs from the previous December recording sessions – *Waiting in the Lobby of Your Heart* and *Don't Make me Cry Again* – were about to be released when the Capitol people called Hank and told him of a phenomenon that was taking place.

The Wild Side of Life had surpassed *Crying in the Deep Blue Sea* as far as radio play, and was beginning to take a life of its own. Also, the jukebox play of the two-sided record was increasing significantly. When *Wild Side* debuted on the charts in March 1952, it was decided that the scheduled March release of *Waiting in the Lobby of Your Heart* and *Don't Make me Cry Again* should be delayed until it could be determined exactly what was going on.

The next few months proved to be some of the most exhilarating of Hank's career as he watched *Wild Side* surge to number one on the Billboard national chart on March 15th. It held that position for fifteen weeks, and stayed on the charts for a total of thirty weeks.

"Nobody was any more surprised than me," commented Hank.

Thus, *The Wild Side of Life* became the third hit song with the same melody.

(Later Johnny Cash made it four versions of the melody when he recorded a song entitled "Flushed from the Bathroom of Your Heart" for his *Live at Folsom Prison* album with a set of lyrics that can only be termed a farce. This version did not become a hit.)

The delayed release of *Waiting in the Lobby of Your Heart* backed with *Don't Make Me Cry Again* occurred in May, and *Lobby* took off well before peaking at number three on the Billboard chart in June, the same time that *Wild Side* was still at number one.

The success of *Wild Side* resulted in some notoriety for Jimmy Heap, who suddenly became semi-famous as the act with the first recorded version of the song.

"We put the song out on the Imperial label, which was a small label then," said Heap in an interview, "and didn't have much distribution. It was good in Texas but that was about all. Texas was the only place we sold it because Hank Thompson picked it up, did it on Capitol, and covered us up with it."

It is interesting to note that, later on, Heap also cut some records for Capitol under the tutelage of Ken Nelson and recorded another notable song entitled *Release Me*, that sold fairly well before Ray Price recorded it in 1954 and sent it up the charts.

The success of *Wild Side* also caused Jim Halsey to practically pinch himself in disbelief. He was barely out of his teens, he had been on the job only a few weeks, and his first and only client now had the number one song in the country. But he rose to the occasion. With an adroit view of the entire playing field, he further expanded the bookings, and was able to get larger fees for nearly each job, albeit in relatively small increments. More importantly, he was earnestly exploring new frontiers for Hank.

As the bookings continued to increase, Hank traded one of the station wagons for a Buick Roadmaster, which he drove to all the jobs. And he had an idea for improving the travel for the band.

In the early fifties, a bus line called the *Las Vegas-Tonopah-Carson City-Reno Stage Line* was operating several twenty-one passenger, short base, *Flexible* brand buses between these cities. The buses were several feet shorter than the standard buses of that era, largely because there were no interstate highways running between these cities at the time, and the buses had to negotiate relatively small, winding, mountain roads. Hence, the short base.

Hank heard that the line was selling off some of the buses at a good price, flew to Nevada, picked one out, and negotiated a price of $6500. He returned to Oklahoma City to arrange for the financing, which ended in a bizarre arrangement. The bank would not consider financing the bus, but they financed Hank's station wagon and the Buick for the $6500. Hank sent Round Boy to Nevada with a cashier's check to pick up the bus. The bus was painted in blue and silver with *Hank Thompson and The Brazos Valley Boys* on each side. It became the band's second home for the next four years.

Hank insisted on an inviolate dress code on the bus, since he felt it was important that The Brazos Valley Boys give a good impression even when just getting on and off. The preferred outfit was nice western pants and shirts and, of course, cowboy boots and hats – outfits that were far better looking than the outfits worn by many *artists* today. And this was before the band members donned their flashy Nudie stage uniforms for the show.

*

The increase in demand for public appearances as a result of *The Wild Side of Life* enabled Jim Halsey to increase the efficiency of the road trips. For example, when Hank and The Brazos Valley Boys were to appear in Los Angeles for a recording session and/or an appearance, Jim would book several jobs between Oklahoma City and Los Angeles. On one such trip, Hank was scheduled to appear at the *Clover Club* in Amarillo, Texas, on a particular Saturday night. Hank arrived at the Herring Hotel in Amarillo in the early afternoon and was surprised to see one of the members of Bob Wills' band, the Texas Playboys, in the lobby. It turned out that they had played in Amarillo the night before and were loading their bus for a trip to their next engagement in Borger.

"Where's Bob?" asked Hank.

"He's up in his room, but he's on the booze again and in pretty bad shape," was the reply. "There's something about Amarillo with Bob. Every time we come here he goes off the wagon. Do us a favor and go up to his room and try to get him to get dressed and on the bus. We need to leave soon, and none of us can get him to go. Maybe you can talk him into it."

Hank went up to the room and knocked on the door. Bob answered the door in his boxer shorts and tee shirt. He and the room smelled like a brewery, and Hank spotted a case of whisky on the floor and a couple of empty bottles on a table. Bob had a drink in his hand and it was very apparent that it wasn't his first. In other words, he was hammered.

"Well hello, Hank," slurred Bob, "Come on in."

"Bob, I know you have got to get going, but we are staying here tonight and I heard you were here. I wanted to come up and say hello."

They sat down and visited, with Hank steering the conversation towards the need for Bob to get dressed and get on the bus. It didn't work. As Hank got ready to leave, he gave it one more try.

"Bob, I know you have got to get ready to go get on the bus, so I had better go," said Hank, as he got up from the table.

A slight pause as Bob lifted his glass and took another sip. He then looked at Hank and tried to focus as he spoke.

"Hank, you're a nice boy, you really are. The only thing I don't like about you is that you are too much like that god-dammed Tommy Duncan and that fucking Leon McAuliffe."

*

Curly Chalker, the newest member of The Brazos Valley Boys, was an enigma. Although an undisputed talent on the steel guitar, he had a dark side, or, at least, a strange side.

He often displayed his mercurial nature when playing with The Brazos Valley Boys. When he made a mistake, he would get infuriated, throw his steel bar down and utter one or more four-letter words. Loud. And, he would often do it at a job with hundreds of people gathered around the bandstand.

"Curly was very inconsistent with his playing," said Hank. "And he got very upset when he would foul something up. But it seemed that when it was really important, he'd come through. On a record session, or at a big concert, he'd play you some of the best stuff you ever heard. For example, he played some outstanding recorded solos as a Brazos Valley Boy when he rejoined the band for two 1963 recording sessions. You listen to those things, such as the song *Reaching For the Moon*, and you'll hear some of the prettiest steel guitar work you'll ever want to hear!"

In the meantime, Hank made some improvements to his J-200. He sent it back to Gibson and had it the original Gibson neck and headstock replaced by with a customized neck and headstock designed by Merle and manufactured by Paul Bigsby[10], a friend of both Merle and Hank. The Bigsby neck had a relatively thin cross-section, and the headstock had the tuners on only one side.

Left to right: Wayne Foster, Hank, Billy Stewart & Billy Gray

---

[10] Paul Bigsby was famous in his own right as the designer of the Bigsby vibrato arm, an industry standard for attaching to an electric guitar, and as the designer and manufacturer of about 50 steel guitars which were highly coveted by musicians. He also produced a few standard guitars which were conceptualized by Merle and had an influence on the Telecaster and Stratocaster solid body electric guitars later produced by Fender. Very few of the Bigsby necks and headstocks for acoustic guitars, such as the one Hank used, are known to be in existence.

Chapter Twenty

Hank Williams pulled a fifth of Jack Daniels from the cupboard, put it on the table, and said to his friend and guest who was seated at the table, "Hank, have a drink."

"Don't mind if I do," said Hank Thompson, "Are you going to join me?"

"No," was the quick reply, "I can't take just one drink. If I start, I'll drink the whole bottle and maybe even one or two more."

Thompson had journeyed to Nashville and was staying with Williams at Williams' apartment on a Friday night in the early fifties. They both were to appear at *The Grand Ole Opry* the next night, Williams as the host and Thompson as a guest. Williams was living in the small apartment by himself during one of his separations from Audrey. The good news was that his *Honky-tonk Blues* and *Half as Much* were currently riding high on the charts, and *Cold Cold Heart* had reached No. 1 the previous year.

As Thompson sipped his drink, Williams pulled out a composition book and started reading from it.

"How do you like these lyrics that I wrote the other day?" asked Williams as he started reading:

Hear the lonesome whippoorwill,
He sounds too blue to fly,
The midnight train is whining low,
I'm so lonesome I could cry.

I've never seen a night so long,
When time goes crawling by,
The moon just went behind a cloud,
To hide its face and cry.

Did you ever see a robin weep,
When leaves begin to die?

That means he's lost the will to live,
I'm so lonesome I could cry.
The silence of a falling star,
Lights up a purple sky,
And as I wonder where you are,
I'm so lonesome I could cry.[11]

"On the several times that we were together, he would often pull out his composition book, as he did in his apartment that night, read some of his lyrics before he recorded them, and ask me my opinion," Thompson recalled. "In fact, he was mainly a lyric writer and used a lot of standard blues tunes and old Jimmie Rodgers' yodels as the basis for his melodies. His lyrics were always tremendous, and I told him so, as I did that night. Often, including this time, he would not yet have a melody for the lyrics. But when I asked about this he usually said 'Aw, I don't worry about the melodies,' which was the same as saying that Fred Rose covered for him on the melodies.

"Like me and others, he often borrowed ideas for songs and improved on them. But this didn't bother me, since *The Wild Side of Life* was also a borrowed melody. Also, it was common knowledge in the industry that, despite the fact that Williams was listed as the writer of *Jambalaya (On the Bayou)*, he bought it from Moon Mulligan who really wrote it. In fact, Moon told me so."

Back in Williams' apartment, as Thompson continued with his drink, Williams suggested that they go to a club in Nashville that night. Williams wanted to hear still another Hank – Hank "Sugarfoot" Garland, one of the first true guitar virtuosos to emerge from the Nashville studios, and who had played on some of Williams' recordings. When Thompson agreed, Williams put down the composition book, got up, and said that he was going to put on a clean shirt. Thompson noticed Williams reach in a drawer and pull out a clean, white shirt. Then, much to Thompson's amazement, Williams put the shirt on over the shirt he was wearing.

"I didn't say anything then, but I thought about that for a long time afterwards," said Thompson, "and the only possibility that I can come up with is that he thought that the two shirts might hide the fact that he was so thin."

That night, the two Hanks enjoyed themselves as spectators at the club, and the next night it was back to business. Williams opened his segment of *The Grand Ole Opry* with *Honky-tonk Blues*, and, as usual, Thompson was very impressed with the performance.

"Unlike most people, I thought Hank Williams was a better singer and entertainer than a songwriter. Normally he was fairly quiet and laid back, but when he hit the stage he immediately took on a new persona and was absolute dynamite. He became very confident almost to the point of being cocky or brash, and his voice had a tremendous projection. He didn't do anything unusual except sing the song, strum his guitar, and pat his foot to the rhythm, but it was as if he was sending a message to the audience, 'I know you people are going to like me, you don't have any choice.'"

As the noise died down from the audience's raucous response to *Honky-tonk*

---

[11] From the Hank Williams song, *I'm So Lonesome I Could Cry*, that has been termed by some critics as "the saddest song ever written". Cover versions of the song have been released by no less than forty other artists.

Blues, Thompson made his way to center stage as Williams introduced him.

"Well friends, we have a young man visiting us tonight that is one of the top folk artists in the whole nation. So let's give a great big welcome to Hank Thompson."

An explanation of the term "folk artist" is in order. In 1944, one Al Dexter released a song entitled *Pistol Packing Mamma* that was as country as it gets by any definition, and enjoyed unprecedented success with respect to radio, record sales and juke boxes. But Billboard Magazine, which at the time was confined to charting the success of "popular music" didn't know what to do with the song. So they started a category they termed "folk records", to accommodate *Pistol Packing Mamma* and all the other folk and country songs that followed. (Billboard did not create a "country and western" category until 1949.) Since Williams had charted no less than eight songs on the Billboard "Folk Records" chart prior to the end of 1949, the most logical and simple explanation is that he was referring to Thompson as a fellow ex-'folk', now 'country', artist.

As the two Hanks stood side-by-side on the stage before Thompson launched into *The Wild Side of Life*, it is doubtful that anyone could have appreciated the significance of this event at the time, for it turned out to be the last time they worked together. Williams' health, drug and alcohol problems spiraled out of control, and his life lasted for only a few more months while Thompson's career would last for six more decades.

Chapter Twenty One

The success of The *Wild Side of Life* gave Hank the opportunity to go to a new level. Fortunately, he had several key elements of a support structure in place that was essential to make this happen.

1. The base in Oklahoma City was firmly established, with the crowds at his appearances in Oklahoma and the surrounding areas already at or near capacity.

2. After over two years of rehearsals, recordings and appearances, The Brazos Valley Boys were turning into a cohesive music-making machine.

3. Jim Halsey was going lights-out on the bookings, which began to include the larger dance halls and clubs throughout the Southwest and California and all stops between.

4. Hank had the energy and desire to undertake a personal appearance schedule that could be described as grueling at the least.

With respect to the band, Hank credits Billy Gray for his immense contributions and professionalism, as well as his strong sense of ingenuity.

"Billy was very creative," said Hank. "And he liked to experiment and try new arrangements and different sounds. From a rhythm standpoint, he was unparalleled. He was not by any means a great guitarist, and he should have been a drummer with his good feel for tempos and rhythm, which was much better than mine. I used to have him kick off the songs because he could nail the proper tempo for each song better than I could. I was concentrating on my vocals; and if I kicked it off, it would often be too fast or too slow. But Billy Gray had an uncanny sense of knowing the proper tempo and pace for every song."

Regarding the personal appearances, Jim not only excelled in making the bookings, his effort to attend every job that he booked for Hank paid extra dividends, since he was able to meet and schmooze each club owner or buyer and pave the way for a return engagement. Just as important, he collected the balance due on each contract. (Each engagement required a down payment with the balance being collected the night of the appearance.)

Two business models emerged which were location-specific. In California, where liquor was sold by the drink, the club owners would make their money on the liquor and beer sales, and therefore could give the band the entire door as long as they brought in a big crowd and worked up their thirst with good dance music. Thus, Jim could usually negotiate the entire door for the band, which, in most instances, was a substantial amount of money.

By contrast, in Oklahoma and Texas, where liquor by the drink could not be sold, the patrons brought in their own. In Oklahoma the only sources of liquor were boot-leggers, and the bottles had to be brought in "brown bags" and placed under the table. Texas was a "county option" state, in which some counties had laws similar to Oklahoma (with the exception that the bottles could be placed on the table), and other counties had the same laws with respect to hard liquor, but permitted beer sales. Thus, the club owners were limited to the sales of set-ups and food (and beer in some Texas counties), hardly a big money-making proposition, and therefore had to make some money on the door. In these scenarios, the band would only get a percentage of the door, usually seventy percent, and the owner would get the balance.

For example, a job at the Trianon would work something like this. Hank would often draw around eight hundred to a thousand people at a cover charge of $1.00 per person. Using nine hundred people as an average, and a seventy percent of the door arrangement, Hank would net about $630[12] before Jim Halsey took his fee.

The Brazos Valley Boys were being paid an average of approximately $100 per member per month. Thus, one night at the Trianon would nearly cover Hank's monthly payroll. Of course, the "take" varied from club to club, but with Jim booking up to five or six jobs a week, it doesn't take a genius to figure out that the financial aspects of Hank's personal appearances had a significant upside.

Hank's dad would be proud. It was becoming apparent that his son could make a living in the music business after all.

*

While playing a job in a club in Hanford, California, after the December 1951, recording sessions in Los Angeles, Hank met Jean Shepherd, who was singing with an all-girl band, *The Melody Ranch Girls*. Jean was a teenager at the time and an Oklahoma native, and Hank was very impressed with her talent. He told Ken Nelson about her and played him a dub of a recording she had made. Nelson listened and, although he was impressed with her voice, his response was underwhelming.

"Girls do not sell in the country music business," said Ken.

Ken's comment was not too long before Kitty Wells' version of *It Wasn't God Who Made Honky-tonk Angels* (an answer to The *Wild Side of Life*) debuted on the charts in July 1952, and then worked its way to number one, a position it held for six weeks. It was the first number one song and million seller by a female country vocalist. (In a touch of irony, her answer song boosted the sales of *The Wild Side of Life*, which had started sliding down the charts, but went back up again when *It Wasn't God Who Made Honky-tonk Angels* was at number one.)

---

12 According to the ultimate authority–the internet– the present value of $1.00 in 1955 is approximately $7.50 after being adjusted for inflation.

The case of Jean Shepherd is a good example of what the success of *It Wasn't God Who Made Honky-tonk Angels* did for female country singers. After turning down Hank's suggestion to sign her, and after observing Kitty's success, Ken Nelson had a change of heart. He signed Sheppard to a recording contract despite some significant legal hassles stemming from the fact that she was underage. However, Nelson pulled it off, feeling that she had the potential to walk through the door that Kitty had opened.

Indeed. The next year, 1953, Jean recorded a duet with Ferlin Huskey, *A Dear John Letter*, that was number one on the charts for six weeks. She then went on to chart over forty songs over a period of twenty-five years, seven of which were in the top ten. She was also a mainstay on Red Foley's *Ozark Jubilee*, joined *The Grand Ole Opry* in 1955, and was named the top female singer of 1959 by Cash Box. The sad news is that her husband, Hawkshaw Hawkins, died in the same plane crash that killed Patsy Cline in 1963.

*

It was a Saturday night in Oklahoma City, and the new home base for Hank Thompson and The Brazos Valley Boys was rocking, with all the usual suspects. Everyone was having a good time and, in a lot of cases, too good of a time.

The Trianon, with a capacity of around eleven hundred people, was located on a very large second floor of a building in downtown Oklahoma City. A large bandstand was located at one corner of the floor, a large concession stand stood at the opposite corner, and the dance floor extended between the bandstand and the bar. A small seating area consisting of benches (which was later expanded to seat around three hundred) was located near the bandstand, and tables were set up in the rear of the dance floor.

The stairs connecting the street to the second floor that contained the ballroom were narrow and steep. Due to Oklahoma's above-mentioned "dry" liquor laws, the patrons would buy booze from their local bootlegger, bring in the bottle or bottles in a brown bag, buy setups at the concession stand, and mix their own at the table. Going up the stairs was often difficult for those patrons carrying numerous bottles of liquor and beer, which was often the case. However, it was coming down the stairs after the alcohol had entered their systems that created the major problems.

A case in point:

As Hank was winding down his performance with his rendition of Merle's classic song *The Nine Pound Hammer*, and with the crowd in an uproar, a reveler (who, for the sake of convenience, will be referred to as "Drunk No. 1") was conscious enough to realize that if he left before the song ended, he might beat the rush out. He made it to the exit and started wobbling down the stairs – a fairly shaky undertaking to say the least.

When Drunk No.1 had negotiated about half the stairs, another inebriated patron, "Drunk No. 2", also started down, but stumbled early on, and began tumbling down the stairs.

Drunk No. 2 hit Drunk No. 1 in the back of the legs and Drunk No. 1 also started tumbling down the remaining stairs.

Drunks No. 1 and No. 2 reached the bottom of the stairs and fell out into the street, prone and disoriented.

It wouldn't be fair to call the third person involved in this saga "Drunk No. 3", although his blood-alcohol level was certainly in the danger zone. But compared to the other two, he was relatively sober. So he will be called "Strong Buzz."

As Drunk No. 1 and Drunk No. 2 fell out into the street, Strong Buzz, having witnessed the whole scene at the top of the stairs, hurried down the stairs without a mishap, pulled a handkerchief from his back pocket, and threw it on the street next to Drunks No. 1 and No. 2, who, in the meantime, had started crawling around the sidewalk, wondering where they were.

Then, with a triumphant look on his face, Strong Buzz shouted for all of Oklahoma City to hear.

"Fifteen yards, clipping!"

*

During Jim Halsey's introductory tour with Hank and The Brazos Valley Boys, he often rode with the band; but on some occasions he would drive his own car – a late model Buick – to the jobs. On one occasion, there were back-to-back jobs in Houston and Dallas, and Jim drove his Buick to Houston. At intermission during the show, he was approached by Hank, who had come to Houston on the bus with the band.

"I've got an idea," said Hank. "Although the band is staying in Houston tonight, why don't we drive your car to Dallas after the job. That way, we can sleep in tomorrow morning, and we won't have to get up early and drive."

"Fine with me," said Jim.

It was about 2:00 A.M when Hank finished signing autographs after his last set that night. He piled in the back seat of the Buick as Jim took the wheel. By the time Jim pulled out of the parking lot, Hank was asleep and didn't wake up until Jim, very exhausted and sleep-deprived, pulled into a motel in Dallas several hours later.

"I thought he said that *we* would drive to Dallas," thought Jim.

Speaking of Dallas, Jim and Hank were happy to note that the response to Hank's appearances in the Dallas/Ft. Worth area increased significantly since Hank moved to Oklahoma City. Hank and The Brazos Valley Boys were now a national act, as opposed to a "local" band.

Chapter Twenty Two

People still have differing opinions on the "classification" of the music played by Hank and The Brazos Valley Boys. Descriptions include "Honky-tonk", "Western Swing", and "Traditional Country". The fact of the matter is that the music The Brazos Valley Boys played, sans Hank, certainly had its roots in Western Swing and meets the definition of "jazz played by musicians in white hats and cowboy boots, and using steel guitars and fiddles." One thing for certain was that the music included precise arrangements, a rhythm section featuring an electric rhythm guitar, a drummer who wasn't shy about a strong rhythm, and fiddles and a steel guitar that were dominant in the intros, instrumental breaks, and closings.

Hank describes it this way.

"When we first started, I didn't want us to sound like Bob Wills, Ernest Tubb or Roy Acuff. I wanted to be more country than Bob Wills, but with more polish and swing. In the early days, we played more honky-tonks than anything else, We were doing the stuff that people who came to the honky-tonks liked best, such as songs by Webb Pierce, Carl Smith, and so on. I think "honky-tonk swing" would describe my music better than 'Bob Wills music' or 'Ernest Tubb music'".

But when Hank hit the stage, things changed somewhat. While keeping the Western Swing foundation, Hank took the music in other directions, resulting in what can simply and better be described as "Hank Thompson Music". A country music historian described Hank's music as follows:

"Thompson's hard-core honky-tonk, Western Swing sound was marked by a strong rhythm section of piano, bass, guitar, and drums; lead and fill parts supplied by twin fiddles, electric guitar, and steel; frequent shifts from 2/4 to 4/4 time; and, above all, his powerful vocals."

Whatever the classification, the music purveyed by Hank and The Brazos Valley Boys gained traction in the early fifties as a result of as many as six jobs a week, year in and year out, which enabled Hank to develop a clear feel of how a show should be presented. On a typical job, the band, without Hank, would kick off at the appointed start time, with Billy Gray fronting. They would play a mix of Western Swing instrumentals, vocals based around country classics, and some country hits of the day, all with a Western Swing foundation. After about an hour or so, the band would take a fairly long break and then hit the stage again and play two or three more songs before Billy would introduce Hank. Hank would sing for about forty-five minutes from a carefully selected play list of his songs based on his past observations of the fans' response to the songs. After another break, the band would come back on, play a few songs; and Hank would come on and close things out.

However, this required an attitude adjustment on the part of some of the club owners and their patrons, who expected the bandleader to be up with the band the entire time. This was especially true in the Southwest, where the patrons were accustomed to orchestras and big bands playing mainly for the purpose of dancing; and in the East, where the patrons didn't dance that much and preferred sitting down and listening to the music. It was also true with Bob Wills and Leon McAuliffe, who were featured instrumentalists as well as bandleaders.

Therefore, when Hank didn't open with the band, people would complain, thinking he was late. Hank and Jim Halsey had to make sure the club owners were tuned to Hank's routine.

"We made sure that the contracts we had with the club owners specified that I would appear only for a portion of the time," said Hank. "We really had an extremely difficult time convincing these people that I was not a bandleader in the traditional sense, but rather a featured act aside from the band."

Another departure from the norm had to be addressed. Most Western Swing bands in Oklahoma and Texas did not take breaks or intermissions. Bob Wills, Johnny Lee Wills and Leon McAuliffe, for example, would play three and four hour jobs without a break, although individuals in the band would slip off the stage at different times, mainly to relieve themselves. One of the main reasons for this was that if intermissions were taken, fights would often break out in the building or outside in the parking lot. But Hank took a different approach.

"I felt breaks were important," said Hank. "This way, we could get off the stage, relieve ourselves, have something to drink, and mingle with the patrons. Some of the club owners would say 'Bob Wills doesn't take intermissions', and I would tell them that if Bob doesn't want to do so, that's up to him, but we are going to do it this way. Also, I bluffed some and told them that we're union musicians and that the union requires we take ten minute breaks every hour."

A major upside of this approach enabled Hank to engage in what became a career-defining activity, one that was not practiced by many artists at the time, nor many artists since. He would seek out and mingle with his fans, whether it be at their tables, around the bandstand, or at the bar.

"I made it a point to go around to the tables, shake hands, converse with the patrons, take requests, and sign autographs," said Hank.

This mingle-and-mix time, coupled with Hank's convivial personality, provided another advantage – Hank was able to meet and learn many of his fans' names and remember them – a trait that has continued throughout his entire career.

It didn't take Jim Halsey long to appreciate the profound effect that Hank's music had on a majority of his fans.

"At all of Hank's shows, I noticed one common trait shared by the fans," said Jim. "The great majority of the people did not have the greatest jobs or income in the world, and their personal lives were often a struggle, not only with respect to finances, but also with raising kids, difficulties at work, health issues, and so on. But, for three or four hours, they could relax, have a drink, forget all of their problems, and become completely engrossed in the music. It was like they were transported to another time and space. And you could see this on their faces and in the way they acted."

This phenomenon was one that Jim observed for the next fifty years.

Jim's introductory tour included a stop at one of Hank's favorite venues – a dance hall in Elk Mountain, Wyoming, a lumbering community that consisted of the dance hall, a hotel, and a combination gas station and grocery store. The local lumberjacks worked hard during the week and partied hard on the weekends, with the parties usually being centered around country music and dancing.

"I remember the hotel," said Jim. "It was a two-story dormitory style, with a big dining room on the ground floor. They served up a family style, real hearty, dinner. Beef steaks, fried chicken, pork chops, mashed potatoes and gravy, green beans, sweet potatoes, and several kinds of pie and cake. The proprietor was eager to show me around, and he told me that the lumberjacks brought their gals or wives to the dance hall and danced hard to every song Hank and The Brazos Valley Boys belted out. This was nothing particularly unusual. But then he advised me to 'wait until intermission – that's when they really have fun!'"

That night, true to form, by the time Billy Gray got through the first verse of the opening song, the dance floor was filled, and it stayed filled until the intermission. Then, nearly all of the lumberjacks and their lady friends emptied into the parking lot, and Jim was astonished when he saw a series of fights break out, almost simultaneously, as if they were choreographed.

"I've never seen anything like this, even in movies," said Jim. "I was mesmerized. After about thirty minutes of organized fighting, The Brazos Valley Boys kicked off the first tune of the second set and the fights stopped as if on cue. Everybody went to a cold stream of water running beside the dance hall, washed the blood and dirt off, came back in, grabbed their bottle and dancing partner and finished their evening of dancing and enjoyment."

By this time, the twelve-inch, 33⅓ RPM LP (for "long play") record format, developed by Columbia Records, was becoming more and more popular since it permitted as much as thirty minutes of music to placed on each side of the disc. Thus, an artist could release ten or twelve songs on a single record, or "album", which changed the playing field throughout the industry.[13] Capitol was on board with the concept, so the game plan for Hank's December 1952, recording session was not only to produce several singles for release in the usual manner, but also to produce some cuts for his first album of original songs in the LP and EP formats entitled *Songs of the Brazos Valley*.

With the recording sessions looming near, there were some major changes to The Brazos Valley Boys. Bob White replaced Johnny Manson on fiddle and teamed with Amos Hedrick to form a dynamic duo. Paul McGhee, whom Hank hired away from Bob Wills, replaced Wayne Foster on drums. Paul was with the band, on and off, for five years, and came to be one of Hank's closest friends. His antics – centered around distilled spirits and parties – were a big help in relieving the tedium of the road. Also, he was a good drummer.

When Curly Chalker informed Billy Gray that he was going to be drafted into the Army in a few months, Gray remembered eighteen-year-old Pee Wee Whitewing whom he had heard when Pee Wee was playing with Lefty Frizzell's band. When Gray found out that Pee Wee was leaving Lefty, he asked Pee Wee to join The Brazos Valley Boys. Pee Wee initially said no and went back to California, but Gray put on a full-court press since he was well aware of Pee Wee's talent and his affinity for Western Swing. Soon Pee Wee was a Brazos Valley Boy and brought with him some new Western Swing arrangements that Gray incorporated into the rotation. It didn't take long for Pee Wee to come into his own and go to the head of his class.

"Pee Wee played with the best tastes behind a vocalist of any steel player that I ever heard," said Hank. "He liked to sing, and so he knew how a steel ought to sound behind a vocalist. Bob Wills said to me one time, 'I don't know who that boy is you got playing steel guitar, but I'm gonna tell you something, son, he lays it right in there for you like it was served up on a platter.'"

Also added to the 1952 band was veteran California Western Swing guitarist Bill Carson, who would become semi-famous later as one of the major figures in designing the Fender Stratocaster guitar. Bill was a "straight picker" (as opposed to a "thumb picker") and stayed with The Brazos Valley Boys about a year.

The first song of the session, written by Hank, was *Rub-A-Dub-Dub*, which returned Hank to his nursery rhyme formula and which turned out to be eminently successful.

"*Humpty-Dumpty Heart* was so successful that I felt we needed another song in the nursery rhyme vein," said Hank. "I thought about the nursery rhyme "Rub-a-dub-dub, three men in a tub" which was very rhythmic, and the song fell into place."[14]

---

[13] Another, less popular, format was the 10-inch EP (extended play) which was essentially the same technology on a smaller disc.

I'll Sign My Heart Away, one of Hank's saddest and most effective ballads, was also recorded and turned out to be the B side of *Rub-A-Dub-Dub*. Since *I'll Sign My Heart Away* was clearly A side quality, it made the two-sided record one of Hank's strongest, if not the strongest. Other highlights included *Yesterday's Girl*, penned by Hank and Billy Gray, along with the traditional *John Henry*. When released about a year later, they also formed a very strong two-sided record.

During this time, Pee Wee had been bugging Billy Gray about a friend of his that should be invited to join The Brazos Valley Boys. But it involved a somewhat revolutionary concept that was a hard sell. Billy finally bought into the idea and then tried to sell it to the boss.

Billy: "I suggest we hire a trumpet player for the band, and I have one in mind."

Hank: "Trumpet? I don't use a trumpet."

Gray: "But a trumpet would be a big boost on some of the instrumentals we do. The guy we have in mind is Dubert Dobson, who has been working around Oklahoma. Pee Wee and Amos know him and say he is a great musician and a real live wire. Plus, he will help load and set up the equipment, drive the bus, and do anything else that might come up."

Hank: "OK, let's give it a try."

Left to Right: Bob White, Dubert Dobson, Amos Hedrick, Paul McGhee, Hank, Billy Stewart, Billy Gray, Bill Carson, Pee Wee Whitewing, Gil Baca

---

[14] Ralph Flanagan, the leader of a very popular big band at the time, apparently agreed with Hank as to the rhythmic appeal of *Rub-A-Dub-Dub*, and recorded an instrumental version of the song, which sold approximately 100,000 copies.

It turned out that "live wire" was putting it mildly. During the next ten years, not only did Dubert's trumpet add depth to the Western Swing instrumentals that The Brazos Valley Boys were playing, but Hank also started using him often for background fills in some of the songs that he sang. Moreover, due to Dubert's personality and antics (especially when imbibing–which was often), and his unrelenting desire to bed down as many female fans as he could, he made significant contributions to the band's bus chemistry and became one of the most popular members of The Brazos Valley Boys.

Opinions could differ as to whether or not Dubert's presence had anything to do with it, but later in the year, Down Beat Magazine selected The Brazos Valley Boys as the number one country and western band in the nation.

Chapter Twenty Three

Hank and Jim Halsey flanking The Brazos Valley Boys.

In early 1953, a novelty song titled *No Help Wanted* by a group called the Carlisles was on a heavy rotation on Oklahoma City radio. Hank started doing it at his shows, the fans loved it, and Hank got an idea. Despite the high radio and juke-box play that propelled the song to a high chart rating, the Carlisles' version was not *selling* all that well since it was on the Mercury label, and Mercury's distribution net-work did not cover the entire United States. Hank felt that the song was well suited for him and The Brazos Valley Boys, and that a well- recorded version distributed through the Capitol national network could sell big time. That is, if they could get it out to the market in time.

He immediately convened the band at the studios of radio station WKY in Oklahoma City, the song was cut in a few minutes, and the tape was overnighted to Ken Nelson in California. Ken found the recording quality acceptable, except that the bass was a little thin, and he augmented it before cutting the master tape and pressing the records.

Capitol put its distribution network in high gear and, in a few weeks, the record was soon going head-to-head with the Carlisles' version on radio and in the jukeboxes. (In those days, it was not uncommon to have two or more different versions of the same song in the Top Ten.) The Carlisles' version stayed at Number one for four weeks, and Hank's version peaked at number nine. The kicker was that, since the charts reflected radio and juke box play only, these numbers did not reveal the fact that Hank's record was smoking the Carlisles' record in terms of *sales*.

*

What started as a routine appearance at the armory in Altus, Oklahoma, ended as a new first for Hank and The Brazos Valley Boys, and a very unpleasant one.

As usual, The Brazos Valley Boys opened the show around nine o'clock to a packed, rowdy crowd of around five hundred people who were not shy about ingesting prodigious amounts of alcohol. Around ten o'clock, Gray introduced Hank; and Hank came on the stage and started strapping on the J-200 as Pee Wee kicked off the opening bars to *Green Light*. A good portion of the crowd rushed towards the stage so that they could drink and watch Hank, while others stayed back so that they could drink and dance. So far, so good.

But just as Hank approached the mike and started singing, a fight broke out in

Bob White dancing to *No Help Wanted*.

Dubert in the air with Billy Gray looking on.

the crowd. Since this wasn't the first time Hank had played to a fight, he kept singing. However, this time it quickly became apparent that this was not a normal barroom-type fight between a few drunks. Rather, this one started out with a large number of people and escalated very rapidly. By the time the song was finished, it looked as if half the room was pitted against the other half. Cursing, fisticuffs, wrestling, broken bottles, and hair pulling. And that was just the women. The men engaged in all of the above, plus chair throwing and table crashing.

"I've seen fights before at my dances," said Hank, "but they would involve only a few people. This fight involved the whole damn crowd and was more like a riot!"

As soon as the song ended, Hank admonished the crowd.

"Please get back to your tables and relax. We're going to take a break until things calm down."

Hank and the band members hurried off the stage; and Hank, with an acute sense of timing, went right to the promoter and insisted that he be paid for the night. The promoter obliged.

The fight(s) calmed down somewhat, so, after about thirty minutes of uneasy tension, Hank went back on the stage with the band, and the music started.

So did the fights.

Again, Hank stopped the music and addressed the crowd.

"You people have a choice. You can either fight, or you can sit down and listen or dance. If you don't behave yourselves and enjoy the music, we're going to stop."

The crowd seemed to relent, and despite the uneasiness in the air, Hank started up with the music.

The fighting broke out again.

Hank looked back at Billy Gray and the boys and said, "Load everything up, we're outta here."

With the fights still going on, it took about fifteen minutes for the band to disconnect the equipment, pack the instruments, and move everything from the stage, out the back door, and into the bus (which, fortunately was parked near the back door). Everybody jumped on board, and as the bus pulled out, the crowd spilled out into the parking lot, apparently looking for Hank and the band.

And they were still fighting.

"That was the only time in my career that I stopped a dance for fighting," said Hank. "On a few other occasions I had thought about it, but I never did."

Later, on the bus ride home, a somber group of Brazos Valley Boys discussed the amazing event they had just witnessed. They could have considered several categories of causation for the near riot, and these would likely have been their findings for each category:

1. Race – Clearly not.

2. Religion – No way.

3. Politics – A possibility, but unlikely under the circumstances.

4. Gender – Very doubtful. For the most part, the women were fighting the women and the men were fighting the men. Besides, the few men that fought women appeared to be losing.

5. Military vs. Civilian – Although an Air Force base existed just outside the city limits of Altus, there was no sign of any military weapons nor were any people in military uniforms fighting people not in military uniforms.

6. Gang War – In Altus, Oklahoma?

7. Drugs – Other than alcohol, the strongest drug in evidence was chewing tobacco.
8. Gay/straight – At a country-dance in Altus, Oklahoma in 1953? Are you kidding?
9. Acute drunkenness – By process of elimination, this had to be it.

*

In May 1953, a few months after *Wild Side* dropped off the charts after a thirty-week residency, *Rub-A-Dub-Dub* debuted and soared to number one. This was especially gratifying for Hank since not only did he collect royalties based on the performance of the song, he was the sole writer.

About this time, Hank made an important business decision. In the past, he had assigned the copyrights on all of the songs he wrote to publishing companies for collection of the "mechanical royalties" earned by the songs when reproduced in any form (such as recordings). These royalties, amounting to a few cents per song as set by law, are paid by the record company to the publisher who, in exchange for its efforts in supervising the collection of the royalties on each song, keeps a share of the royalty and pays the balance to the songwriter (typically a 50/50 split).

Now, with his portfolio of written songs building up, Hank formed his own publishing company – the *Brazos Valley Music Company* – instead of signing over the songs to a third-party publishing company. He thereby became the publisher of all of his songs as well as some songs written by other artists. Hank also bought back a catalog of some of his earlier songs from one of his first publishing companies and assigned it to the new company. In this manner, in the case of songs that he wrote, he had three bites at the apple. He would receive a percentage of the sale of each record based on his role as the recording artist, the songwriter, and the publisher.

*

Hank has often been asked about a certain fact of life on the road. A typical question, usually from a male, would go something like this.

"Hank, with you and The Brazos Valley Boys on the road for weeks at a time, performing on stage with good looking western outfits in environments conducive to alcohol and dancing, there must have been a lot of good looking, available girls all over the place."

"There were," understated Hank.

The Brazos Valley Boys, ever aware of Hank's admonition to be nice and friendly to the fans, took their responsibility very seriously, especially in connection with the females. With the very high testosterone levels that were developed on the road, and with a cornucopia of attractive females awaiting them at every job, the only real decisions that had to be made were in connection with selecting the females who liked to party, using the word in an all-encompassing sense. To provide the proper setting for these activities on the road, the band established The Brazos Valley Boys Invitation Only Fun and Games Unwinding Parties, which were often held after the job at the motel where the band stayed. And good parties they were. The routine would be something like this.

During the dance or show, which served as a pre-party, The Brazos Valley Boys would carefully screen the female fans, usually over a drink or two before the dance, during intermission, and/or after the dance. Then a select group of the more suitable guests would be invited on the bus to continue partying with the band before they drove to the motel. At the motel, everyone would gather in one room, and the drinking would shift into high gear as the social aspect of the evening hit a crescendo. Close friendships were formed; and, as the raucous part of the party died down, the newly formed couples would try to find some privacy where they could couple. This was sometimes difficult, since two or more band members stayed in each room; but it didn't seem to bother Dubert, who was a league leader in conquests.

"It was very hard to find any privacy with that bunch," remembered Pee Wee, "but Dubert didn't really care where he performed or if anyone was watching."

Thus, by the mid-fifties, The Brazos Valley Boys had developed an excellent network of very special female fans who didn't consider a night with Hank Thompson and The Brazos Valley Boys complete unless they bedded down one or more of the band members. Although the great majority of the invitees were locals, several groupie-types evolved who were not adverse to traveling to the various locations throughout the Southwest so that they could offer their special services to the band members at every location. They became charter members of The Brazos Valley Boys Groupie Society and deserved, and received, special recognition.

More prominent members of the society were Black Rider, Willa Lou, Yo-Yo, Squirrelly, and Yolanda. All were attractive, voluptuous, and eager. For the most part, they specialized in The Brazos Valley Boys and, according to one school of thought, they had at least an informal exclusive arrangement. At any rate, they would follow Hank and the band to venues throughout the Southwest, attend the dance or show, and set up shop at the motel afterwards. And they were willing to service the entire band, preferably on the same night (the word "gang-banging" comes to mind, but perhaps it should be "band-banging").

Willa Lou, an exceptional-looking and very conscientious member of The Brazos Valley Boys Groupie Society, received special recognition from Hank. He would often sing a song entitled *Jelly Roll Blues,* and he revised the lyrics to mention Willa Lou and others. One line of a verse went like this:

I know a gal, her name is Willa Lou and I don't know nothing that she can't do.

Hank also modified the standard lyrics to one of his most popular songs, *John Henry,* to include Willa Lou.

Willa Lou had a surprising reaction to this. One night she came up to Hank between sets at a club.

"Hank, I wish you would quit using my name in all your songs."

However, it was generally accepted that a brunette from Oklahoma City was at the head of the class. Paul McGhee named her "Black Rider" from an old Bob Wills tune, since she was always dressed in black. She was attractive, and distinguished herself in several ways, one of which proved to be embarrassing to Hank.

"She was a cute and sweet girl," Hank recalled, "but she would often embarrass me at shows. For example, she would stand in line for an autograph and then give me a personal item, such as a towel, or the like, that had 'Hank, I love you' embroidered on it."

But this was just the tip of the iceberg for Black Rider, as Hank and The Brazos Valley Boys later discovered.

Chapter Twenty Four

With the professional partnership between Hank and Jim Halsey firmly established, they created a five year plan for the promotion of Hank and his music that included several revolutionary concepts.

"Hank was the first to explain to me how important it is to be *first* because it only happens once," said Jim, "and it piqued my interest in a couple of ideas I had in the back of my mind. We started planning to do things that nobody else had done and thought were impossible. One goal was to get a corporate sponsorship."

In an era in which "corporate sponsor" and "country artist" were hardly ever used in the same sentence, Jim went to St. Louis and met with the Falstaff Beer people, and hit a home run. Here, in Jim's written words, is his account of his meeting with the Falstaff people in 1953.

In thinking about how to expand on the popularity of Hank Thompson and his Brazos Valley Boys, I was inspired by the television cowboys, Gene Autry, Roy Rogers, and Hopalong Cassidy. They endorsed, commercialized, and appeared before audiences for a host of marketed products – cereals, dog foods, others. There had to be money there. Why not take my own "cowboy", Hank Thompson, connect a product with his endorsement, and expand from there.

After a quick study of many of the clubs and ballrooms Hank was playing, it was obvious beer was as big a commodity as selling the tickets. Many of our jobs were judged successful equally by how much beer was sold as to the amount of gate admission.

The obvious was a beer company. One of the biggest beers in the Southwest at that time was Falstaff. It was sold at many of the ballrooms and nightclubs we played. Wouldn't it be great if I could get Falstaff to sponsor Hank Thompson?

As I learned early in life – write it down. This is just what I did. I filled several legal pads with ideas and notes of ideas I wanted to present to Falstaff. Refining those notes and with the additional creative genius help from Hank, I perfected a presentation to Falstaff.

Still not knowing for sure what I was doing, I called the president of Falstaff Beer in St. Louis seeking an appointment to make my pitch. I was quickly turned over to the Director of Sales and Marketing. Disappointed and feeling I was being given the brush off, I continued the pursuit. I was thrilled and a little bit surprised when I was given an appointment. Traveling to St. Louis for the meeting with great excitement and anticipation, I reviewed my honest but unprofessional presentation. Press kits were provided that included pictures, bio material, reviews from newspapers and trade magazines, photocopies of the Billboard and Cash Box charts, and some letters of praise from fairs and rodeos where we recently had appeared.

Arriving a few minutes early of my appointed time, I spent the time reviewing the proposal and how I would make it. Preparing myself mentally, emotionally and spiritually, I took several deep breaths and then it was time to walk in. The Director of Sales and Marketing, Director of Advertising, Director of Public Relations, and a couple of others, all were waiting around a highly polished official looking conference table – and all eyes focused on me. I took another deep breath. I waited another moment or two, giving time for silence in the room. Then I spoke.

All had a copy of my presentation as I talked about Hank, and how important his endorsement of Falstaff would be and how we could tie our appearances in with clubs that would agree to feature Falstaff on the night of our appearance. Our posters that advertised our performances would carry the Falstaff logo. Even the uniforms of Hank's band would blazingly bear the Falstaff logo embroidered on their shirts (these costumes were created and executed by the famous designer and tailor, Nudie). Falstaff was suggested to buy accompanying radio spots advertising our performance, tagged by Falstaff. Where legal, contests were to be held. And the final "piece'd resistance", a radio show series by Hank to play on a network.

This was embellished by the enthusiastically-received idea that Hank Thompson and his Brazos Valley Boys would appear, sponsored by Falstaff Beer, at the annual State Fair of Texas (entire run of 21 days) on the Magnolia Bandstand at the head of the midway. What a promotion! And talk about impressions! The State Fair of Texas admissions ran over 100,000 people daily.

I was overwhelmed. My presentation was well received. No decision was to be made that day. It took several more trips and on-site visitation of the various sales and marketing decision makers before they made the deal. I didn't get everything I asked for, nor all of the money requested. But, it was enough, and that began a relationship that lasted for years…That fateful day changed my inexperience into a successful reality. Understanding the positive belief of making an intelligent presentation, I realized just how important a corporate sponsor can be to an artist's career (and to the bottom line).

I was lucky. I felt I made a decent presentation, and Falstaff was interested in what I had to say – they realized (probably before I ever got there) what a big name like Hank could do for their product.

Thus began a relationship between a country artist and a corporate sponsor that was unprecedented in the industry, and one that lasted for nearly twenty years

To start things off, Hank was given a check for around $20,000, and The Brazos Valley Boys were outfitted with Falstaff-branded western outfits made by Nudie.

The following October, and for the next thirteen Octobers, Falstaff also sponsored Hank and the band on the main stage of the State Fair of Texas. With about a hundred thousand people milling around the fair during peak times, it's safe to say that the crowds that actually attended the concerts were some of the largest of Hank's career.

Another goal in the five-year plan was national radio exposure. Jim dovetailed the Falstaff sponsorship with a national radio show sponsored by Falstaff and starring

At the State Fair of Texas

Hank. It was broadcast over the Mutual Radio network through more than six hundred and fifty stations throughout the country, three times a week. This radio exposure was buttressed when, soon thereafter, the Light Crust Flour Company came on board and sponsored another radio show. For fifteen minutes, five days a week, Hank and The Brazos Valley Boys became *The Light Crust Doughboys*. What was unusual about the *Light Crust* deal, and what highlights Jim Halsey's power of marketing persuasion, was that the Light Crust Flour Company didn't sell flour in Oklahoma!

For both series of radio shows, Hank would bring The Brazos Valley Boys into the studios at WKY in Oklahoma City on a week day where no personal appearances were booked and record a series of the fifteen minute shows, with Hank usually doing the commercials. Often they could knock out about two weeks' worth of Falstaff shows in one session, and would record ten Light Crust shows in one setting every other week.

These two radio shows gave Hank much more exposure to Mr. and Ms. record buyer than all the artists on *The Grand Ole Opry* put together. Thus, the gut-wrenching decision that Hank made less than four years earlier to leave Nashville and head for Texas turned out to be justified, to put it mildly.

*

Edward "Wahoo" McDaniel was a Choctaw-Chickasaw Native American who achieved fame as a professional football player and later as a professional wrestler. He also was a big Hank Thompson fan.

Despite being a problematic teenager, he had been accepted by Oklahoma University to be part of Bud Wilkinson's football program. Although his college career was somewhat marred by injuries early on, by his senior year Wahoo was one of the top players on the team, despite many antics that made it clear that he preferred a curriculum of mixed drinks and The Trianon Ballroom to the curriculum offered him at OU.

One such stunt involved a night at the Trianon with Hank holding forth, where Wahoo and several friends drank heavily, early, and often. By the time Hank was closing out the evening, Wahoo was in a severely altered state – like horizontal and comatose. Two of his friends, who were probably teammates on the football team, had the dubious task of removing Wahoo from the premises but came to the realization that they were in no condition to carry his large and heavy body anywhere, much less down the steep stairs of the Trianon. However, another college student in the crowd – possibly a physics major – suggested that this could easily be accomplished using the law of gravity.

With a crowd of friends and supporters gathered around offering encouragement and advice, the friends dragged the still-unconscious Wahoo to the top of the stairs and positioned him so that his head was on the top step and the rest of his body extended down the stairs. Then they simply pulled down on his legs and Wahoo slid down the full flight of stairs under his own weight.

But there was a problem. Each time a step was traversed, Wahoo's head hit the step with a significant amount of force and bounced back up before encountering the next step. And so on down the steps.

When he reached the sidewalk he appeared to be no more unconscious than he was when he began his journey down the stairs; so his friends, who were in no condition to perform a medical evaluation, drove up to the curb, loaded him in the car and drove him back to the campus in Norman.

The next morning, word of the latest Wahoo McDaniel story spread quickly around the campus, and some people were concerned whether or not he was *alive*. But those who called the athletic dorm were assured that Wahoo woke up the next morning with what he thought was no more than a normal hangover.

After his career at OU, Wahoo played professional football for the Denver Broncos and the New York Jets, once making twenty-three tackles in a single game for the Jets. His wrestling credits included competing for championships in connection with several wrestling organizations too numerous to mention, and the magazine *Pro Wrestling Illustrated* selected him as the Most Popular Wrestler of the Year in 1976.

*

Despite the fact that The Brazos Valley Boys were at the top of their game, music wise, Billy Gray would continue to call for practice sessions at the Trianon, especially before an extended tour or a recording session. These sessions added to the existing heavy load on the band, and Pee Wee Whitewing remembered feeling the strain.

"It was tough, with all the personal appearances, recording sessions, radio shows, and rehearsals," said Pee Wee, "but if you wanted to play music, The Brazos Valley Boys was the band for you."

Despite this, Pee Wee and Dubert found another outlet for their musical talents. Pee Wee, in addition to playing steel guitar, was an accomplished jazz/blues guitarist.

So after a job at the Trianon, he would borrow Hank's Super 400, Dubert would take his trumpet, and they would go to the black section of Oklahoma City and sit in with the black musicians at an "after hours" blues/jazz club.

"Often we were the only white people in the club, but we really enjoyed playing music with those guys," recalls Pee Wee. "They were very good players."

But there was even more work on the horizon. Jim Halsey was developing some other promotional concepts for Hank, helped in no small way by the fact that Hank encouraged him to think out of the box and gave him carte blanche on all business dealings.

"In my early years of working with Hank," said Jim, "I was very pleased to learn that he, too, was a visionary thinker and wanted to expand his scope beyond the norm. Our partnership would become a magical one, and we became pioneers – being first at so many events and opportunities."

To pave the way for implementation of the additional promotional concepts, Jim stepped in and started coordinating the efforts of several team members that Hank already had in place, including Capitol Records, Ken Nelson, and a prominent music attorney. Also, when he was not on the road with Hank, Jim often traveled to New York and Los Angeles for various activities on Hank's behalf, not the least of which was face-to-face meetings with the Capitol executives.

"Back in those days, nobody associated with country music ever went to New York or Los Angeles to do business," said Jim. "Their approach was that if it wasn't done in Nashville, it wasn't worth doing. But I was able to book Hank in places that these people didn't even know about. Also, another vision I had for Hank was the international market. At that time, nobody in country music even thought about this."

*

During the time that Hank was filling the airwaves with his radio shows, fifteen-year-old Wanda Lavonne Jackson, who loved to sing country music, had landed her own radio show on station KLPR in Oklahoma City after winning a talent contest sponsored by the station. Hank heard her show on several occasions and was impressed by her singing. After one show, he picked up the phone, called the station, and got Wanda on the line.

"Wanda, this is Hank Thompson."

"Yes," said Wanda, wondering if she should believe it.

"I really enjoy your radio show – you are a great singer. We're playing at the Trianon Saturday night. Why don't you come over and sing with the band?" asked Hank.

A pause from Wanda, as she tried to gather herself.

"I'll have to ask my mother," she finally replied.

With her parent's permission, Wanda joined The Brazos Valley Boys on stage the next Saturday night at the Trianon and for several jobs that followed.

"I was amazed that Hank, with all his talent and charisma, would take the time to let a high school girl come to the Trianon and sing with his band," remembered Wanda. "He was always very nice to me, and he had so many neat friends and was always gracious enough to introduce them to me."

Later on that year, Hank came across a song in connection with his publishing company called *You Can't Have My Love*. The song was written for a "boy-girl" vocal and Hank suggested that Wanda do it with Billy Gray. They cut a demo of the song backed by The Brazos Valley Boys at Hank's home studio in Oklahoma City, and Hank sent the demo to Ken Nelson, with the hope of getting Wanda a recording contract with Capitol. Ken declined for two reasons. He felt her voice lacked maturity, and he also remembered the legal hassles with the underage Jean Shepherd.

"I don't want to get in that bucket of worms," Nelson told Hank.

Never mind. Hank was able to land a Decca recording contract for Wanda and she recorded *You Can't Have My Love* with Billy Gray in 1954.

*

Hank was asked to headline Cliffie Stone's *Hometown Jamboree* in El Monte, California, before a crowd of two to three thousand people and a large television audience. After one of Hank's performances, Cliffie, an accomplished musician, bandleader and radio host, pulled Hank aside and complimented him and The Brazos Valley Boys.

"You and your band are the most professional I have ever heard," said Cliffie. "Your arrangements are perfect, everybody is in tune and well rehearsed, and the musicianship is first rate. I've got the best country musicians in California playing with me, and compared to you and your band, they sound like they are playing in a jam session."

Later that same evening, Hank was squatted down on the side of the stage, signing autographs, a necessity in those days since there were no booths or tables where the artists could sign autographs and sell merchandise. By this time, he was getting a lot of "Do you remember me?" questions from his fans, a clear result of Hank's meet-and-greet policy at his shows. This night he was trying hard to participate in the conversations, but he was tired and getting very sore in his squatting position.

A couple was in line and, when they worked their way to the front, the man looked at Hank and said, "Hi Hank, do you remember us?"

Hank recalled that, about this time, he was so tired and sore that he almost said. "No, I don't", and let it go at that. But he took a closer look and realized it was Doris Ricky's parents, the couple from Redondo Beach that had been so good to him during his Navy days when he was dating Doris.

"Thank goodness I didn't put them off," said Hank. "If I had, I would never have forgiven myself. I learned a good lesson that night, and from then on I tried to be as polite as possible to all of my fans, no matter what the circumstances. The toughest thing is the question that I get all the time, 'Do you remember me?', especially when the fan is referring to a conversation I had with them years, even decades, in the past. I try to be as honest as I can with the answer and sometime ask them to give me a clue before I try to answer."

Chapter Twenty Five

Jim Halsey continued to tour the country with Hank and the band as they polished their Western Swing skills at each job. He noticed that they played several classic big-band popular songs, such as *String of Pearls*, *Tuxedo Junction*, *Jersey Bounce*, *Sunrise Serenade*, and *The Johnson Rag*. He also noticed that this music was not all that far removed from the popular big band versions of the songs that he had enjoyed so much in his youth and which were still being played. Still another thing that he noticed was that the crowds loved this music.

"As a big band enthusiast, I had become a fan of Woody Herman, Glen Miller, Duke Ellington, Count Basie, Tommy Dorsey, Stan Kenton, etc.," said Jim. "I even remembered the names of the ballroom locations where they played. I read about them in Down Beat Magazine, and I heard them broadcasting late at night, from magical locations such as The Prom Ballroom in St. Paul, Minnesota; The Terp in Austin, Minnesota; The Trianon Ballroom in Chicago; The Pla-Mor in Kansas City; and The Surf in Clear Lake, Iowa. Granted, these bands did not have steel guitars and fiddles, and The Brazos Valley Boys did not have saxophones and trombones. But the music was essentially the same."

A light went on, and Jim went to Hank.

"Your music will hold its own with the big band music now being played in the main-tier ballrooms throughout the country," said Jim. "The trouble is that never, never, have any of these locations even thought of playing country music, much less the music of Hank Thompson and The Brazos Valley Boys."

He then outlined what will be termed The Halsey Crossover Plan to Hank.

"It was my goal for Hank to became a real crossover artist and play many venues that had only booked pop or big name band attractions," said Jim. "The fact that Hank was one of those rare individuals who had a 'nothing was impossible' philosophy that coincided with mine was a revelation to me and a strong factor in our achieving the things that we did."

Jim started the initial steps to put The Halsey Crossover Plan into effect.

*

It was about two in the morning after a gig in Austin, Texas, when the bus, filled to capacity with Hank, the band, prominent members of The Brazos Valley Boys Groupie Society and their colleagues and associates, and an impressive assortment of bottled liquid, pulled into the parking lot at the Stephen F. Austin hotel on Congress Avenue in downtown Austin. Another Brazos Valley Boys Invitation Only Fun and Games Unwinding Party was about to begin.

However, there was a potential bump in the road. They had been kicked out of several hotels and motels in Austin in the past, and this may have been one of them. So Hank, ever concerned about providing housing for his employees and even more concerned about the fact that he had a bus full of revelers in hormonal overdrive, had an idea. He called Pee Wee over and outlined a plan.

Approximately two minutes later, the night clerk of the Stephen F. Austin, who also happened to be the night manager, was sitting at the front desk when a young-looking, small, skinny kid wearing western clothes came in the front door of the hotel and headed to the desk.

"Sir, I'm with the softball team out in the bus," said Pee Wee, having a hard time keeping a straight face, "and we need to check in."

The reply was immediate. "Softball team, my ass. You are The Brazos Valley Boys and we kicked you out the last time you were here. No deal."

Pee Wee put on his young, innocent sad look.

The manager relented somewhat. "But I'll tell you what I can do. I know there's going to be rip-roaring party – The Brazos Valley Boys are famous for it. We have a mezzanine floor that has no rooms on it, and I'll rent the whole floor to you for the party. I'll also rent regular rooms to you and your group. BUT NO PARTYING IN THE ROOMS."

Pee Wee couldn't reply fast enough.

"That's a deal."

In the meantime, the party was well underway in the bus. When Pee Wee gave Hank the good news, everyone filed out of the bus and into the hotel, delighted with the prospect of adjourning to the new Brazos Valley Boys Party Room at the hotel. If the night manager had bought the softball team story, he would have been amazed at the looks, the physical profiles, and the form-fitting fifties dance hall gowns of their cheerleaders.

The party room was very elegant and even had a marble floor and full curtains extending from the floor to the ceiling. With this type of playing field, it turned out the party was one of the biggest The Brazos Valley Boys had hosted in a week or two. Dubert and Gil Baca, the piano player, who had already established their credentials with respect to conquests, maintained their rankings that night.

"Dubert was relentless in his pursuits," said Pee Wee, "and the women were attracted to Baca for another reason. He was so well endowed, we called him 'tripod' – if he walked through the sand he would leave three tracks."

The next morning Pee Wee went by the mezzanine floor on the way from his room to the coffee shop and looked in the party room, which, needless to say, was a shambles. The room was empty except for one person – a female fan passed out on a pool table and wearing only one of the curtains.

"I can't repeat some of the things that went on that night," said Pee Wee, "but I can say that the elevators from the mezzanine to the individual rooms were running all night." Later, when Pee Wee and Hank checked out, the desk clerk had a message for them indicating that this stay at the hotel would be their last.

The hotel is now called *The Inter-Continental Stephen F. Austin Hotel* and is billed as "an historic landmark hotel". We now know why it is historic. It was the first hotel to provide a special party room for Hank Thompson and The Brazos Valley Boys and their guests, and the first to permanently ban them.

The next time Jim Halsey tried to book Hank and the band in Austin, he was unable to find *any* hotel or motel that would accept them. So, he had to book them in a motel in a town fairly close to Austin so the band could drive there the same night after the job. This put a damper on the band's social life in Austin, but it turned out to be workable, since the Austin cheerleaders were more than willing to travel.

Throughout the years, Hank Thompson and The Brazos Valley Boys won a lot of awards and accomplished a lot of "firsts", and this was a notable one – they were the only musical group ever to be banned in Austin.

*

Weldon Allard, a local Amarillo, Texas, musician, had a country music show on a local radio station; and Johnny Hathcock, the program director at the station, often collaborated with Weldon in writing songs. In early 1953, Hank received a tape from Weldon that had several songs on it for Hank to consider recording. Hank got with Billy Gray and they listened. The first five or six were not impressive; but the last song, entitled *Wake Up Irene*, was an upbeat, frivolity-laced answer to the Gordon Jenkins pop hit *Goodnight Irene*, and it got their attention.

"I thought it was a really cute song," recalled Hank, "and it wasn't your typical 'answer' song, since it had a completely different melody and a catchy rhythm."

Hank and The Brazos Valley Boys were playing in Amarillo about two weeks later and Hank went to the radio station for an interview. Afterwards, he had a conversation with Allard and Hathcock.

"I got your tape," said Hank. "Man, that last song is dynamite."

"What song is that?" said Allard.

"*Wake Up Irene*."

"*Wake Up Irene*? Was that on the tape?

"It sure was."

Allard and Hathcock exchanged looks of amazement. And embarrassment.

"Oh my gosh!" said Allard. "We didn't mean to include that song. We wrote it as a gag for my radio show and made an audio tape of the show. Then we taped over the show to record the songs we sent to you. I guess we didn't get to the end of the show on the tape, and that last song stayed on. Hell, I had forgotten that we had even done the song! And, you really liked it?"

"Yes, and I'm going to record it!" was Hank's reply.

A few months later, before a scheduled recording session in Los Angeles in June 1953, Hank visited Merle Travis at his house in North Hollywood. They were enjoying some beverages and talking shop when Hank mentioned to Merle that he was going to record *Wake Up Irene*, and explained that it was a rhythm tune that needed a thumb picking type of lead guitar.

"You mean like this?" said Merle, as he picked up his guitar and starting playing *The Wildwood Flower*, using his thumb picking style that Hank liked very much.

"That's exactly what I mean!" exclaimed Hank, who was very familiar with the popular arrangement of the song by the Carter family, featuring Maybelle Carter's 'drop-thumb' guitar licks that were not dissimilar to Merle's thumb picking.

"How about coming to the session and doing it on the record?"

"Why, sure," was the reply.

The next day, Hank brought Merle to the recording session, but had to talk Ken Nelson into doing *Wake Up Irene*, since Ken wasn't keen on "answer" songs.

"I had to convince him that the song was not, in a true sense, an 'answer song,' said Hank, "but rather a stand-alone song with original lyrics and a melody that did not remotely resemble the original, *Goodnight Irene*."

The synergy between Merle, Hank, and The Brazos Valley Boys at the session was very palpable as Merle easily nailed the guitar lead for *Wake Up Irene*. Hank was right. The song, although written as a gag by Weldon Allard and Johnny Hathcock, had a gravitas that worked.

Things went so well with *Wake Up Irene* at the session that Hank and Ken asked Merle to stay and play on several other songs including *A Fooler, a Faker* and *Breaking the Rules*, two other class-A tunes that ended up charting high, along with *Wake Up Irene*.

This session with Merle Travis enabled a new sound to be sprinkled into the Thompson arrangements. Thus began a long musical collaboration between Merle and Hank that continued through substantially all of Hank's recording sessions for Capitol and one that was the most important of his career.

Over fifty years later, Hank ran into Weldon Allard in Ruidoso, New Mexico, and they reminisced about the song that wasn't meant to be sent.

Chapter Twenty Six

In July 1953, *Down Beat Magazine*, which was a prominent jazz publication, sponsored a huge outdoor live music show at Soldier Field in Chicago featuring several jazz and pop artists. In this context, the following multiple-choice question is offered for music trivia buffs:

Question – Of the musical acts, listed below in alphabetical order, which one did not play at Soldier Field that night?

Ray Anthony and his Orchestra
Louis Armstrong
Eddie Fisher
Ella Fitzgerald
Norman Granz's Jazz Band featuring Oscar Peterson and Gene Krupa
Julius La Rosa
Ralph Marterie and his Orchestra
Patti Page
The Sauter-Finegan Jazz Band
Hank Thompson and The Brazos Valley Boys
June Vali

Answer: *None of the above.* <u>All</u> *of these acts played at Soldier Field.*

This came about when Jim Halsey, in an attempt to implement the Halsey Crossover Plan, mustered the courage to go to Chicago and meet with Norman Weiser, the publisher of *Down Beat*. Jim was extremely nervous when he met Weiser, and even more nervous when he told him of The Brazos Valley Boys' capabilities with respect to big band popular and jazz music. Then he practically held his breath when he suggested to Weiser that Hank and The Brazos Valley Boys be added to the July 1953 show.

No problem. It turned out that Weiser was a big Hank Thompson fan and Hank was added to the bill despite the fact that *Down Beat* had never been associated with country music. Hank and the band were well received at Soldier's Field; and, from that time forward, Weiser became another mentor of Jim and opened a lot of doors for Hank.

*

It was about an hour before The Brazos Valley Boys were to take the stage on a Saturday night at the Trianon, and the tables on the main floor were filling up fast. Although many of The Brazos Valley Boys hadn't even arrived, Dubert and Paul McGhee were all dressed and ready to go. That is, go and hustle.

Dubert, armed with a large plastic cup filled with ice but void of liquid, would start at the front of the ballroom, to one side, and work his way through the tables and towards the back. If he spotted a bottle sitting on a table (which was often the case even though the bottle should have been in a brown bag under the table, according to Oklahoma law), he would head that way. If the brand of liquor did not meet his fairly high standards, he would continue on. If it did meet his standards, he would go up to the table, greet the people at the table, and shake the ice in his cup – a fairly blatant sign that he needed a "refill". Usually the patrons, thrilled that a Brazos Valley Boy was at their table, would offer him a drink. If this didn't happen, Dubert would quickly move on the next table.

At the same time, Paul was doing the same thing on the other side of the room.

As soon as one would score a drink to his liking, he would wave to the other to join them at the table and also partake in the fruits of the labor. And as soon as the cups were fairly quickly drained, they would continue their mission. Needless to say, the two musketeers were certainly primed and ready to go (and about half-way in the bag) when the band hit the stage.

*

124

Left to Right – Bob White, Amos Hedrick, Dubert Dobson, Billy Gray, Paul McGhee, Pee Wee Whitewing, Wanda Jackson, Hank, Bobbie White, Billy Stewart, Donny McDanial

Wake Up Irene was released in late 1953, debuted on the Billboard chart in December of 1953, and went to number one in early 1954. Thus, Hank had a streak of three number one songs three years – The *Wild Side of Life* in 1952, *Rub-A- Dub-Dub* in 1953, and *Wake Up Irene* in 1954.

*

During this time, Hank and Billy Gray were disappointed when Pee Wee Whitewing gave his notice that he was quitting the band and moving back to California. Not only was Pee Wee a top notch steel guitar player, he had made significant contributions to the big band Western Swing arrangements that the band was playing with increasing regularity. Gray quickly hired a young steel player named Bobbie White (no relation to Bob White, the fiddle player) but also put on a full court press to persuade Pee Wee to come back. A few weeks later, Pee Wee relented. Gray didn't want to fire Bobbie White, so he was on the horns of a dilemma. But he came up with an idea and went to the boss with a new concept.

Gray told Hank that he had persuaded Pee Wee to come back and then dropped the punch line.

"Let's use two steels," said Gray. "Two fiddles are working fine, and we'll also make it work with the steels."

"O.K., let's give it a try," said Hank.

As the band transitioned from one steel guitar to two, Pee Wee and Bobbie became fast friends. Pee Wee brought Bobbie up to speed with the arrangements of the songs. But as time progressed, both Hank and Billie Gray looked to Pee Wee to take the instrumental break when they were singing, and it was apparent to all that Bobbie felt left out. Pee Wee devised a plan where Bobbie would play harmony on a

Kate Smith presents Hank with the Cash Box Magazine award for the
number one country and western singer of 1953.

lot of the songs, not unlike the fiddle players. The plan worked.

"The sound was so much better with the two steel guitars playing those parts,"
recalled Pee Wee.

It must have been. In late 1953, *Billboard Magazine*, which had just started giving awards, selected The Brazos Valley Boys as the number one country and western
band of the year. Also, Hank and the band made their debut on national TV on The
Kate Smith Hour, a variety show on NBC-TV. On the show, Kate presented Hank
with his biggest honor to date – the Cash Box Magazine award for being the number
one country and western singer of the year.

In the meantime, Jim Halsey was busy parlaying the success of the Soldier Field
gig into bookings at other venues previously confined to big band popular music. One
was the Terp Ballroom in Austin, Minnesota. The show was heavily promoted, and
everyone was delighted when it broke the attendance record set by Glenn Miller and
his orchestra in the late 1930's.

Another breakthrough venue was Johnny Betera's Holiday House, which was
located about twenty miles outside of Pittsburg, Pennsylvania. It was a supper club
that catered to the biggest pop names of the day – Perry Como, Patti Page and the
like – and could not have been further removed from country music. But that was
before Jim secured a week's engagement for Hank and The Brazos Valley Boys.

Jim remembered it well.

"This was really a gamble. We had to make sure the show would be successful. We
got Capitol Records solidly behind it and a country DJ in the area to plug it on the
radio. Hank did interviews for the newspaper and radio stations, and even did a spot
on a Pittsburgh television newscast. It was quite an interesting departure for the
Holiday House, and it was news."

The television news spot was on the local news in Pittsburg a few hours before the first show was to begin. After the spot, Hank and Jim took a taxi from the television station to the Holiday House, and as the taxi got closer to the Holiday House, they saw flashing lights from the police and the highway patrol. When Hank inquired about a possible wreck or delay, the driver explained,

"No, it's just a traffic jam caused by people trying to get to the Holiday House. They've got some cowboy band from Texas out here tonight and everybody is curious."

Jim also recalls the job from another standpoint.

"It was a supper/night-club setting, and I caught every show that week. The food was terrific, and I especially enjoyed their famous seafood stew, with rich portions of crab, lobster, shrimp, various fish, plus some secret spices and herbs that made it one of the best I have tasted to this day. However, on my last night, walking through the kitchen, I noticed that as the waiters and bus boys cleared the tables and brought the plates back into the kitchen, they would stop at a big thirty-gallon pot that was simmering with the stew. They would empty any uneaten portion of lobster, crab, shrimp, fish into this pot for further enjoyment of some unsuspecting, yet-to-be, diner."

Despite the issue with the stew, Hank's engagement was a solid success.

*

As Hank's popularity increased, the road trips became more frequent and often extended over longer distances, which increased Hank's determination to purchase a private plane that he could fly to the jobs. In the meantime, he continued his pilot training by attending a flying school in Oklahoma City to get his instrument rating, also under the GI Bill of Rights. In 1954, he fulfilled the long desire and purchased a Cessna 180, a single engine model, called a "tail dragger" and "sky wagon". Thereafter, except on very short hauls, Hank would fly the Cessna to each appearance, usually taking one or more of the band members with him.

Hank in the Cessna 180 greeting Nudie, Roy Rogers & Rex Allen.

"I enjoyed flying, and it afforded me the opportunity to get more utility for my time," said Hank. "Instead of having to be on that bus and drive all night to the next job and then all the next day to get home, I'd fly right in to any place that had some kind of an airport. I could hop in my plane; and in a couple or three hours, I'm at the job. Afterwards, I would fly home and have the whole day ahead of me."

Although Hank was often reminded that plane accidents ended the lives of other country music singers including Patsy Cline, Cowboy Copas, Hawkshaw Hawkins and Jim Reeves, this didn't bother him.

"It wasn't a matter of luck, it was a matter of judgment. I was a very skilled pilot, I had a damn good airplane, and I knew how to fly it. I knew what I couldn't do in bad weather, and when to get the plane on the ground. As a result, I never had any problems."

He continued flying his own plane to most of his personal appearances for the next thirty years.

*

Hank had a job in San Diego at the Bostonian Ballroom, and Merle Travis agreed to help him close out the second set that night. Hank flew into the airport at North Hollywood, Merle picked him up, and they drove down to San Diego. On the way, they picked up a bottle of Seagram's finest and, upon arriving at the Bostonian, had a couple of sips backstage while The Brazos Valley Boys opened the show.

After Hank finished his set, he and Merle had a couple more drinks after the intermission and during the time that The Brazos Valley Boys played a few songs to start the second set. Then Hank went out, did three or four tunes that didn't last over fifteen or twenty minutes, and introduced Merle.

As Merle came on stage, Hank handed him his guitar but was shocked to see Merle stagger around as he tried to strap it on. As the staggering continued, Merle started stepping on the strap and stumbling, until Hank and Billy Gray finally got the guitar strapped on. Then Merle said in a drunken drawl, "I'm going to do John Henry" as he hit a chord that Hank describes as follows:

"That was the worst sound coming out of an amplifier that I ever heard. The club owner rushed on stage, and we got Merle off. After I finished the set, I went backstage and there was Merle calmly sitting there, as sober as a judge. In fact, later he drove us to his house in North Hollywood. I've never seen anybody get so drunk, and then sober up, so fast!"

*

Joe Lehr, the owner of the famous Rainbow Ballroom in Denver, was a jazz/big band guy and knew absolutely nothing about country music. Nor did he care. Despite Lehr's high degree of skepticism, somehow Jim Halsey convinced him to book Hank into the ballroom on a prime Saturday night. Hank and Jim flew into Denver on the Friday before the job and decided to go to the ballroom and check it out. They were pleasantly surprised when they learned that Lionel Hampton, a jazz bandleader, percussionist and vibraphone player who ranked among the great names in jazz history, was playing there that night.

Jim and Hank entered the ballroom during intermission, with Hank wearing a

Nudie overcoat and suit, cowboy hat, and pink-and-light-blue cowboy boots. One can only imagine the reaction of the Lionel Hampton crowd to this outfit. Jim happened to see Lionel walking across the room and took Hank over to introduce them. Lionel was somewhat vertically challenged, especially when compared to Hank; but this was a good thing since it gave him a better view of Hank's boots. After Jim made the introduction, Lionel's eyes got big as he looked down at the boots.

"Man," said Lionel, "those are crazy shoes."

The next night the ballroom was filled to the rafters, and Joe Lehr became a believer.

After the job in Denver, it was from one extreme to the other as Hank played at a small honky-tonk in Pueblo the following Monday. Although the club held only two hundred people, it was worth it from a financial standpoint, since Monday was usually an off day, and even a small job would help defray expenses.

After the show, the owner came up to Hank. "You boys did a great job. Do you know anybody else that we could book in here?"

"Try Lefty Frizzell," Hank replied. "He's a real hot act and may come here for you."

About a year later Hank was back at the same club and asked the owner about Lefty.

"Yes, we booked Lefty in here," was the reply. "It was unbelievable. He and his band showed up carrying more liquor than equipment. The bottles of scotch were stacked up high like a cord of wood. They weren't shy about consuming it either, but they managed to make it through the show."

Chapter Twenty Seven

The success of *Wake Up Irene* got Hank another *Grand Ole Opry* guest shot in 1954, which led to a controversy caused by the narrow minds that ran the *Opry*.

The day of the appearance, Hank and The Brazos Valley Boys arrived at the Ryman auditorium in Nashville in time to set up the equipment, including Paul McGhee's full drum set, and ran through a rehearsal in front of some *Opry* types, including the director, Jack Stapp. Afterwards, Stapp came up to Hank and reminded him that drums are not allowed on the stage. Hank told him, if that was the case, they would have to do another song because the whole flavor of *Wake Up Irene* depended on the "drum roll" effect that Paul created by hitting the drumsticks against the side of the snare drum. Stapp didn't buy this, but since he wanted Hank to do the song, a compromise was reached. Paul was permitted to bring only the snare drum on stage, and play it while standing up behind Hank.

"It looked like the Revolutionary war painting of 'The Spirit of '76', with that snare drum, and Paul standing behind it," said Hank, "but we did the song."

This created a mini-controversy involving *Grand Ole Opry* history concerning the first use of drums on the stage of the *Opry*. There are two versions for consideration.

Version No. 1 (the Minnie Pearl version)
Minnie, who was a member of the *Opry* from 1940 until her death in 1996, told Hank that his rendition of *Wake Up Irene* that night on the *Opry* was the first time a drum was played on the *Opry* stage. Jack Stapp obviously supported this version, and Hank also agrees.

Version No. 2 (the Rich Kienzle[15] version)
Around 1944, Bob Wills went through the same drill with the *Opry* people in

---

[15] Rich Kienzle, a noted country music historian, authored the excellent liner notes for Hank's above-mentioned Bear Family box set.

connection with his first appearance on the *Opry*. This time a compromise was reached that involved allowing Bob's drummer to play behind a curtain. However, after he was introduced, and just before the opening song started, Bob threw open the curtain and shoved the drum set out on the stage.

"Whichever version is accurate doesn't really make that much difference to me," said Hank. "In any event, it is now commonplace to have drums on the stage of the *Opry*, and it was not commonplace back then."

*

As she finished her high school career, Wanda Jackson continued to appear with Hank and The Brazos Valley Boys at the Trianon and at some jobs on the road.

"For the most part, my father would take me to the various jobs with Hank and the band, or I would fly." said Wanda. "On some occasions, he let me ride on the bus, especially if it was in the daytime and there was no sleeping on the bus. In fact, my father appointed Bob White (the fiddle player) to watch over me. (A sage decision on the part of Mr. Jackson since Bob was the least rambunctious of The Brazos Valley Boys and usually not a participant in the debauchery at The Brazos Valley Boys Invitation Only Fun and Games Unwinding Parties.)

As Wanda honed her singing skills on stage with The Brazos Valley Boys, she looked to Hank as a mentor to help her with her stage presence and performance. For example, early on she was having a difficult time staying in time with the band, and went to Hank for help.

Hank with Wanda Jackson

"Don't worry about it," said Hank. "Your guitar is probably throwing you off. I had the same problem. You have to learn to sing to the time of the band, not to your guitar. Let the band's rhythm dominate. Just keep working at it, and you'll come around."

She did, and she did.

Speaking of guitars, Hank decided to switch from his J-200 acoustic to an electric guitar during his personal appearances. As The Brazos Valley Boys grew into a large dance band requiring huge speakers and amplifiers that created very high sound pressure levels, the J-200 just didn't work. Thus, a Gibson L-5 solid body electric guitar joined the family. Hank would often do his first set with the J-200 and concentrate on his ballads and medium tempo vocal songs; and then bring out the L-5 for the second set that enabled him to do some up-tempo tunes, some blues-type songs, and instrumentals.

Another reason for the switch was Merle's increasing influence on Hank's sound. Hank realized that, to fully render the sound of his studio recordings at live venues, he had to learn to play the thumb picking style.

"I leaned it little-by-little by practicing often, watching Merle, and asking Merle questions, although I didn't want to bug him too much," said Hank. "Merle was always glad to answer my questions, but he wasn't that good of a teacher."

But Hank became a skilled disciple of Merle's thumb picking style, which turned out to be especially fortuitous the next year when he hit the charts with an instrumental version of *The Wildwood Flower*. Although Merle did the lead guitar work on the recording, Hank played a comparable version at his appearances.

*

In 1954, much to everyone's disappointment, Paul McGhee resigned from the band and was replaced by Kermit Baca who, in turn, was replaced a few months later by John "Jack" Greenbach. Jack distinguished himself fairly quickly in a manner that had nothing to do with playing the drums. On a road trip to the western states, Hank and the band were booked in a motel in Jackson Hole, Wyoming, and Pee Wee, Bobbie White and Greenbach were sharing a room. One morning Bobbie was brushing his teeth and let out a roar.

"What is this stuff on my toothbrush? It tastes awful!"

Pee Wee had no idea, but Greenbach looked sheepish.

"I'm sorry Bobbie, I used it last night to apply some ointment to my crabs."

"Your CRABS!" Bobbie said as his face turned red and he almost lost it. But he took a deep breath.

"Well you get your ass downstairs and buy me a new toothbrush. And make sure its identical to this one."

Greenbach hustled out the door and found a standard motel-issue toothbrush that was identical to the one he had just contaminated, and brought it back to Bobbie with another apology.

The next morning Bobbie was brushing with the new toothbrush and it also had the same awful taste.

"What the hell?" shouted Bobbie. "This new brush has the same ointment on it!"

"Oh shit," said Greenbach. "I thought I was using the old one last night, and I must have used the new one."

When he heard the story, Pee Wee commented, "No wonder! Jack was the Southwest distributor for the crabs."

Chapter Twenty Eight

Merle made the introduction, and Hank fell in love. The object of Hank's affections had a well-portioned body, nice hips, and a long neck. Hank was in Los Angeles for a March 1954, recording session and was hanging out with Merle at Merle's house in North Hollywood when Merle showed him his new guitar. It was a version of Gibson's Super 400 electric arch-top guitar that had been customized for Merle at the Gibson factory. Included was a custom headstock, a neck with Merle's name inlaid in western-style mother-of-pearl letters, a gold-plated Bigsby vibrato tailpiece with an unusually long arm, and a redesigned pickup. Merle paid Gibson $1,070 for the custom version, which was the most expensive guitar the company had produced to date.

In the meantime, Hank had briefly replaced his Gibson L-5 with another Gibson solid body and had also tried a Fender solid body, but he was not totally satisfied with their sound. After the introduction to Merle's guitar, Hank placed a call to the president of Gibson in Kalamazoo, Michigan, and ordered an identical version of the Super 400 including all the custom features. Gibson agreed to do it with the exception of the headstock, which had been custom-made for Merle by a third party and was no longer available. Later, Hank went to the Gibson plant in Kalamazoo and selected the wood and certain trim; and he was promised the guitar in a few months.

At the recording session, some of the focus was to record another album in the EP and LP formats to be titled *North of the Rio Grande* containing a few old standards and traditional numbers, a few new tunes, and a couple of instrumentals. Included were Sister Rosetta Tharpe's gospel standard, *This Train*; the traditional *The Little Rosewood Casket*; the Cindy Walker composition, *Dusty Skies*; and *Gloria*, a song Hank had heard Tommy Duncan sing when he was with Bob Wills and The Texas Playboys.

"Sometime after *Gloria* was released by Duncan and Wills, I was in a restaurant in Dallas, and heard it playing on the juke box, but it wasn't by Tommy Duncan," Hank recalled. "I rushed over to the juke box and found out it was the original recording of the song by the Mills Brothers, and I loved it. I went out and bought the record, learned the song, and started singing it. I turned out to be a big Mills Brothers fan, and I discovered that many of their songs adapted real well to my sound." (In 1971, he recorded an album of Mills Brothers tunes.)

Hank wrote *I'd Do It Again* for inclusion in the album and teamed with Billy Gray for *A New Deal Of Love*. Also, Weldon Allard and Johnny Hathcock, of *Wake Up Irene* fame, contributed *When Your Love Burns Low*; and Hank and Dorothy co-wrote the good-natured *Baby, I Need Lovin'*, another number with a rare piano break from Gil "Tripod" Baca.

Then, it was singles time, highlighted by three strong Thompson/Gray numbers – *We've Gone Too Far*, (which peaked at number ten on the charts), *If Lovin' You Is Wrong* (number twelve), and *Annie Over* (number thirteen). The last song is notable because it is one of the first songs in which Hank switched from his trusty 2/4 beat into 4/4 time for the instrumental break, a technique he used in many of his later-recorded songs.

Also recorded was a ballad, *Tears Are Only Rain*, also written by Allard and Hathcock. Shockingly, Nelson later overdubbed The Norman Luboff Choir as background to Hank's vocals in an attempt to create the same sound that permeated a huge hit by Ferlin Huskey entitled *Gone*. Hank was underwelmed.

"It was a little too fancy or churchy, too formal, and not in character," said Hank.

Four songs were updated – *Tomorrow Night, Today, A Lonely Heart Knows* and *Green Light* which was renamed *The New Green Light*.

The New Green Light was no departure lyrically from *The Green Light*, but the arrangement in the new version was light-years ahead of the old and provided a good measure of The Brazos Valley Boys' improvement over the previous seven years. The new version would become the definitive rendition of the song, one that in the fall of 1954 would chart even higher than the original, peaking at number three and remaining on the charts a total of twenty weeks. It also became one of Hank's signature songs.

"The reason we called it *The New Green Light* was the fact that it had much better sound, and we didn't want people to think it was a reissue of the same recording," explained Hank.

The final recorded song, *Honky-tonk Girl*, like *The New Green Light*, would become one of Hank's best-known numbers. He co-wrote it with Waco bandleader Chuck Harding who had worked at KWTX when Hank was there just after returning from the Navy.

"Chuck wrote good songs, and I really liked this particular one despite the fact that the lyrics had some problems," remembered Hank. "But, I used to sing it all the time. Ray Price heard me do it at a personal appearance, and he said, 'Man, you ought to record that thing. That's a good song.'"

Hank went to work and rewrote the lyrics and added a new verse. The song was released later in the year, debuted on the charts in July and peaked at number nine. More importantly, it had good staying power.

"Every time I get royalty statements, it includes some based on *Honky-tonk Girl*," added Hank.

The session featured the new sound of the two steel guitars interweaving with Merle's lead guitar, and, at least initially, Hank was pleased.

"It gave us three guitar sounds, and they would alternate playing choruses. We also tried to use the two steel guitars in harmony like we did with the twin fiddles."

Looking back at the unprecedented number of quality songs produced at these sessions, it is clear that the sessions found Hank, as well as Billy Gray's well-oiled unit, at the top of their game and demonstrated just how far their sound had matured and developed over the past several years. But that wasn't all that was recorded.

Some additional songs were recorded for a very unusual, but logical, reason. Jim

Halsey, in implementing the Halsey Crossover Plan, talked Ken Nelson into having The Brazos Valley Boys record an entire session's worth of big-band, or Western Swing, instrumentals, all of which were staples on their dance jobs. The main purpose wasn't to release the songs commercially, but to provide some custom pressings to send to the ballroom operators to give them an idea of what the band was capable of playing, and to possibly dissuade them from any prejudices against hillbilly music. Hank footed the bill for the session, and several of the popular big-band songs that were recorded included three associated with Glenn Miller – *Jersey Bounce, Sunrise Serenade,* and *The Johnson Rag.* Everything went so well that the executives at Capitol, after hearing the finished recordings of the instrumentals, decided to release them as singles.

The day they cut the instrumentals was a busy one for several of The Brazos Valley Boys. After the sessions, they went a few doors down from Capitol to the Decca studio to record five songs for Wanda Jackson for the Decca label, including her first hit single, the above-mentioned *You Can't Have My Love,* the duet with Billy Gray, that went to number eight on the charts.

Later on in the year, *Billboard Magazine* selected The Brazos Valley Boys as the best country and western band for the second straight year (and for the third straight year, counting the 1952 *Down Beat Magazine* award). They would receive the Billboard award for the next eleven years.

"It was almost automatic because there was no one close to us," Hank said, recognizing that only Bob Wills and Leon McAuliffe could afford to carry decent bands but simply did not have the level of popularity to tour the entire nation.

*

To the best of everybody's recollection, one of Hank's most infamous fans, nick-named the "San Antonio Rose", forged her image into everybody's consciousness at the Trianon one Saturday night in the mid-fifties. It could be called her coming out party, and auspicious it was.

Nicknamed by The Brazos Valley Boys for the famous Bob Wills tune, the San Antonio Rose was not particularly young but was able to attract attention at the Trianon by her fashion statements. A typical outfit consisted of a body-clinging crepe

Hank with Wanda Jackson and Billy Gray

dress (usually red) complemented by obviously dyed jet-black hair and heavy make-up including an overabundance of rouge.

"She wasn't a bad looking gal," said Hank, "but she wore more make-up than a Hollywood starlet and had a loud voice that could penetrate a war zone."

This particular night, she was decked out in her game-day outfit and obviously had consumed an enormous quantity of alcohol. Hank was on stage for his first set, had just finished a song, and was about to introduce another, when he heard a loud and distinct voice from the large group of people standing behind the sitting area a few yards from the bandstand.

"HANK, I WANT TO HEAR THE SAN ANTONIO ROSE!" was Rose's request, very loud and clear.

Hank ignored her.

In the lull between the next two songs, the actual verbiage of the request changed somewhat, but the meaning remained the same, and it was just as loud.

"GODDAMNIT, HANK, PLAY THE SAN ANTONIO ROSE!" This time it was even louder and clearly audible to a majority of the other people in attendance.

She apparently didn't know that Hank did not do that song (although, on occasion, The Brazos Valley Boys would do it when Hank was not on stage, with Billy Gray usually doing the vocal).

Two songs later, when Hank was just getting ready to kick off another song, Rose's impatience became even more clear when she uttered the infamous punch line that nearly everyone in the room heard directly or heard *about* later.

"HANK, ARE YOU GOING TO SING THE SAN ANTONIO ROSE, OR ARE YOU JUST GOING TO STAND UP THERE LIKE YOU'VE GOT A HARD-ON?"

*

A few weeks after Rose's performance, The Brazos Valley Boys were on the bus headed for Los Angeles with several jobs along the way. A general conversation started up, and the topic was groupies in general and the San Antonio Rose (the person, not the song) in particular. One of the newer band members, who was impressed with Rose's performances at the Trianon, yet was well aware that she wouldn't win any beauty contests, wondered out loud if she was on the preferred groupie rotation.

"Has anybody screwed her?" asked another.

Silence.

Finally, someone suggested that no one would *want* to screw her.

"Not even Dubert?" someone asked.

Chapter Twenty Nine

One of the main frontiers that Jim Halsey wanted to conquer in the Halsey-Thompson five-year plan was a relatively new medium that, in his view, had tremendous potential, and that was television.

"I knew that if I were to succeed with Hank in a big, spectacular way, he had to be exposed to the mass audiences of America on a regular basis." said Jim. "That meant television. Enlisting the help of my acquaintances at Capitol Records, I asked for introductions that would help in booking Hank on some of the most popular network television shows."

However, he had to look no further than Oklahoma City for a television opportunity, albeit on a local level. In 1954, a deal was secured with Channel 9, the CBS affiliate in Oklahoma City (and, at that time the only television station in Oklahoma City), for Hank to do a live, local television show on Saturday afternoons. The format of the show was not a lot different from that of the radio shows. Hank would sing a few songs, The Brazos Valley Boys would do an instrumental and a vocal or two, and a guest artist would do one or two songs. Hank readily adapted to the new medium, and the shows went well.

A few months later, Channel 4 opened in Oklahoma City as a NBC affiliate. They had their own country show entitled *The Big Red Shindig*, featuring some local musicians and sponsored by a huge furniture store in Oklahoma City, the Big Red Warehouse.

After a few months of the two shows going head-to-head, Halsey engineered a deal whereby Hank was to take over the *Big Red Shindig*. A deal term was that Hank was to paint his bus with the Big Red Shindig logo. A more important deal term was that he was to be paid more money than he received for the Channel 9 arrangement.

During this time, a game of musical drummers took place. Johnny Migetto replaced John Greenbach; and, in December 1954, just prior to the recording session scheduled in Los Angeles, everyone was pleased when Paul McGhee asked to rejoin the band. Request granted.

*

The December 1954, recording session at the Capitol studio proved to be one of Hank's most productive, from a hit record standpoint.   In addition to Paul on the drums, the remaining lineup for The Brazos Valley Boys included Merle and Billy, Bobbie White and Pee Wee on the steels, Round Boy on bass, and fiddlers Amos Hedrick and Bob White. Pianist Donnie McDaniel took over when Gil "Tripod" Baca left the band, creating a loss that had a negative impact on The Brazos Valley Boys Invitation Only Fun and Games Unwinding Parties.

The session was highlighted by two of Hank's best all-time ballads – *Most Of All* and *Breakin' In Another Heart*. *Most of All*, a lament for an unrequited affection, reached number six, was one of Hank's personal favorites, and became a staple of his personal appearances for the next six decades. *Breakin' In Another Heart* was based on an idea Dorothy gave to Hank and Hank co-wrote with Billy Gray. It peaked at number seven.

Simple Simon, penned by Hank, Gray and Bud Auge, again returned to the nursery rhyme motif, and the Ned Fairchild/Merle Travis honky-tonk *Too In Love* was never issued as a single, and appeared only on the *North of the Rio Grande* album.

"On *Two in Love*, we originally recorded it as a ballad," recalled Hank. "But on the jobs, we'd kick the tempo up and the thing really did swing, and we worked up a little better musical arrangement." He liked it so much he recorded it again later in the more upbeat style.

The evening session again returned the band to instrumentals, beginning with the Glenn Miller favorite *String of Pearls*, a burning arrangement of Bob Wills' 1940 big band instrumental *Big Beaver*, and the 1949 Leon McAuliffe hit *Panhandle Rag*. The latter two instrumentals also wound up on the *North of the Rio Grande* album.

There was time left for one more recording, and Hank definitely had one in mind.

"I heard Merle play around with *The Wildwood Flower* one time," said Hank, remembering the time Hank had told Merle about the need for a guitar part in *Wake Up Irene*, "and I thought that it would make one heck of a good band arrangement." At the studio, as Hank outlined his arrangement and the band prepared for the recording, Ken Nelson, who was becoming fascinated with tape splicing, said, "Just go in there and cut it about three or four times. I can splice the best parts together if necessary."

They did just that. Merle nailed the song on nearly every take, and Ken went to work with the razor blade to produce the finished product, a flawless rendition of the song and a good example of the Travis technique at its best. But Hank remembered that Merle brought more than just his resourceful guitar parts to the session and to all of the other sessions that he worked with Hank and The Brazos Valley Boys.

"He was such a good musician and had such good ideas for turnarounds, fills, etc., that he would have been an asset to our recording sessions even if he didn't play the guitar," said Hank. "He could do so many things and had so many good ideas. He would think of little garnishments such as a different chord, or he would say 'Why don't you let so and so do this right in here?', or 'Tell the bass player to play this particular way right in there.' They weren't all that complicated, but nobody else thought of them. But he did, and they all improved the recording. He was that creative, and he worked so well with Billy Gray and me. The three of us kind of complemented one another; and what one didn't think of, the other one would."

The Wildwood Flower was released in 1955 on the flip side of *Breakin' In Another Heart*, climbed to number five, and thus became Hank's biggest instrumental hit of all. Hank expected the song to be popular because of its sheer quality, but he never thought it would become the hit that it did.

Thus, with *The Wildwood Flower*, *Most of All*, and *Breakin' In Another Heart*, Hank sent three songs up the charts within two months of each other, and each made it to the top ten.

North of the Rio Grand was released a few months later and became a huge commercial success and one of Hank's best-selling albums. It was also one of his best.

Hank with Merle

Hank with Merle

In connection with the switch to WKY for *The Big Red Shindig*, Hank planned to have Wanda Jackson on the show and expressed another idea to Jim Halsey.

"There are two guys that call themselves *Jude and Jody* that had a show before mine on Channel 9. They are very good and are popular as hell. Let's get them for the new show. I'll pay the two of them twenty-five dollars a show."

"Twenty five dollars doesn't sound like a lot now, but it was back then," recalls Hank.

Jude (his name is J.D. Northcutt) remembered that he got a call from Halsey offering the job, and he accepted it on the spot.

"I jumped at it. As far as we were concerned, Hank Thompson was number one in the nation and we were honored to be on his show. I don't recall us rehearsing much with the band on some of the early things we did on the television show, since The Brazos Valley Boys would often come in from the road just in time to set up and go on the air. But we played an upbeat style of country rock and Paul (drums) and Round Boy (bass) easily picked up on what we were doing. Hank also asked us to play some jobs with him at the Trianon and surrounding areas, and after a few weeks, the whole band was in the groove behind us. We learned a lot about the road, the music, and the business, and we had a lot of fun."

The Big Red Shindig, starring Hank Thompson, opened on WKY with Hank, acting as host/emcee and handing the ball off to Wanda, Jude and Jody, selected band members, and other special guests. The show became a big success.

But that wasn't the only television exposure for Hank, as Halsey stood firm in his conviction to get Hank on national television.

"We were able to secure appearances on the Kate Smith Show, which opened the door for other national network appearances," said Jim. "Hank was thus able to perform *The Wild Side of Life* for millions upon millions of viewers. And he was able to use The Brazos Valley Boys, which was a big feat at that time."

Fortunately, Hank took delivery on his custom Gibson Super 400 in time for his debut on WKY, and he could have not been more pleased. He used it as one of his performing and recording guitars for the next five decades.

Since the second J-200, with its Bigsby neck and headstock, was no longer Hank's go-to guitar and was fairly banged up, Hank sent it to Gibson for refurbishing. Hank was horrified when Gibson sent it back with a new Gibson neck and headstock and returned the Bigsby neck and headstock in the case. Since he was using the Super 400 full time, he decided to defer dealing with Gibson again for the time being, and put the J-200 in its case for storage.

*

On a Saturday night in 1955, Gordon Lingo, a highly-ranked member of the Hank Thompson fan club, brought a delegation of Hank's fans from his hometown of Wewoka, Oklahoma, to see Hank play at the Cimarron Ballroom in Tulsa. Without an abundance of disposable income, the delegation pooled their resources and barely came up with enough money to buy two essential items – gas for the car to get them to the dance, and bottled liquid to refresh them at the dance.

The twenty-two hundred-seat Cimarron Ballroom was a former ornate theater and opera house complete with minarets and elaborate murals. It also featured a large dance floor, a balcony for extra seating and a broadcast booth for live remote radio shows. It was home to Leon McAuliffe and his Western Swing band and was also used as a ballroom for all genres of music, including the popular big bands of the day.

Perhaps because of its history with classical music, the dress code at the Cimarron was different from that of the standard country music honky-tonks, clubs, and some of the dance halls of the era. When Gordon and his crew checked in at the ticket counter at the Cimarron that night, decked out in Levis and sports shirts, they received a shocker – they were in violation of the Cimarron's dress code, which expressly prohibited jeans, and they were not allowed in.

Undaunted, they worked their way to the back of the building and were relieved to see Hank's bus with some of The Brazos Valley Boys and friends inside indulging in a pre-dance party. Gordon knocked on the bus door, got the attention of Dubert and Amos Hedrick, and told them about their experience at the ticket counter.

Not to worry. Dubert and Amos put down their drinks, headed straight for the baggage compartment of the bus, came up with an assortment of The Brazos Valley Boys' stage uniforms, and handed some of the pants to Gordon and friends. Five minutes later, everyone was in the bus imbibing, and the issue with the dress code was history.

"I had hoped that Dubert or Amos would simply slip us in the backdoor of the Cimarron still wearing our Levis," recalled Gordon fifty years later, "but they apparently respected the dress code enough to let us wear those neat western pants."

Hank confirms the story:

"Back then, jeans were considered to be only work clothes for the oil fields, ranches, etc. and were not acceptable in some of the ballrooms and dance halls."

*

In 1955, Billy Gray decided to quit the band and go out on his own. During his six years' association with Hank, and starting from ground zero, he had helped Hank mold The Brazos Valley Boys into the best Western Swing band in the country, an achievement that was recognized by all. With Hank's blessing, he formed a new band known as the Western Okies, and made several records for Decca.

The gap left by Billy was filled, in at least some respects, by Merle Travis, whose chemistry with Hank and The Brazos Valley Boys was well-established, and who was already an unofficial member. Since Merle had enough star-power in his own right, Jim Halsey was able to book him as a solo artist along with Hank and The Brazos Valley Boys at many jobs during the mid-fifties. On these dates, Merle would perform as a solo act, and then would remain onstage with the band as a featured instrumentalist during Hank's portion of the show.

*

The sponsorships that Jim Halsey secured with both Falstaff Beer and Light Crust Flour enabled him to establish valuable relationships with many advertising agencies across the country. As a result, several agencies sent their executives to Oklahoma City to sign Hank up to do some radio advertising recordings and Jim made sure to schedule their trips around one of Hank's appearances at the Trianon. For the most part, the executives had never been west of New York City, and Oklahoma was *real-*

ly out West by their standards. Needless to say, at least from their standpoint, the scene at the Trianon was something to behold.

For example, executives from the Dancer-Fitzgerald-Sample advertising agency in New York spent a few days in Oklahoma City supervising Hank's recordings of several commercials for two pesticides for farmers. (The pesticides were so deadly that they are now illegal.) Halsey timed their visit and the recording sessions so that Hank would finish recording the commercials by Saturday afternoon to enable the New Yorkers to visit WKY for Hank's television show and then attend the dance at the Trianon that night.

The New Yorkers, aware that Oklahoma was a dry state at the time, were simply not prepared for what they saw when Jim escorted them, dressed in dark suits and ties, into the Trianon that night. The place was packed, the music was loud, and The Brazos Valley Boys, who had opened about an hour earlier, had worked the audience into a semi-frenzy. A large portion of the raucous crowd was drinking, hollering, and dancing on the dance floor, another portion was drinking and hollering at the tables, and another portion was drinking, hollering, and standing around the bandstand waiting for Hank to come on. But what really shocked the New Yorkers was the amount of alcohol being consumed and the amount that had obviously *already* been consumed. But they were in for still another surprise.

The New Yorkers were seated at a VIP table near the bandstand along with Jim and several personal friends of Hank, Jim, and the band. When Hank closed out the show, he came over and joined them in a post-dance beverage, which was about the same time that some trouble started. Apparently, patron A had been dancing with patron B's girl friend which riled up patron B (patrons A and B were both males). Patron B started after patron A, and patron A's friends started after patron B. Almost simultaneously, patron B's friends started after both patron A and his friends. Before you could say "Altus riot", a brawl erupted that could have been filmed as a sequence out of one of the old saloon scenes from a western movie. The honored New York City guests were horrified and turned pale. And this was *before* the main event occurred.

One of the fight participants, who happened to be dukeing it out with an adversary near the end of the VIP table, took a hard right to the jaw that propelled him across the full length of the table, wiping it clean of glasses, ice buckets, whiskey bottles, beer cans, ash trays, popcorn, handbags, and everything else.

A few minutes later, after everyone had regained their composure and poured a fresh one, Halsey commented to Hank loud enough to be heard by the New Yorkers, "Well, this was a fairly slow night at the Trianon – no shooting or knifings!" as Hank nodded in agreement.

"We heard from the New Yorkers about that trip for a long time," said Jim. "Sure, we continued to do a lot of business with Dancer-Fitzgerald-Sample, but they never visited us in Oklahoma again. One of their VP's later claimed that a night at the Trianon with Hank Thompson appeared to them to be more deadly than the pesticides Hank had promoted in his radio commercial in the first place!"

Chapter Thirty

In the mid-thirties, Bob Wills had held an "Old Time Fiddlers" contest each year in Tulsa. (The expression "Old Time" referred to the music, not the age of the fiddlers.) One year, the contest drew sixty-seven entries, and a young man by the name of Julian Franklin "Curly" Lewis won the contest. He was ten years old.

By 1955, Curly had just completed his tenth year with the Johnny Lee Wills band based out of Tulsa when he got a call from his friend, Paul McGhee. Paul informed him that Hank and The Brazos Valley Boys would be passing through Tulsa the next day on the way to Oklahoma City. He asked Curly if they could stop in Tulsa and talk to him.

At the meeting, Paul and Hank told Curly that fiddler Bob White was leaving the band and they asked Curly to sign on. Curly remembered backing Hank when Hank sang *Humpty Dumpty Heart* in April of 1948 on the *Johnny Lee Wills Show* in Tulsa, the day after Hank's marriage to Dorothy, and Curly came away with a positive impression. Also, the pay he was offered was slightly greater than he was earning at the time.

Curly was thus on board for the recording session at the Capitol Studios in June of 1955. With Merle Travis the only outside musician joining them, Hank and The Brazos Valley Boys laid down four numbers in the first session – *Honey, Honey Bee Ball, Quicksand, Don't Take It Out On Me* and *You Can Give My Heart Back Now*, all written or co-written by Hank.

Session number two yielded three instrumentals, one of which was of interest from a non-musical standpoint. Although the expression "politically correct" had not been coined at that time, the song *Red Skin Gal* certainly would have raised some eyebrows in the modern era. It was an old fiddle tune that Bob Wills had previously recorded under the name *Brown Skin Gal*. The decision to change the title was Hank's.

"When we decided to record it," recalled Hank, "Ken Nelson suggested that we change the title for obvious reasons. Since we lived in Oklahoma, I suggested that we call it *Red Skin Gal* as a tribute to the Native Americans."

Years later, the subject came up in a conversation Hank had with Bob Wills, during which Hank explained that they changed the name so as not to offend the black people.

"Isn't that odd?" Wills replied. "The original name of the song was *Red Skin Gal*. We were in Oklahoma, and we changed it to *Brown Skin Gal* because we were afraid we might offend the Indians!"

*

A few months after the successful debut of the *Big Red Shindig* on WKY, NBC started feeding some color transmissions to their affiliates and the people at WKY invested in color cameras and related equipment for producing and transmitting their own local shows in color. One of the first shows they wanted to do in color was the *Big Red Shindig*. This turned out to be a mixed blessing.

On the positive side, the show went over well, and Hank chalked up another first – the first musical act to have a regular television show telecast in color. The negative side had to do with the technical aspect of the show.

In those days, of course, there was no video-recording technology, and all the shows were live. Since the cameras contained a fair share of vacuum tubes, they required at least a two-hour warm-up before they could be used. When warm, they generated a more than generous amount of heat around the studio, which was exacerbated by the brilliant lighting that had to be used for color.

Therefore, a fairly bizarre routine had to be followed before each show. A couple of hours before air time, the lights in the studio were turned off and the studio had to be chilled down and kept at a relative cool temperature as the cameras warmed up. Make that a relatively *cold* temperature. This precluded any rehearsals; so Hank, The Brazos Valley Boys, Wanda, Jude and Jody, and any other guests would have to set up and tune their instruments in the cold and the dark, put together a schedule, and wait until just a few minutes before show time to take the stage as the lights were turned on.

"It was so cold, you could hang a side of beef in that studio when we started the show," said Hank. "But by the end of the show, we were all sweating with the heat generated by the cameras and the lights. Also, since the stringed instruments were tuned in the cold and used in the heat, they would get way out of tune and we would have to tune them between songs."

Wanda experienced some other difficulties in connection with her first three shows.

"On the first show, I completely forgot my lines in the middle of a song. Even though it was live television, everybody kind of laughed like it was no big deal. But when it happened on the show the next week, I was so afraid that Hank was going to say, 'You're out', that I was almost in tears. But he came over and hugged me with a big grin on his face, and he wasn't upset at all.

"As the third show was drawing near, I was getting very nervous so I wrote the key words to the lyrics on the inside of my left hand and up my arm. During the song, I would stretch out my arm to view the lyrics as I was singing, and it worked. At the end of the song, with the live cameras still trained on me, Hank came out and pointed the cameras to my arm and explained my technique to the audience, and everybody got a big kick out of it."

As the show gained in popularity, Wanda, like Jude and Jody, was often booked with Hank at his personal appearances across the country, which also resulted in some other uneasy moments. For example, during a tour with Hank in the mid-fifties, Wanda made a remark on stage at a show in a theater in Indianapolis that she remembers vividly today.

During the show, Hank sang a few songs, introduced Wanda, and left the stage.

The theater had a microphone on a stand that had an adjustable height that could be controlled remotely, something Wanda had never seen. Naturally, the mike was at a very high elevation for Hank and, as Wanda prepared to start her first song, she looked up and saw that the mike was so high she couldn't even reach it. Then miraculously, as Wanda looked on, the mike started lowering until it got to a height that was perfect for her. She made a spontaneous remark that caused The Brazos Valley Boys and the audience to break out in laughter.

"My goodness, I've never seen something go up and down like that without first having to do something to it!"

She couldn't figure out what everybody was laughing about, but found out from a band member after she finished her set.

"I was scared to death that Hank was really going to get on to me to be more careful," said Wanda, "but here he came towards me laughing, literally picked me up, and said 'That's the best one yet!' In fact, he never reprimanded me for anything and always told me that everything was OK, and it was just an experience that I can benefit from."

Jude also remembered a potential snafu that he created on a tour that he and Jody made with Hank and The Brazos Valley Boys in the late fifties.

"Hank was really hot in the Northwest, from California up through Oregon and Washington, and we would play to a very responsive, packed house at nearly every job."

With Jude and Jody on board, the presentation changed somewhat. The Brazos Valley Boys would start each show as usual and play for an hour, and Hank would come on and sing for thirty to forty-five minutes. After a break, Jude and Jody would open the second set in front of The Brazos Valley Boys, and then Hank would come on and close things out.

This schedule was especially fortuitous for Jude and Jody, since it gave them ample time to quench their thirst and hustle the girls after they had completed their segment and before Hank closed things out. One night, they played to a packed house at a big club in Eugene, Oregon, and Jude and Jody's segment was very well received. Afterwards, as Hank was holding forth, Jude was having a drink and conversation with some friends while surveying the scene for prospects. Low and behold, an attractive female came up to him. Make that an aggressive, attractive female.

"Hi Jude, I'm Sally and my mother owns this club. You sure are a great performer and a good-looking guy. I sure would like to get a little of you. Can we go somewhere?"

Jude took a sip, and started thinking fast. He marveled over the good fortune that had apparently just come his way, and he reminded himself that he was single and of age. "Sure, why not?" he replied. With the deal thus sealed, he started thinking about the logistics.

Since Hank and the band were still on stage, he knew that if he got his newfound friend back to the hotel where they were staying, they would be assured of some privacy in which to consummate the deal, yet they could probably finish in time to still make the start of The Brazos Valley Boys Invitation Only Fun and Games Unwinding Party, which he didn't want to miss. So Jude and friend hurried out of the club and to the hotel, got to Jude's room, and started up.

So far, so good. Until the phone rang.

"Like a fool, I answered," said Jude, "and it was her mother wanting to know where her daughter was. I don't know how she got the number, but I handed the daughter the phone and heard her assure her mother that everything was OK. Then the daughter hung up, and we were able to finish our business."

Later at the party, Jude started feeling guilty, and he went up to Hank.

"Hank, I had the club owner's daughter in bed in my hotel room about an hour ago, and the mother called my room. I hope it doesn't jeopardize any future bookings at the club."

"Don't worry about it," said Hank. "The mother was just pissed off because she wanted to make it with me and I turned her down."

Chapter Thirty One

The Big Red Shindig ran from 1954 through 1957 and required Jim Halsey to alter the road schedule somewhat to insure that Hank and the band would be back in Oklahoma City nearly every Saturday for the show.

One road trip in Canada ended just in time for The Brazos Valley Boys to drive the bus back to Oklahoma City by Saturday, with one stop for a job in Liberal, Kansas. With a couple of days of constant driving, the dress code on the bus was relaxed. Everybody neglected to shave, and, in general, everyone looked fairly grubby.

About an hour before they were to stop for lunch, Billy Gray noticed that Amos Hedrick was sound asleep. This gave Billy an idea that he passed on to the others.

Everybody with the exception of Amos quietly cleaned up, shaved and dressed for lunch and, when the bus pulled up at the lunch stop, went in.

"I'll bet it's so quiet in the bus that he will wake up before we leave," predicted Gray as they ordered their lunch. This was essential for phase two of the plan to take place.

Sure enough, a few minutes later, Amos came in wearing an old tee shirt and jeans and looking for his band mates. He was languid from the long nap, unshaven, and looked terrible.

As he headed toward the group's table, Gray called the waitress over.

"I don't know who that bum is, but he stinks. Please keep him away from us," he said.

The waitress summoned the manager, who promptly kicked Amos out of the restaurant. After The Brazos Valley Boys quit laughing, Gray told the manager about the joke, and Amos joined the band for lunch.

On another road trip, Hank and the band played on a Friday night in Bandera, Texas, after which the band drove the bus back to Oklahoma City. The next day, Hank had the occasion to check the bus and found a stranger in the bus, where he had apparently spent the night.

Before Hank could utter a word, the stranger took the initiative.

"Hey, chief, my name's Ben Dorsey and I'm your new road manager," he said. "The Brazos Valley Boys hired me last night. You don't have to pay me anything. I'll sleep here on the bus and work for free, and The Brazos Valley Boys are going to give me a little money to eat on."

Sure enough Ben joined the group as the roadie and turned out to be a full-fledged character who added to the bus chemistry. He also became the go-to guy for getting things done, no matter how insignificant or difficult.

"He was the best I have every seen about getting things done," Hank recalls. "For example, we'd be in some small town late at night after a job when everything was closed, and I would ask him to get me a hamburger. And, sure enough, about thirty minutes later he would come back with a hamburger. He very well could have talked someone into making one for him."

Another amazing achievement for Ben occurred one year when Hank and the band were playing at the State Fair of Texas. Hank and a few friends – not including Ben – had tickets to the Oklahoma-Texas football game at the Cotton Bowl at the fairgrounds. The stadium held about sixty thousand fans at the time and had been sold out for months. (Despite being an alumnus of the University of Texas, Hank was a Sooner fan.)

"It turned out that, after the game started and we were seated, Ben had to talk to me about something that was urgent," said Hank. "He had no ticket and didn't know where we were sitting, but yet he got into the stadium and found me among about sixty thousand people! I called him 'America's number one band boy', and I had a pair of white coveralls made with *Ben Dorsey, America's No. 1 Band Boy with Hank Thompson and The Brazos Valley Boys* embroidered on the back."

As it turned out, Hank was the one who reimbursed Ben for his meals.

After working as Hank's road manager for several months, Ben resigned but reappeared in Tulsa a few months later. Hank was playing at the Cain's Ballroom, and Ben came up to him at intermission to say hello. He was dressed up in a suit and tie.

Hank noticed the makeover and gave Ben an admiring look.

"Hank, my wife passed away and left me some insurance money, and I've got enough money now that I don't have to carry these damn speakers and amplifiers around any more," said Ben.

"Good for you!" was Hank's reply.

After the dance was over, Hank was backstage visiting with some friends and saw Ben. He had his suit jacket off, his tie loosened, and was helping the band members load the bus with the speakers and amplifiers.

Hank: "Ben, what the hell are you doing?"

Ben: "I know chief, I know. But it's a force of habit!"

Later, Ben's money apparently ran out, and he worked for Ray Price, Waylon Jennings, and, for the last several years, Willie Nelson.

"Willie is a good-hearted guy," said Hank, "I know Ben's in good hands."

*

In 1955, Hank headlined a package show that toured the south and included Carl Perkins, Johnny Cash, and several other performers. Once, during the afternoon show, one of the other performers came up to Hank backstage and told Hank about a problem he had.

"My records so far are not really country, although I want to be a country singer," said the young man. "I have written two country songs and would like to sing them for you and get your opinion on them."

"Sure," said Hank.

During the lull between the afternoon show and the evening show, the young man sang the songs to Hank, accompanying himself on the guitar.

"I have to be truthful," said Hank, after the songs were finished. "Those are not good enough to distinguish yourself in the country field. However, I noticed the audience's reaction to your performance at the afternoon show, and I think you can be successful with what you are doing. So my advice is to stick with it."

Elvis took the advice.

A couple of days later, on the same tour, The Brazos Valley Boys were backstage with the other performers, and a seven or eight-year old kid was wondering around with pencil and pad in hand looking for Elvis to get his autograph. He went to Paul McGhee, who was somewhat rotund.

"Hey fatso," said the kid. "Where's Elvis?"

Paul dismissed the kid as the other Brazos Valley Boys joined together in laughter at Paul's new nickname. Then Paul rolled his eyes and uttered, "That little son of a bitch!"

*

In the mid-fifties, despite a successful reign at the Bob Wills ranch house in Dallas, Bob got restless again and moved his operation to Sacramento, California, where he opened up Bob Wills Point, a country music dance hall a few miles out of the city. Bob didn't like to travel much, especially cross-country, and this location let him tap the lucrative California market and yet reduce his travel. Hank and the band were booked for several days at the California State Fair in Sacramento, and Hank took the opportunity to call Bob and suggest that they meet for lunch at Hank's hotel. Bob accepted.

Bob showed up in his usual attire – a western suit, boots, a cowboy hat, a big diamond ring, and a cigar. And he was sober.

During lunch, the conversation drifted towards the music and the musicians.

"Bob," said Hank, "you know that I have had a hell of a turnover in fiddle players, yet you seem to keep the same ones, year end and year out."

"Yeah," replied Bob. "I have been able to keep three guys in rotation, although I only hire two at a time. But when one would leave, there would be one that would be ready to come back."

Hank wanted to broach another related subject – drummers. This was a sensitive area, since Hank had hired three from Bob's band – Paul McGhee, Jack Greenback, and Johnny Migetto. Make that three in a row.

Hank decided to take the bull by the horns.

"I want to talk to you about your drummers," said Hank with a grin.

"What's the matter?" said Bob as he bit down on his cigar. "Ain't I learning them good enough for you?"

*

After the California trip, Hank and the band played one Friday night in Bartlesville, Oklahoma. After the show, Hank and Billy Gray took Hank's car back to Oklahoma City and The Brazos Valley Boys were to drive back in the bus. After the dance ended, an especially attractive, fully figured female fan, who had not gone unnoticed by the trained eyes of the band members, asked for a ride on the bus back to Pawhuska, which is about twenty-five miles from Bartlesville and on the way to Oklahoma City. A deal was struck, and she hopped on the bus and quickly and efficiently serviced all willing members of the band before they arrived in Pawhuska. Assuming that the bus traveled at a relative low rate of speed of, say, fifty miles an hour (a reasonable assumption, given the circumstances), that's approximately one Brazos Valley Boy per five or six minutes. As far as anybody could tell, it set a new record.

The next afternoon at the WKY studios, before the *Big Red Shindig* was to go on the air, Hank was tuning up and saw Willa Lou backstage hanging with some of The Brazos Valley Boys. Willa Lou, by this time, had established herself as a prominent member of The Brazos Valley Boys Groupie Society.

"Willa Lou," said Hank. "I hate to see records broken, but those things happen. I know it took you a fairly long time to fuck all The Brazos Valley Boys. Last night there was a gal that did them all in one night."

Chapter Thirty Two

Hank joined the songwriter's association, ASCAP, which policed the industry and collected fees based on the playing of their client's songs, and which was more advantageous from a financial standpoint that the other songwriter's association, BMI. However, at that time, he was writing a lot with Billy Gray, who was a BMI writer. ASCAP would not pay a BMI writer, and BMI would not pay an ASCAP writer. Enter "Orville Proctor", a name that Dorothy remembered from a childhood friend. Hank registered the name with BMI and used it as a pseudonym to avoid the problem in connection with the songs he wrote with Gray and other BMI writers.

Orville was a co-writer of one of the songs, *I'm Not Mad, Just Hurt* which was recorded at a January, 1956, recording session in Los Angeles. *It Makes No Difference Now*, a cover of the Floyd Tillman-Jimmy Davis honky-tonk standard was also recorded, along with *Anybody's Girl*, a Thompson-Gray effort; and *Taking My Chances*, penned by Hank and Charlie Mills. There were about fifteen minutes left in the session (not unlike the famous session in which The *Wild Side of Life* was recorded), and Ken Nelson again asked Hank if there was anything else he wanted to try in the next few minutes.

"Well, there is one," Hank replied. I've been working on it but have held back on it since I'm not all that keen about it. See what you think."

Hank sang *The Blackboard of My Heart* for him and Ken said, "Hell, that's a good song. Let's do it!"

After the recording they listened to the playback and Hank said, "You know, you are right. That's not a bad song!"

Session number two went back to instrumentals, and they recorded the 1947 hit of the Mills Brothers, *Across The Alley From The Alamo*. Hank wrote the arrangement; and then Merle played lead on an instrumental of the traditional country number *Bury Me Beneath The Weeping Willow*, which, like *The Wildwood Flower*, was a guitar driven number long associated with the Carter family. It didn't have nearly the impact as *The Wildwood Flower*; but Hank, who had become very proficient at the

Travis thumb picking style, performed it regularly on his shows. *Prosperity Special*, one of Hank's favorite fiddle tunes, was also recorded.

The recording emphasis then shifted to the task of re-recording some of Hank's oldies for the album *All-Time Hits*. Getting the makeover treatment were *I'll Be Your Sweetheart For A Day, Standing On The Outside Looking In Now, My Front Door Is Open,* and *Swing Wide Your Gate of Love*. The second session brought remakes of *Humpty Dumpty Heart* and *Whoa Sailor* along with original versions of *I Find You Cheatin' On Me, The Grass Looks Greener Over Yonder,* and an odd, Latin-flavored version of *You Remembered Me*.

The *Blackboard of my Heart* turned out to be the most popular song of the sessions, debuting on the charts in March 1956 and peaking at number four. Thus, beginning with *The Wild Side of Life* in 1952 and ending with *Blackboard*, Hank sent twenty songs up the charts, all of which landed in the top fifteen, with eighteen out of the twenty ascending to the top ten.

*

Hank and Jim Halsey frequently went to New York City to attend meetings with the Capitol Records executives, Hill and Range Publishing Co., and some advertising executives. Hank, with his imposing height enhanced by his cowboy boots and cowboy hat, made quite an impression.

"He practically touched the ceiling everywhere we went," said Jim. "And with that deep, resonate voice of his, his large vocabulary, and his precise enunciation of words, he was totally different from what most people expected. As a result, when he made a presentation, he took command of the meeting and made a terrific impression. This, coupled with his ability to focus on the goals we had established, set me up in good stead with all these people and paved the way for the deals I was able to make on his behalf."

Jim would often book Hank and the band in New York City to coincide with some of these meetings. Pee Wee remembered one occasion when they stayed at a hotel near Times Square. After they checked in, Pee Wee and Dubert rode the elevator up to their room – a fairly long process since the elevator was old and required an operator, and since their room was on an upper floor of the hotel. During the ascension, Pee Wee engaged the elevator operator, a dignified older gentleman, in some small talk while Dubert stayed quiet and looked bored. As the elevator reached their floor and the operator reached for the door, Dubert spoke for the first time.

"Does this hotel have any whores?"

Later in 1956, Pee Wee, who was tired of the road and being away from his family, quit the band again and moved back to California where he enrolled in barber school.

"We played over three hundred one-nighters my last year with the band, not including the television shows and rehearsals," said Pee Wee, "and I was burned out. But I very much enjoyed working with Hank. He was a tremendous influence on me because he was a smart guy, and I paid attention to a lot of things he said. Also, The Brazos Valley Boys were a tight group and good friends, and we stood up for each other. We also made a lot of friends throughout the country, some of whom I still see today. We partied pretty heavily, and I drank nearly every night, but after I resigned from the band I quit drinking altogether. In fact, I have never even thought about drinking."

Bobbie White, who had come into his own after starting with The Brazos Valley

Boys in 1954, was now the sole steel guy. Amos Hedrick also resigned about the same time as Pee Wee; and Keith Coleman, a top-rated Western Swing fiddler who had done his training as a Bob Wills Texas Playboy, stepped in.

Also in 1956, with about twelve hundred hours logged on the Cessna 180, Hank upgraded his airplane. The new arrival was a four-seat, twin engine, Piper Apache that served him well for the next five years. Also, he bought a new customized twenty-nine-passenger bus for the band, which included convertible bunks, a power plant, and a Falstaff sign on the front.

"It was as about as good as you could get back then," said Hank.

*

There is no question that the infamous, alcohol-induced near-riot in Altus will go down in history as the biggest fight at a Hank Thompson dance. However, year-in and year-out at Hank's dances during the fifties, The Cotton Club in Lubbock, Texas, was the epicenter of alcohol consumption taken to the extreme.

Drinking at The Cotton Club didn't resemble social drinking, where friends at a table would mix and sip as they visited, danced and listened to the music. Rather, it was very clear that the main purpose of the liquor and beer that the customers hauled in by the gallons was to simply get themselves as drunk as they could, as quickly as possible. As a result, The Cotton Club also led the league in the number of fights.

"The patrons would bring in fifths of whiskey and quarts of beer, stack them up by their tables, and start in," recalled Hank. "They obviously weren't planning on taking any of it home. They sometimes used set-ups at their table, but often would simply drink straight from the bottle. When they left the table, they would carry the bottle – usually a fifth – around with them and guzzle from it at every opportunity. The men would hold their dance partner with one arm and cradle a bottle in the other. And, boy, they would get drunk! And then, when we took a break between sets, one or more fights would usually break out."

*

In April 1956, construction was completed on The Capitol Records Tower, one of the most distinctive landmarks in Hollywood, located just north of the intersection of Hollywood and Vine. It was the world's first circular office building, and had wide, curved, awnings over windows on each story, along with a tall spike emerging from the top of the building that combined with the awnings to give the appearance of a stack of 45 rpm records on a turntable. A blinking light atop the tower spelled out the word "Hollywood" in Morse code.

A few weeks before their first scheduled recording session at Studio B at the Tower, Hank was driving his car from Tulsa to Oklahoma City with some friends. He heard a recitation of a poem by Annie Christie on the car radio, which reminded him of another poem entitled *The Congo*.

"That gave me the idea for a song with a rock flavor based on *The Congo*," remembered Hank. "I thought it would be good to get into this rocking type of thing they were doing at the time and have it about animals dancing and rocking all night long. I had one of the guys finish driving to Oklahoma City so I could get in the back and write the song while I had it fresh on my mind."

The song *Rocking in the Congo* was recorded, along with several others designed for Hank's soon-to-be-released LP entitled *Hank!* Included were *I Don't Want To Know*, which stands up today as one of Hank's best, and *Old Napoleon*, written by Hank and Billy Gray, a very effective novelty number that was a major departure from the standard Thompson/Gray model.

The second session yielded *I Was The First One*, an excellent rhythm tune with a rock flavor that had to have pleased those fans of Hank who also leaned towards rock.

"I liked that thing that Elvis Presley did called *I Was The One*," said Hank, "and wondered why it wasn't more popular than it was. So I used *I Was the One* as a basis for *I Was the First One*, but ending up changing most of the ideas. And I did it with that type of a rock beat thing they were doing at that time."

In fact, *I Was the First One* suited Elvis' style so well that it would have been interesting if Elvis had recorded it.

Speaking of Elvis, Hank remembered a change at his personal appearances.

"We really had resurgence during the Elvis thing. Our crowds increased because people would come out and say, 'By God, it's good to hear some good country music, because you sure as hell can't hear it on the radio anymore.'"

Rocking in the Congo, backed with *I Was the First One*, debuted in early 1957 and peaked at number thirteen.

Meanwhile, back at Studio B, to fill out the album, a Western Swing favorite was recorded – Bob Wills' *Hang Your Head In Shame*, along with two pop standards – the 1946 Ink Spots hits *The Gypsy* and *Don't Get Around Much Anymore*, and Ernest Tubb's *Don't Look Now (But Your Broken Heart Is Showing)*.

Then it was back to the basics with two songs that were released as singles – Hank's *I Didn't Mean To Fall In Love* and *A Girl In The Night*. The former debuted on the charts in late 1959 and peaked at number twenty-two; and, inexplicably, the latter, a marvelous, honky-tonk weeper that showcases Hank's talent as a balladeer, failed to make the charts, even thought it turned out to be one of Hank's best and most requested ballads, and one he sang often at his appearances.

*

In the meantime, Jim Halsey continued to meet and deal with many important people in the business.

"I was able to establish a network of contacts in the business," said Jim, "not just people that we could use, but people that we respected and had respect for us. Therefore we were able to establish relationships that resulted in a mutual benefit to us and to them. And this happened time after time."

For example, he was able to secure an engagement for Hank to appear at The Golden Nugget, the famous casino/hotel in Las Vegas, one that was unprecedented in the industry. It lasted over a twenty-six week period on a "two weeks on-two weeks off" schedule. Hank would play six forty-minute shows a night on Monday, Tuesday and Wednesday, and five shows on Thursday, Friday, and Saturday, with a twenty-minute break between shows. The engagement was successful despite the fact that many other country acts had experienced less than stellar results in Las Vegas, and the arrangement continued over the next several years.

By this time, Wanda Jackson, now a high school graduate, had recorded several songs for Decca records and wanted to start a full-time singing career. Jim and

Hank got Wanda a recording contract with Capitol, and Jim went to work on the bookings.

*

None of the "firsts" that Hank Thompson and The Brazos Valley Boys accomplished throughout the years was more interesting than the "first" they achieved after a job in Portland, Oregon, in 1956.

It all started with a routine Brazos Valley Boys Invitation Only Fun and Games Unwinding party at a room in their hotel after the dance. The hotel was one of the nicest in Portland, which turned out to be a mistake. On this particular night, most of the band members were well hydrated around midnight, and this was *before* the party started. In fact, when they and their eager guests arrived at the hotel to start the party, Curly Lewis and Amos Hedrick were already mellow enough, and decided to go to their rooms and go to bed. Despite losing two teammates, the rest of the group, led by Dubert and Paul, stepped up and carried the ball, and got the party off to a rip-roaring start in their room a few doors down. A few minutes later, after Curly had just nodded off to sleep, the phone rang in his room. It was a Brazos Valley Boy.

"Curly, pack up, we just got kicked out of the hotel and we're moving to another hotel down the street."

The party-timers didn't miss a beat at the new hotel, and were able to regain the momentum from the first party. This time, Curly and Amos joined in, and the party lasted about an hour and a half before word was received from the hotel security people that their presence was no longer desired at the hotel. The time was approximately 4:00 A.M.

Someone had sufficient presence of mind to realize that the downtown Portland hotel circuit was not exactly suited to The Brazos Valley Boys, so plan C was immediately hatched and implemented. This led them to a motel on the outskirts of town. By 5:00 A.M., they had loaded their belongings into the bus, driven out to their new quarters, and checked in. This time everybody went to bed, but there was a problem.

"By that time," Curly recalled, "it was almost time to get up and go on to the next job."

Thus, the Brazos Valley Boys garnered another "first" – The First Country Band To Stay In Three Different Establishments On The Same Night. Looking at a bigger picture, perhaps that should be "The First Band...".

Today, Curly regrets that they didn't win still another award.

"We won the best band award for fourteen years, and we also should have won an award for getting kicked out of the most motels and hotels."

But, this distinction did not go unnoticed by everybody. Later, just after Lefty Frizzell and his band got kicked out of a motel in Boise, Idaho, Lefty drove by the office of the motel, rolled down his window and hollered at the motel manager:

"Hey, you son of a bitch, you think we're bad – we're going to send Hank Thompson and his Brazos Valley Boys here, and they'll *really* take care of your fucking motel!"

Chapter Thirty Three

If it looks like an orgasm and sounds like an orgasm, then it must be an orgasm. Black Rider was in the middle of one, with all the attendant pelvic movements and moans as she built to the final climax. Of course, this was nothing unusual for Black Rider. But, what was unusual was that she was in the front row of the seating area at the Trianon, seated just under the bandstand with Hank performing on stage trying to get through *The Wild Side of Life*. Several hundred people were gathered around the seating area watching the performance (her's, not Hank's), and several hundred other people in the background were *wishing* they could get close enough to see her.

"I like to gauge my performances by the crowd reaction," said Hank, "but in this case there was very little crowd reaction to me, since all of it was diverted to Black Rider. The band was also completely diverted and, in fact, even *I* had a hard time concentrating on the music."

This event, which happened more than once, gave new meaning to the term "public display of affection", and cemented Black Rider's status as an important player in The Brazos Valley Boys Groupie Society, and as one of the principle characters in the lore of the Trianon Ballroom.

*

Tex Ritter was still going strong with his dual career as a western movie star and a recording artist. In 1952, he recorded the title-track song from the movie *High Noon*, thought by many to be the best western movie ever made. The song became a mega-hit and, after he sang it at the first-ever televised Academy Awards ceremony in 1953, it received an Oscar for best song.

Hank had maintained his friendship with Tex and was forever grateful for the help that Tex had given him in signing with Capitol records. By then, Jim Halsey was also booking Tex; and Hank and Tex worked several jobs together. After the success of *High Noon*, Tex, naturally, had to sing it at his appearances. This created a dilemma, since the chord pattern and metering of the song were very difficult to play on the guitar and were certainly beyond Tex's three-chord limit. (In fact, Capitol had brought in Merle to play on the original recording.)

In 1956, Tex and Hank were booked at a concert (as opposed to a dance) in Kansas. Tex was to open for Hank but did not have his guitar player to accompany him, so he approached Hank.

"Hey, dog ass," (a term of endearment for Tex) Tex said to Hank. "Can you help me out on *High Noon* tonight?" Hank agreed, and Tex outlined a plan.

When Tex opened that night, an astute observer would have noticed a very long guitar cable extending from the amp on stage to an area behind the curtain behind the stage. When Tex launched into *High Noon*, Hank's guitar was on the other end of the cable and Hank did the accompaniment.

*

Prior to the September 1957, recording sessions in Studio B at the Capitol Records Tower, fiddler Keith Coleman resigned and was replaced by Billy Armstrong. Also, because Merle wasn't available at the time, a new guitarist was bought in for the first day of the sessions – versatile L.A. studio musician Bob Bain, who later worked for years on the 'Tonight Show' with Johnny Carson's studio band. Otherwise, all the usual suspects were in attendance, and the sessions were fruitful in many respects. The agenda included recording some singles and some vocals and instrumentals for a forthcoming album entitled *Dance Ranch*.

Four honky-tonk standards were initially recorded – the Bob Wills favorite *Bubbles In My Beer*; Ted Daffan's *Headin' Down The Wrong Highway*, Jerry Irby's boozing anthem *Drivin' Nails In My Coffin* (a 1946 hit for Floyd Tillman), and Merle's *Lawdy, What A Gal*, a favorite of Hank.

The next day, Bob Bain was replaced by longtime Travis pal and guitar partner Joe Maphis, who, although basically a flat picker, could play the Travis thumb picking style by using a flat pick between his index finger and thumb on the bass strings and the middle finger of his right hand on the treble strings. A star of the *Town Hall Party* TV show and a Columbia recording artist in his own right, he was an extremely capable guitarist who was getting considerable attention as a studio guitarist.

Two songs of note were recorded in the first session – *I Wouldn't Miss It For The World* and *If I'm Not Too Late*. The latter, written by Hank, was as close to a pop recording as a Hank Thompson recording gets, and included background vocals by two of The Brazos Valley Boys who sounded like one of the many popular male vocal groups of the times.

Also recorded was *Just an Old Flame* which, like *A Girl in the Night*, was a honky-tonk weeper that failed to make the charts even though it turned out to be one of Hank's best and most requested ballads.

The tape machines kept rolling on the third day as four instrumental tracks were laid down, all of which had been played by the band on numerous occasions. One of the latter songs was the *Bartender's Polka*, the song that Hank remembered his Dad playing on the car radio back in Waco when Hank was a kid. Hank had decided to record it earlier and, on a trip back to Waco to see his parents, he drove to the same radio station in Temple that had played it a decade earlier and got a dub of the record from a transcription at the station. However, trying to arrange it for a Western Swing band proved to be a challenge.

"It's a pretty tricky tune that was written for the accordion, which made it kind of difficult to transpose to fiddles and guitars," said Hank, "and it didn't come out as smooth as I would have liked."

Dance Ranch was released in 1957 and is considered to be one of Hank's best albums.

*

Dubert often played a special role during The Brazos Valley Boys opening set at the large dance halls. When they played a song in which he had a lead part, such as *String of Pearls*, *Milk Cow Blues*, or the like, he would slip off the bandstand before the song started, sneak over to the opposite end of the hall, stand on the bar or a table, and play his part.

"It sounded like stereo," said Jude, who often sat in the audience. "The crowd would be focusing on the bandstand and when Dubert would play his part to their rear, they would jerk their heads around in amazement."

*

One winter in the mid-fifties, Hank and Merle were booked together on several jobs in the northern states. Merle flew with Hank to the jobs, and they were scheduled for one more show in a fairly small town in Missouri on their way back to Oklahoma City. Wanda Jackson had made an appearance on the *Ozark Jubilee* in Springfield, Missouri, the previous night; and Hank had agreed to fly into Springfield, pick her up, and fly her back to Oklahoma City with Merle after the Missouri job. But when they landed at a small secluded airport in Missouri on the afternoon of the show, Merle was so sick that he couldn't get out of the plane, much less make an appearance that night. Since the illness appeared to be no more than the flu, a plan B was hatched.

The promoter was contacted, and it was agreed that Wanda could substitute for Merle on the bill. It was very cold, and Hank and Wanda left Merle in the plane with several blankets and coats, with the understanding that they would be back in about three or four hours after the show.

The show went well, and Hank and Wanda hurried back to the airplane in what was then *very* cold weather. Hank opened the door to the plane and found Merle wrapped up in the blankets with only his head sticking out, looking like an Eskimo.

"Are you all right?" asked Hank.

"Let me put it this way," replied Merle, in a soft voice. "A few polar bears came by a few minutes ago, knocked on the window, and asked if they could come in here where it was good and cold."

Soon after this, Wanda was on the bill with Hank for a show in the Midwest that included an afternoon performance and an evening performance. Wanda got the flu and couldn't make the afternoon performance, but she mustered the energy to go on for the evening performance. One of the cables connecting a fiddle to an amplifier was extending about two inches above the floor, and, as Wanda finished her closing song and started walking away from the mike, she tripped over the cable and fell on her face. But, with some help, she got up and limped off the stage.

After the evening show was over, the promoter refused to pay Hank for either show (including Hank' performances), claiming that Wanda was so drunk she missed the first show and fell down during the second show.

*

In sports, it is well accepted that the home team usually has an advantage, but not so with The Brazos Valley Boys. It was harder for them to score at home than on the road, especially since several of them lived in Oklahoma City and had wives and/or serious girl friends. This was never more evident than on one particular night at the Trianon.

A friend and fan of Bobbie White was at stage front, trying to get Bobbie's attention. This was easy, since the fan was a very attractive girl with whom Bobbie had already forged a relationship during several jobs in nearby Seminole. Bobbie, who lived in Oklahoma City, had been careful to confine the liaisons to road trips, since it's safe to say that this particular fan was not a topic of conversation between Bobbie and his wife over morning coffee.

Bobbie's special fan's presence at the Trianon that night surprised Bobbie, but he had to ignore her because his wife was also in attendance and, in fact, was sitting at a table not far from the bandstand.

During the break between sets, Bobbie's fan came up to Hank with a frustrated look on her face and said, "Hank, I went up to see Bobbie a few minutes ago and the sumbitch wouldn't even say hello." It was apparent to Hank that she was fairly well anesthetized with alcohol.

"Cool it kid," was Hank's reply. "Since Bobbie is here with his wife, I strongly suggest that you wait until the next time we come to Seminole." With this admonishment fresh on her mind, she staggered over to Bobbie who was sitting next to his wife at the table with several other people. After thrusting her head between Bobbie and his wife, she faced Bobbie, and slurred in a voice that no one at the table had trouble hearing, "Bobby, how come you won't talk to me. Is it because your old lady is here?"

*

During this time, Hank took a vacation and asked Merle and Tex Ritter to take his place on consecutive weeks. They were to host the *Big Red Shindig* on Saturday, and also fill in for him for any personal appearances that were booked. Tex, still basking in the success of *High Noon*, flew into Oklahoma City on a Friday; and that night, he and The Brazos Valley Boys journeyed to Clinton, Oklahoma in the bus to appear at the Sooner Inn.

The show went well, and Tex was well received by the Sooner Inn patrons, so much that it was about an hour after the show before Tex finished signing autographs.

In the meantime, an extra convivial atmosphere prevailed backstage as The Brazos Valley Boys entertained several fans, mostly female, with a little frivolity and a lot of liquid. However, since they were driving home in the bus that night, they could not have a Brazos Valley Boys Invitation Only Fun and Games Unwinding Parties at a motel.

Never mind. The band members were kind enough to ask some of the more special guests at the backstage party to join them on the bus, and the party was in full swing by the time Tex finished his autograph session. Paul McGhee had made quick friends with a very attractive black lady who was sitting next to him on the bus sharing conversation and drink when Tex boarded. Tex walked on the bus, stood at the front, and surveyed the scene. A hush came over the bus as everybody fixated on Tex. Then he uttered a line that, from a dramatic impact standpoint, eclipsed the lyrics to *High Noon*.

"Godallmighty," said Tex, in his booming voice. "It looks like The Brazos Valley Boys have done fucked all the white girls in Oklahoma and are now starting in on the blacks."

Chapter Thirty Four

There were some changes to The Brazos Valley Boys. The good news, at least for The Brazos Valley Boys, was that Billy Gray returned to the fold. Although he had given it his best shot as a solo act from 1955 through 1958, he had never gained any significant traction despite his considerable talents.

But Curly Lewis decided to resign and join Leon McAuliffe, who was based out of Tulsa (which was also Curly's hometown) and who had a much less stringent road schedule than Hank. Curly was replaced by Tommy Camfield, who, in addition to being a good fiddler, distinguished himself in two other areas – he was a eager consumer of cold beverages and he had an exceptional, albeit warped, sense of humor. This was in evidence one night after a job in Lawton, Oklahoma, when The Brazos Valley Boys decided to stop and have a bite to eat before the bus ride back to Oklahoma City. Tommy was aboard and had a few pops before, during and after the show. To the other band members, this was a good thing, since the alcohol seemed to bring out the best in Tommy.

The bus pulled into the only establishment that they could find that was open at that hour – an all night truck stop with a restaurant, using the latter term in its broadest sense. It was a hot night, and the neon lights of the truck stop attracted a lot of bugs.

As the band was leaving the cafe after consuming a meal of dubious quality, a car-load of fans pulled up and started to go in the restaurant. One of the fans recognized Tommy.

"Hey Tommy, great show tonight," said the fan. "How is the food in here?"

"It must be good," was Tommy's reply. "Ten thousand flies can't be wrong."

A few weeks later, Tommy was on stage at the Trianon with the rest of The Brazos Valley Boys, warming up the crowd prior to Hank's first set. The place was packed, the atmosphere raucous, and the amplifiers were turned up high to overcome the crowd noise. To say that the music was loud, especially around the bandstand, would be a gross understatement.

During the middle of a tune, a fan came up to the bandstand and motioned to Tommy, so he went over and bent down so he could hear.

"Tommy, the fiddles are too damn loud," shouted the fan in an attempt to overcome the amplified music.

Tommy rose up and gave the fan a puzzled look. "What did you say?" he asked as he bent down again.

"The fiddles are too loud!"

Tommy raised back up with the same puzzled look, then bent down again and shouted to the fan, "Sorry, hoss, I can't hear you. The fiddles are too loud!"

*

In addition to music, Hank and Merle Travis also had a common interest in hunting. They would often fly Hank's plane to Alaska and stay at a friend's lodge near Stoney River to hunt moose and brown bear. On one such trip in the mid-fifties, Merle combined business and pleasure and took a job at the fairly famous Malamute Saloon in Ester, Alaska, and Hank came along to spectate. Merle was backed by a three-piece house band who, before Merle took the stage, played a song entitled *Squaws Along The Yukon*. The song got the attention of both Hank and Merle, and afterwards, as they checked out the other bars and saloons in the area in the interest of research, they discovered that the song was being played by the house bands in most places.

Another hunting venue was the One-Shot Antelope Hunt in Lander, Wyoming, that was, and still is, a historic event that draws celebrity sportsmen from around the country to try to harvest a pronghorn with a single bullet. Hank and Merle were in attendance for the event in the late fifties; and, one night after the hunt and a few drinks, they had a conversation that did not involve hunting or music.

"Hank", said Merle, "the next time you go to Los Angeles you are going to meet this gal. Her name is Hurricane Shirley and she's something else." This got Hank's attention, since Merle was usually pretty laid-back on such matters.

"How will I know who she is?" asked Hank.

"Don't worry." was the reply. "She is going to look you up, and there will be no mistake, you will know who she is when you see her."

Hank's interest in hunting landed him several guest appearances on *Celebrity Outdoors*, a television series on The Nashville Network. Hank was the guest host on several of the televised hunting expeditions, including a dove-hunting trip in Mexico and a goose-hunting expedition in Maryland.

Also, there was one memorable hunting trip in the late fifties that, fortunately, was not televised. Hank, Round Boy, and a friend were antelope hunting in Nebraska, near the Wyoming border. While driving along in a station wagon, they spotted an antelope across the state line in Wyoming. Despite the fact that hunting season had not yet started in Wyoming, they opened a gate at a fence along the border, drove into Wyoming, and shot the antelope. Hank got out his knife and started to gut the antelope when Round Boy suddenly got excited.

"Let's get this sumbitch in the station wagon right away!" called out Round Boy. "There's a Wyoming Fish and Game Warden driving this way!"

They threw the antelope in the station wagon and took off, with Hank's friend doing the driving and the Game Warden in pursuit. When they got back to the gate, Round Boy jumped out and opened it to let the station wagon through into Nebraska. He then closed the gate, wrapped some wire around it, jumped in the station wagon and they headed out. When they got to the top of a nearby hill, they looked back and saw that the Warden was still trying to untangle the gate, and they knew they were home free.

Later that night the three escapees were quenching their thirst and replaying the day's events, this time from a more humorous standpoint.

Hank had a confession.

"If the Game Warden caught up with us, I was going to say, 'Look, I was just a total stranger standing on the side of the road and these guys picked me up. I don't know anything about what these damn guys have been doing.' Of course this might have been a difficult sell since a half-gutted antelope was in the back and I was the one with the bloody hands and knife."

Everybody got a good laugh, and it occurred to Hank that it would make a good basis for a song. Soon the song, *Total Strangers*, centered around a hunting incident with a couple of twists, was a reality.

Meanwhile, back at the home base, Junior Nichols replaced Butch White and turned out to be one of the best drummers in the history of The Brazos Valley Boys. Despite this change, and several others through the years, The Brazos Valley Boys had a relatively low turnover of musicians by industry standards, due in no small part to the way Hank treated his musicians – a policy shared by some, but not all, of the performers of the day.

"I tried to treat the guys right, and I never was a slave driver," said Hank. "I did not criticize anyone, but rather treated them like I'd like to be treated. I paid them as well as I could, and I was fully aware that they had to make a living and were working hard for it. I gave out a lot of bonuses, Christmas gifts, and other things to make them appreciate their jobs, while trying to instill into them the pride that they were the best."

He also made sure that all The Brazos Valley Boys shared his positive attitude especially during the long road trips. Hank and Billy Gray looked carefully at this when they were recruiting, and any candidate that managed to pass the interview but later turned in to a chronic complainer and/or malcontent had a short career with the band.

Jude and Jody were clearly with the program and, when Jim Halsey packaged them with Hank (and sometimes Wanda) for a tour, they greatly enjoyed the life on the road with Hank and The Brazos Valley Boys.

Also, after several tours with Hank and The Brazos Valley Boys, Jude also came away with a great respect for the shenanigans at The Brazos Valley Boys Invitation Only Fun and Games Parties in general, and for Dubert's conquests in particular.

"On many of the jobs, the local Falstaff distributor would make sure that there was a big tub of iced-down Falstaff beer in one of our suites at the hotel after the show. Often, during the party, Dubert would be engaged with someone on the bed, there would be a dice game in one corner of the suite, and everybody else would be gathered in another corner drinking and telling lies. Or watching Dubert.

"On other occasions, when we were somewhere in the sticks after a job and it was too far to our motel or hotel to have a party, we would park the bus in a field, turn on the headlights, and play softball. This, of course, was after we had drunk enough to think that we were great athletes. I remember a tour in Calgary and Edmonton in Canada when this happened on several occasions.

"Also in Canada, we discovered that we could buy the best liquor we had ever tasted – Seagram's Crown Royal and VO – at very reasonable prices. It was so much better than the rot gut we had been buying from the bootleggers in Oklahoma that we were astounded. In fact, every time we went to Canada, Bobbie White bought two or three cases of it, put it on the bus and sold it to the people in Oklahoma, including the band members, for about twice what he paid for it."

Bobbie White was also excelling in areas not related to marketing Canada's finest.

"Bobbie was an outstanding member of the organization," said Hank. "In addition to being a great steel guitarist, he was the consummate team player and helped me in other phases of the business including collecting the final payment on the contract at the jobs."

*

For an April 1958, recording session at the Capitol Records Tower, Ken Nelson suggested that Hank consider recording an album of instrumental waltzes. Nelson, who knew pop music and had even worked with classical music in his days in Chicago radio, reminded Hank that he had done very few waltzes in his career.

"I was aware that some of the biggest songs of all time were waltzes," said Hank. "But I never did write much in three-quarters time. So I agreed that we should record some."

It wasn't all that easy. The Brazos Valley Boys had a hard time mastering some of the arrangements, particularly in the fiddle section.

The next day Hank sang four waltzes – Clyde Moody's popular *Shenandoah Waltz*, Cowboy Copas' *Signed, Sealed and Delivered*, the pre-World War I pop favorite *In The Valley Of The Moon*, and the Cindy Walker honky-tonk favorite, *The Warm Red Wine*.

When waltz-time was over, and before the next session, Merle was warming up in the studio and called Hank over.

"Do you remember that song we heard in Alaska, *Squaws Along The Yukon?*" asked Merle as he started playing it on the guitar. "I've rewritten some of the lines and you may also have some ideas about updating it and recording it."

"Good idea," said Hank. They huddled for a few minutes, reworked the song some more, came up with an arrangement, and committed it to tape.

Several other singles were also added to the portfolio including *You're Going Back To Your Old Ways Again* and *I've Run Out of Tomorrows*, evidencing that Hank had brought his A game. Also recorded was *Gathering Flowers*, a guitar instrumental not dissimilar to *The Wildwood Flower*, in which Hank did the arrangement and Merle nailed the guitar work.

I've Run Out of Tomorrows peaked at seven, but *Squaws Along The Yukon* turned out to be Hank's highest charted song since *Wake Up Irene*. *Squaws* climbed to number two after debuting on the charts in the fall of 1958, which, by pure coincidence, was the same year that Alaska was admitted to statehood.

Chapter Thirty Five

After several straight years of appearances, Hank and The Brazos Valley Boys had become a fixture at The State Fair of Texas which was one of the highlights of the tour schedule each year. During the fair one year in the late fifties, a female from one of the nearby fair booths took a liking to Hank and the band and began hanging around the bandstand during the shows. She was very attractive and had a state-of-the-art profile. Since no one remembered her name, we'll call her Voluptuous.

"Boy, was she good looking!" said Hank. Very high praise indeed, considering that his tastes were in the stratosphere regarding such matters.

The band members, who were always looking for new talent to induct into The Brazos Valley Boys Groupie Society, readily extended Voluptuous their friendship. She countered by giving Hank and each band member a cigarette lighter – one of the prizes offered at her booth. Moreover, each lighter was engraved with the recipient's name.

Hank was so impressed by the handsome presents that he made a special announcement during one of his shows, expressly thanking Voluptuous for them. Since Dorothy was back stage, Hank soft-pedaled the announcement to something like this:

"We would like to take a minute to thank a very sweet young lady from a near-by booth for the wonderful gifts she gave to me and each member of The Brazos Valley Boys."

During intermission, Hank was at the side of the bandstand talking to Dorothy when he saw Voluptuous walking toward them. Thinking quickly, he started the introduction before Voluptuous got close enough to say anything.

"Hi, this is my wife, Dorothy. Dorothy this is the person that gave us the cigarette lighters."

After Voluptuous left, Dorothy gave Hank a concerned look and a sarcastic remark. "Is that the 'sweet young lady' you were talking about? Don't give me that shit – she looks more like a Hollywood starlet!"

Later on that evening, Billy Gray and his wife Billie Faye, who were living in

Dallas, hosted a poker game at their house for Hank, Dorothy, Round Boy and his wife, Juanita. All of the guys were drinking and smoking cigars or cigarettes; and, as the game progressed, Dorothy noticed that Hank, Round Boy and Billy all were using their engraved cigarette lighters, which were lying on the table.

"Aren't those the lighters that that 'sweet young lady' at the State Fair of Texas gave you boys?" asked Dorothy, making no attempt to hide the sarcasm.

Billy and Round Boy, with sheepish looks on their faces, nodded in the affirmative.

Billie Faye to Billy Gray: "But you told me you got yours from a radio station!"

Juanita to Round Boy: "You told me you got yours from the Falstaff people!"

With that, Dorothy picked up the lighters, went to the front door, opened it, threw all three lighters into the yard across the street, went back to the table, sat down, and said:

"OK, deal!"

*

Another year during their engagement at the State Fair of Texas, Hank and The Brazos Valley Boys stayed at a motel that was near the fair grounds. It was also fairly close to the Musician's Union Hall in Dallas where the musicians could meet and engage in several activities such as jamming, telling stories, and, most importantly, keeping themselves well hydrated. One evening, after the State Fair show, Dubert and Paul headed for the Hall and partook in the activities, comfortable with the fact that it was only a short walk, or crawl, back to the motel.

Much later on, after the bar at the Hall closed down, they headed on foot for the motel – a questionable proposition considering that they both had a difficult time putting one foot in front of the other. As they progressed down the street, Paul announced that he had to take a leak. He noticed a large, high, wooden construction fence, or barricade, along an area of the sidewalk in front of a large multi-story building that was being remodeled. He found an opening in the fence, asked Dubert to wait for him, and headed through the opening.

Dubert waited and waited. And waited. He finally decided to go look for Paul and went through the same opening, took a few steps and discovered that he was inside the lobby of a building that was having its front façade replaced. He also noticed a security officer sitting behind a desk in the lobby.

He tried to walk the straightest line possible as he approached the desk.

"Are you with that other guy who came in here?" asked the security guard.

Dubert gave him the soberest sounding reply he could muster.

"Yes."

Wrong answer.

"You're in the lobby of the Dallas City Hall," was the sharp reply. "Your drunken friend just came in and started pissing in our lobby. We have him in a jail in the back. You have two choices – you can either join him, or you can get the hell out of here."

Fortunately, Dubert was able to logically process the two choices. "I think I will leave," he said as he turned around and carefully walked out.

He escaped, and Hank bailed Paul out the next day.

Soon after that, Paul left the band, and was replaced for a short time by Butch White. Of all the band members, Paul was Hank's closest friend.

"Paul was probably as good a friend that I had in the band," said Hank, "we had a nice rapport." But Hank and Paul remained close friends and saw each other on occasion when Hank was on the road.

*

In 1947, Roy Hogsed recorded the original version of *Cocaine Blues*, a song about a hophead who shoots his woman down, and it ascended to number fifteen nationally. But it was so explicit and violent that it got little radio airplay and, in some cases, was only sold under the counter. During the April 1958, recording sessions, Hank suggested to Ken Nelson that he record the song for release as a single.

"Hank, there's not a way in the world you'll ever get any airplay on that thing," cautioned Nelson. "However, if you really want to do it, we might be able to put it in an album."

After the April sessions, Hank starting thinking about Ken's suggestion for *Cocaine Blues*. What if he put it in an album along with several other songs of the same genre? It's almost as if he were thinking "If Ken Nelson thinks *Cocaine Blues* is bad, wait until he hears this!" As a result, he came to the December 1958, sessions armed with a collection of raucous honky-tonk songs written by others and dealing with a major-league lineup of grossly politically incorrect subjects.

The entire album was recorded in two days, was released in 1959 under the title *Songs For Rounders*, and was one of several "firsts". It was Hank's first recording in stereo (and one of the first country albums to be recorded in stereo), and it certainly was one of the first "concept albums" in country music. But probably most significant, the album has to be one of the most politically incorrect in the history of *music*. It was this last characteristic that had the suits at Capitol records concerned; but they let it be released and, surprisingly, it received little criticism, became a big commercial success, and is one of Hank's most popular albums.

The song lineup included *I Left My Gal in the Mountains* (drinking, murder and prison), *May I Sleep in Your Barn Tonight Mister* (adultery), *Deep Ellum Blues* (drinking and promiscuous women), *Drunkard Blues* (too much drinking), *Roving Gambler* (gambling, murder and prison), *Teach 'Em How To Swim* (drinking), and, of course, *Cocaine Blues*.

But the bell ringer was the song, *Little Blossom*. Based on a poem written by Martha J. Bidwell in 1873, the song is about a drunken father who comes home to his young daughter who is by herself and, in a drunken rage, kills her. (Dolly Parton and Mac Wiseman also recorded the song.)

There is also a story behind the photo shoot for the *Rounders* album cover. Hank, dressed in a white Nudie outfit, is shown playing poker with two extremely attractive and scantily-clad dancehall girls. After recording the songs about drinking all day, Hank and several of The Brazos Valley Boys decided to stay in character and have a drink or two after the session ended. They took a couple of the Capitol guys to a bar down the street from the Capitol Tower for that very purpose.

"We walked in the bar, and I was pleasantly surprised to see one of the girls from the photo shoot," said Hank, "but was she bombed! She had apparently been in there drinking ever since the photo shoot that morning. I said to her, 'Hi, how you doing?' and got no response. I don't even think she recognized me!"

The next day, with the *Rounders* album in the can and everybody's thirst quenched, the attention was directed to recording some singles. The first song recorded was *Lost John*, a song that Hank had heard performed by Merle, Wayne Raney and the Delmore Brothers. Then came two exceptional ballads – *I Guess I'm Getting Over You* and *What Made Her Change*. *Total Strangers*, the song that Hank penned based on the nearly ill-fated hunting incident in Nebraska/Wyoming, was also recorded and was released in early 1959 as the B side of previously recorded *Anybody's Girl*. *Total Strangers* peaked at number twenty-five, and *Anybody's Girl* at number thirteen.

At the final sessions, The Brazos Valley Boys recorded instrumental versions of the pop tunes *Coconut Grove* and *Tuxedo Junction*, the latter being a million seller for Glen Miller. *Give The World A Smile*, another guitar driven piece selected to showcase Merle's talents, was recorded with background vocals supplied by the gospel-singing Stamps Quartet, a group that Hank had heard singing over WFAA in Dallas. The song ended up as the flipside to Hank's vocal 1961 hit, *Hangover Tavern* and, along with the instrumentals, wound up on the 1962 Brazos Valley Boys LP entitled *Number One Country and Western Band*.

Chapter Thirty Six

One night in 1959, Hank and Billy Gray were in their dressing room between sets at the MB Corral in Wichita Falls, Texas, a huge dance hall that was one of Hank's more popular venues. Jerry Miller, one of the members of the Miller Brothers, the Corral's house band, came in and started a conversation.

"Hey, I've got a hell of a song for you guys. The opening line goes like this:

Hey, mister bartender, please don't be so slow,
I've got time for one more round, and a six pack to go.

What do you think about that?"
"Sounds like a good idea," said Hank. "Did you write it?"
"Yeah," was the reply.
"Please send me a tape of it."
Several weeks later, Billy Gray had a question for Hank.
"Did you ever hear from that old boy about the six pack song?"
"No, I never did," replied Hank.
It turned out that this was the backdrop for a bizarre confluence of coincidences that led to Hank's recording of *A Six Pack to Go*.

Coincidence No. 1
A few weeks after the Wichita Falls job, Hank and the band were making plans to go to California for a scheduled recording session in Los Angeles in December 1959. Some jobs were booked on the way to Los Angeles, one of which was for a private party on a Friday night in Grants, New Mexico, followed by a Saturday night dance at a hall in Flagstaff, Arizona. About a week before the scheduled jobs, Jim Halsey got some bad news – the hall had burned down.

When Hank got the news, he was concerned.
"That's a bad deal, especially since it's on a prime Saturday night," Hank said to

Jim. Hank didn't have to remind him that The Brazos Valley Boys were being paid regardless of the jobs they had.

"I'll come up with something," said Jim, knowing full well that there was not a lot he could do in December, on such short notice, as far as dance halls in Arizona and New Mexico were concerned. But a few days later, Jim informed Hank that he had, indeed come up with a possibility for the Saturday in question.

"It's a door deal at the American Legion Hall in Holbrook, Arizona."

"Where?"

"Holbrook, Arizona. It's due east of Flagstaff and between Flagstaff and the Arizona/New Mexico border. The hall seats several hundred people, but advertising is going to be difficult since there's no radio station in Holbrook, they only have one weekly newspaper, and we've missed this week's issue. Our only hope is to advertise on a radio station that is closest to Holbrook. Don't expect a big crowd, but at least it's a job.

"Ok, we'll take it."

Coincidence No. 2

Johnny Lowe, a country music artist, was based out of Cairo, Illinois, which is located at the southernmost tip of Illinois. During the late fifties, the town was replete with honky-tonks, bars and dance halls, and Johnny and his band got so much work that they seldom went on the road. But one rare road trip included a job in a club in Holbrook on the same Saturday night that Hank was booked at the American Legion Hall.

Coincidence No. 3

Included in the surprisingly large crowd that showed up at the American Legion Hall in Holbrook to see Hank was an old friend of Hank's – a rodeo trick rope artist by the nickname of "Buffalo". He owned the club where Johnny Lowe was playing that night, but he came to the Legion Hall to see Hank. During Hank's break, Buffalo came up to say hello.

"Hey, Hank, I own a club not far from here. We stay open late, and you ought to come by after your last set. The drinks are on the house."

Later on, Hank and Buffalo were enjoying a drink at the club with Johnny Lowe and his band holding forth. After a song finished, Johnny announced from the bandstand:

"Well it looks like its closing time. We want you all to come back and see us again real soon. We'll close things down with some good advice from a song that goes like this:

"Hey, mister bartender, please don't be so slow...."

Hank cut short his conversation with Buffalo, diverted his full attention to the bandstand, and said, "Hold it just a minute, I need to go talk to that guy."

As the song ended, Johnny Lowe looked over and saw one of his biggest idols standing at the edge of the bandstand, looking right at him. Buffalo had told Johnny that Hank might be in the audience, but Johnny was not quite prepared for his presence at the bandstand and didn't know what to think or do. The one thing he was fairly sure of was that Hank wasn't there to get his autograph. Johnny took a step towards Hank as Hank held out his hand.

"Hi Johnny, I'm Hank Thompson."

"Well...yes I know," said Johnny, still wondering why Hank was there as he grasped Hank's hand.

"May I ask where you got that last song you just did?" asked Hank.

"I wrote it with Dick Hart, a buddy of mine," was the somewhat cautious reply.

"Do you have it copyrighted?"

"Yeah."

"I sure would like to talk to you about it. Would you mind joining me at that table over there?"

Johnny and his wife joined Hank and Buffalo at the table. After a brief discussion, Johnny got his guitar and sang the song at the table while his wife wrote down the lyrics and gave them to Hank. Hank assured them he was going to record it and ordered a round of drinks for everybody.

The next day Hank handed the lyrics to Billy Gray, and said, "Remember that *Six Pack To Go* song that Jerry Miller, the old boy in Wichita Falls, mentioned? Well, this is it. A guy named Johnny Lowe wrote it; I met him last night at a club. Miller used to play in Johnny's band and was blowing smoke when he said that he wrote it."

Later, Hank worked over the lyrics slightly, changed the arrangement and couldn't wait to get to Los Angeles to record it.

"I knew that song was going to be a hit. I was never more sure of anything in my life," recalled Hank.

*

As the fifties wound down, the Thompson organization was also coming to the realization that even in the Southwest, Rocky Mountains and Pacific Northwest – which had been fertile grounds for Hank and The Brazos Valley Boys for most of the decade – Western Swing was on the decline. Despite Jim Halsey's stellar and creative booking efforts, it was difficult to keep a positive cash flow. The playbook had to be retooled.

One major move involved Hank's turning over the care and feeding of the band to Billy Gray. The band was reduced in size by eliminating the piano, keeping only one steel player, and using only one or two fiddle players. Gray would pay the band members, take care of personnel changes and hassles, and be responsible for equipment and transportation. Hank would hire the band on an "as needed" basis from Gray, the band would perform as The Brazos Valley Boys, and Hank would pay Gray a per-night fee for use of the band. In the meantime, Gray could also book the band on other jobs under his own name.

Billy, realizing that he would need a featured vocalist when the band was not playing with Hank, hired nineteen year old Curtis Potter, an accomplished vocalist and rhythm guitarist who was a fixture at an NCO club in Abilene, Texas, where Hank and The Brazos Valley Boys played one night in the late fifties. During the gig, Billy asked Curtis to come on stage and sing with the band and, afterwards, offered him a job. Curtis readily accepted.

Hank also sold the bus to Roy Acuff, who, later on, sold it to George Jones, who in turn, sold it to Ray Price. Later, in Corpus Christi, Texas, the bus was raided and the raiders uncovered an amount of narcotics sufficient to cause the bus to be confiscated. With the confiscation, the bus had to be put up for auction, and Ray had to go buy back his own bus.

Chapter Thirty Seven

Ann Williams was underwelmed by Lubbock, Texas, when she moved there from Ft. Worth in the late fifties. Ft. Worth was still a country town at the time, but it paled in comparison to Lubbock, which, at least to Ann, appeared to have nothing but pick-up trucks, cowboy hats, and country music, none of which she found especially appealing. Although she was single, attractive and in her early twenties, she had to make an effort to establish a social life in Lubbock. Therefore, one Saturday night soon after her move, she readily accepted an invitation to go with some friends to a dance at the NCO club at Reece Air Force Base in Lubbock.

"Who's playing?" asked Ann.

"Hank Thompson and The Brazos Valley Boys," was the answer.

"Never heard of them," replied Ann.

"Well, you are in for a treat."

"Why not?" Ann thought.

Later, when Billy Gray kicked off the opening tune that night, Ann had a very positive initial impression of The Brazos Valley Boys, but it was not based on the music.

"All of The Brazos Valley Boys were so cute, dressed in their Nudie outfits and white cowboy hats," remembered Ann.

After the first set, Hank was making his usual rounds schmoozing with the patrons. He dropped by Ann's table, said hello to everyone, and was introduced to Ann.

Later, Ann was at the water fountain at the club, and Hank walked by. Ann looked resplendent in a tight, white strapless dress, a sight that did not go unnoticed by Hank's trained eye as he walked by and said hello again.

Hank: "Are you having a good time?"

Ann: "Not particularly," as she thrust her hips to one side and put on a defiant expression.

Hank: "Why not"

Ann: "I don't like hillbilly music."

Hank's negative reaction was palpable. "We don't play hillbilly music, we play Western Swing, and there's a big difference."

"Whatever," said Ann, as she did a one-eighty and headed back to her table, giving Hank an ample opportunity to view her backside.

Which he did.

*

The early days of television had interesting characters. One was Cal Worthington, a new and used car salesman extraordinaire. He claims on his web site today that his operations have "probably sold more cars than anyone in the country over the past 52 years". In the fifties, sporting a fourteen-karat smile, a comb-over, and a Nudie suit, he was the star in countless bizarre television spots in southern California. Cal would cavort with a zoo's worth of animal sidekicks, including a lion, an elephant, a water buffalo, a gorilla, a tiger, a rhinoceros, assorted snakes and a killer whale (which he rode at Sea World), while hammering home his main theme of "I'll stand on my head to beat anybody's deal." In one commercial, he stood on his head on the roof of a car with a live tiger by his side as he extolled people to buy his cars.

Rather than buy television ad spots, Mr. Worthington bought entire *programs*. Every Saturday and Sunday, he hosted a three-hour variety show broadcast live on a Los Angeles station from one of his dealerships, where he combined the music with his tasteless pitches for selling cars. Throughout the years, the show featured a Who's Who of country music including Hank, Johnny Cash, Buck Owens and Roger Miller. These performers put on their shows in front of a boisterous crowd that, in exchange for free admission, put up with Cal's car pitches between acts. The consumption of alcohol was not discouraged.

Hank was booked in for a Sunday afternoon show in December 1959, just prior to a scheduled recording session at the Capitol Records Tower. He was standing backstage visiting with some friends before his set when a nice looking, well-proportioned blond made her way towards his group. He instantly knew that she was the girl Merle Travis had mentioned earlier – Hurricane Shirley! And he was right. She introduced herself to Hank, and Hank introduced her to some of the band members. She immediately became the Brazos Valley Boys' new best friend, especially later that night when she made her very successful band-banging debut at the Brazos Valley Boys Invitation Only Fun and Games Unwinding Party at the bands' motel.

The next day at Studio B, Hank went up to Ken Nelson and handed him the paper with the lyrics to *A Six Pack to Go* and said,

"Ken, here's our next hit song."

Ken looked it over and said, "Let's do it!"

But the first item on the agenda was to record songs for another LP, to be titled *This Broken Heart of Mine* and include several remakes of Hank's most popular songs for the main purpose of recording them in stereo.

"There were a lot of remakes during that period, since there was a dramatic change in the sound you were able to get from stereo as compared to mono," said Hank.

Before the session, Billy Gray called Pee Wee Whitewing in California and hired him to help out on the steel. The sessions started off with four remakes and several new songs for the album that strengthened Hank's canon of quality songs – *Hangover*

Heart; How Do You Feel; Those Things Money Can't Buy; Give A Little, Take A Little Love; Take a Look At This Broken Heart Of Mine, and *A Fooler, A Faker.*

Finally it was singles time, and *A Six Pack to Go* went down without a hitch with Merle bringing a world-class guitar break to the party. Highlights of the other songs included *She's Just A Whole Lot Like You* and *Teach Me How To Lie,* both of which stand up today as two of Hank's best.

It turned out that these last recording sessions of the decade were some of the most productive, from both a quality and quantity standpoint.

In fact, looking at the big picture, the fifties was the most productive decade of Hank's career from a recording standpoint. He sent thirty-one songs up the charts, with three landing at number one, seven others landing in slots two-to-five, and ten others landing in slots six through ten.

Jim Halsey later reflected on this success, and especially on the experience he had gained in his nine years on the job.

"In a business replete with unscrupulous people, shady deals and under-the-table payoffs, Hank was always on the up-and-up, and his integrity was impeccable and an integral part of his philosophy of life. I also discovered what a keen intellect he possessed. Not only was he a brilliant, intelligent person, he was also a very positive person. As we would experience successes and failures, he was quick to point out that they were basically part of the same learning process, since even some of our greatest failures would lead to some of our greatest successes."

Chapter Thirty Eight

The momentum from the previous year carried over to Hank's third decade with the release of *A Six Pack to Go*. Hank's statement to Ken Nelson at the recording studio about the expected success of *Six Pack* proved to be prophetic. The song climbed to number ten early in 1960, followed by *She's Just a Whole Lot Like You*, which reached number fourteen in the early fall.

But merely stating that *A Six Pack to Go* was a hit song is not doing the song justice. It became an instant standard in Hank's repertoire and one of the most requested songs at his personal appearances throughout the next four decades. In fact, it became an anthem for the legions of people who planned their weekend activities around country music and a cold one. Hank fully recognized this and made it a staple at his personal appearances, often concluding a set, or show, with the song.

"*A Six Pack to Go* was popular when it was first released and has stayed popular through my entire career," said Hank. "It, along with *The Wild Side of Life*, are my two most requested songs."

*

A few months after Billy Gray agreed to take over The Brazos Valley Boys, Hank and Billy changed their previous arrangement to one in which Billy and the band would back Hank on an exclusive basis. When Billy learned that Round Boy was going to leave the band, he had a talk with Curtis Potter.

"Curtis, now that we are backing Hank exclusively, we don't need another vocalist."

"Oh shit," thought Curtis, "that's it for me."

But Billy went on. "However, in a few weeks we will need a bass player."

Curtis: "But I can't play bass.

Billy: "That's OK. We want you to continue singing when Hank is not on stage. And don't worry about playing the bass. We're going to California soon, and we'll introduce you to Merle Travis. Merle can teach you, and it shouldn't take too long."

Curtis: "OK, I'm willing to give it a shot."

Billy ordered a new electric bass from Fender, and Curtis spent two days with Merle at his house in North Hollywood.

"Merle was a musical genius," said Curtis. "He took his time with me, showed me the simple steps, and taught me how to play the bass in two days. Soon thereafter, Billy inserted me in the starting lineup with the Brazos Valley Boys at a dance and Hank couldn't believe how much I had learned."

Between 1960 and 1972, Curtis was the bassist/vocalist for the Brazos Valley Boys with two exceptions. He took a hiatus for a few months in 1961 and again in 1965, and was replaced by Round Boy on both occasions.

*

It was around two in the morning after a dance in Ada, Oklahoma, when Hank, with three passengers, took off in the Apache from the Ada airport. Soon after takeoff, Hank discovered that his landing gear would not retract, so he immediately circled back and landed. It turned out that an electrically-operated switch that controlled the landing gear had malfunctioned but could fairly easily be fixed. While he was underneath the plane doing the repairs, Hank heard some noise and looked up into the barrel of an automatic rifle. After crawling out from under the plane, he found himself surrounded by three military types, including an army lieutenant and a sergeant. Hank produced his ID and explained who he was and what he was doing there. The lieutenant, who apparently was not a country music fan, asked Hank and the three passengers to accompany them to a military office in Ada for further questioning.

Hank restrained his anger as he and the three others were taken to the office and interrogated. Hank finally insisted that he be told exactly what was going on.

"We have received word from the Air Force Base at Tinker Field in Oklahoma City that unidentified flying objects were seen flying this way," replied the lieutenant.

"Did you confuse my plane with a space ship?" asked Hank. "Do we look like little green people from Mars?"

That evening, the radio and television stations in Oklahoma City and Tulsa reported that radar experts were confirming that unidentified flying objects were, in fact, picked up on the radar at Tinker Field that day, heading generally towards Ada.

The story died the next day.

*

In the meantime, Billy Gray was looking for another steel player to replace Bobbie White, who had decided to resign from the band and start a club in Oklahoma City. About ten candidates contacted Gray, and he held out for a young man who had played with Jim Reeves and currently was with Ernest Tubb. Bobby Garrett, a Dallas native, got the call. He gave Ernest his notice that night and was on a bus for Tulsa the next day in time to join the band for a job that night. Bobby had used a Sho-Bud pedal steel and played a C6 tuning with Ernest. But to better capture Hank's sound, he altered the tuning to B-flat sixth, something Curly Chalker had started in the band, and thus continued a tradition of the Brazos Valley Boys.

The Thompson sound continued.

About a year after Hank met Ann Williams at the NCO club in Lubbock, Ann moved to Midland, Texas, which was similar to Lubbock with one exception. Although there was plenty of country music in Lubbock there was *nothing but* country music in Midland, and she had no choice but to become a convert. A few weeks after her move, she heard that Hank was playing at The Melody Club in Odessa, a few miles from Midland, and she decided to go. She didn't have a car, but she did have a plan.

"Guess what?" Ann said to her roommate, who had a car but didn't like country music. "There's a jam session in Odessa next Saturday night. Why don't we go?" Ann knew her roommate liked jam sessions.

"Sure," said her friend, who apparently didn't know or care who was playing what kind of music.

On the Saturday night, as the two roommates wheeled into the parking lot of *The Melody Club* for the "jam session", Ann gulped. The Melody Club made The Cotton Club in Lubbock look like a five-star resort. The roommate appeared to have the same reaction.

"Who's Hank Thompson?" said the roommate, in a skeptical tone of voice, as she read a sign on the front door of the Melody Club.

"He's really cute and he plays country music," said Ann. But this didn't seem to bring the roommate out of her funk.

"I almost lost a roommate that night, but since we had driven that far, she agreed to go in with me," said Ann.

Later that evening, Hank was signing autographs during the intermission, and Ann got in line. She was wearing skintight gold-lame pants. When she reached the front of the line, Hankís trained eye again took in the whole package and sent a very positive signal to his brain.

"I remember you," he said with a smile.

"I didn't think there was any way he would recognize that smart mouth from Lubbock," remembered Ann, "but he did."

"Well, have you learned to like Western Swing?" asked Hank. Obviously, he had remembered the Lubbock encounter, but Ann's current outfit apparently trumped the memory of the smart mouth.

"Yes, I like it now," replied Ann.

All was well.

But they did not see each other again for nearly five years.

Ken Nelson, who was awaiting Hank and the band at Studio B in the Capitol Records Tower in December 1960, was not the type of producer that came to a recording session loaded with suggested songs to be recorded. This was especially true when he was recording Hank, who not only showed up with plenty of material but with demo tapes of the arrangements. Therefore, over the course of their working relationship, Ken only brought a very few songs, most of which were submitted to him by friends. In each case, Hank listened to the song and told Ken he couldn't do it.

"That's OK," said Ken. "Now I can tell my friend that I gave it to you."

However, Ken had a different approach for this session. As Hank was warming up with several of the Brazos Valley Boys, Ken pulled Hank aside and told him that Capitol was going to release an album of old favorites done by the original artists.

"Do me a favor," said Ken. "Jack Guthrie, Woody's cousin, had a hit in 1945 with a song called *Oklahoma Hills*. We are going to do an old favorites album and we were going to put Jack's recording on the album, but the sound quality is so poor that we can't do it. We need a new recording of the song. Will you do it?"

"I've been singing that song on and off for several years," said Hank, "and I'll be glad to do it."

The song was recorded, but not without some difficulty. Bobby Garrett remembered it well.

"This was my first recording session with Hank, and I quickly learned what perfectionists he and Ken Nelson were. I remember on *Oklahoma Hills*, we did nineteen takes."

Later, Hank was pleasantly surprised when Capitol told him that they were going to release *Oklahoma Hills* as a single.

And for good reason. It sold like hotcakes, peaked at number seven in the summer of 1961, and became another one of Hank's signature songs. It was a natural "introduction number" and he soon began opening his shows with the song, and continues to do so today.

Meanwhile, back at the recording session, several songs were recorded for an upcoming LP, *An Old Love Affair*. Included was a tune *I Keep Meeting Girls Like You*, a Thompson-Bud Auge composition that stands up today as one of Hank's best ballads. The song had an interesting history.

"I had done a demo version of the song and had taken it to a previous recording session, maybe a year or so before," said Hank. "Ken Nelson listened to it and said, 'No, I don't think you ought to do that song because it's a put-down to females.' I understood what he was saying and didn't think any more of it. But I brought it back out for these sessions, and Ken said, 'Boy, that's a good song! Let's do it!' I didn't tell him that he didn't like it the first time."

Johnny Lowe, the co-writer of *A Six Pack to Go* sent Hank a song entitled *Hangover Heaven*, written by Johnny and his wife Mary, who had come up with the idea. Hank was concerned about the negative religious implication of juxtaposing Heaven with a booze binge and changed the title to *Hangover Tavern*, along with attendant changes to the lyrics that focused only on the booze binge. It was a number twelve single in the fall of 1961.

One evening during the recording sessions, Hank went over to Merle's house for beverages and a visit. He was surprised to notice that Merle had a twelve-string guitar sitting in the corner of his living room that appeared to be identical to the Stella twelve-string that Hank used back in 1941. The only difference was that it had a Bigsby neck and headstock not unlike those that were on Hank's second J-200, with the exception that the headstock had six strings on each side.

"That looks like a Stella twelve-string that I had back in the forties," said Hank, "except for the Bigsby neck and headstock."

"Why don't you take it?" said Merle, "I have too many damned guitars anyway."

"Are you kidding?" asked Hank.

"No, go ahead and take it," was the reply.

Hank immediately picked up the guitar and started out the front door with it.

"Where are you going?" asked Merle.

"I'm going to lock it in the trunk of my car before you change your mind," answered Hank.

The gift was much appreciated. Although Hank did not use it when performing, he kept it and, approximately thirty years later, had it refurbished. It now sits in the living room of his home in Keller, Texas.[16]

While Hank and the band were in at Capitol Towers, a shocking news item circulated among the band members – Black Rider was moving her operation to California! A debate ensued as to whether or not she would form an alliance with Hurricane Shirley (probably causing the band to salivate over the possibility of a tag-team band-bang) or go into competition with her. It turned out that two of the highly ranked members of The Brazos Valley Boys Groupie Society were going into competition.

---

[16] This Stella is the only twelve-string guitar known to be in existence that has a Bigsby neck and headstock.

Chapter Thirty Nine

In the early sixties, Louie Prima, Keely Smith, and their band were taking Las Vegas by storm with their high-octane stage act that juxtaposed sheer musical talent with crazy stage antics. They often performed "after hours" (which, by Las Vegas standards, was *very* late) so that the other Las Vegas acts, as well as the casino employees, could see the show after they got off work. A cult following developed, the general public caught on, and their show became the hottest ticket in town. Hank would often go by to see them if he could score some tickets, which was very difficult. Capitol Records got on the bandwagon and decided to do a live recording of their act and the Capitol engineers were able to make a first class recording directly from the stage – one of the first of its kind – and the album was a commercial success.

In the meantime, Hank, playing on the success he had already enjoyed in Las Vegas, suggested the possibility of recording a live show in Las Vegas using the Prima/Smith model, and the idea was sold to Capitol. He was already booked at The Golden Nugget in downtown Las Vegas, and it was decided to do the recordings there in March 1961, during the first weekend of one of the engagements.

Before the sessions, Billy Gray called Curly Lewis, who was still working for Leon McAuliffe in Tulsa, and asked him to come to Las Vegas for the Nugget recordings. Billy wanted an A team, and Curly not only knew all of the arrangements from his previous stint with the Brazos Valley Boys, but he was one of the best Western Swing fiddle players on the planet.

In addition to Curly, the lineup consisted of Gray, Bobby Garrett on steel, Dubert on trumpet, Bob White on the other fiddle, and Junior Nichols on drums. Also, Curtis Potter had taken a leave of absence from the band for several months and Round Boy was the bass man. With Merle on board, this was arguably one of the strongest lineups in Brazos Valley Boys history.

The recording sessions were set for the Friday and Saturday of the first week, when the Nugget was jammed with patrons. The stage was located adjacent the casino, and the main floor was well dampened, a ploy by their sound engineers to prevent the music from interfering with the sound of the gambling tables. Although this did not give a lot of resonance to the instruments and Hank's voice, it made it easy to get good isolation on the microphones and yet pick up the ambience, including the sounds of roulette wheels, telephones, slot machines and even some drink orders.

With six shows a night during the week and five shows a night on the weekends, the schedule was not exactly a walk in the park. During the first four days in front of the Nugget crowd, Hank and the band were able to polish the songs to be recorded. Since there were five chances on Friday and five on Saturday to get what they wanted, they decided to start doing the songs on the first show on Friday with the tape machine running, and to continue to do each song on successive shows until they felt comfortable with the take. Hank and Ken Nelson would listen to the tapes between shows and decide whether or not a song needed to be redone.

The system worked to perfection. On the Friday and Saturday nights in question, all the planets were aligned – Hank and the boys brought their A game, the crowd could not have been more responsive, the song selections and sequencing were right on, and Capitol nailed the recordings with just enough crowd and casino background noise to provide the right ambiance. The documented result provides an excellent representation of Hank and The Brazos Valley Boys at their peak.

The opener on the album was the 1954 hit, *Honky-tonk Girl*, with Dubert's muted trumpet providing the instrumental turn-around, a departure from the original studio recording. Two ballads followed – Hank's original *I Guess I'm Getting Over You* and Johnny Bond's *I'll Step Aside*, a 1947 hit for Ernest Tubb. Then the fiddlers went to work with a blazing *Orange Blossom Special*, the perfect instrumental to arouse the rowdy Vegas crowd, after which Hank brought things back to the present with his 1960 ballad, *I Really Didn't Mean To Fall In Love*. Next on deck was a driving version of the traditional *John Henry*, a staple of Merle's repertoire, giving Hank (vocally) and Merle (instrumentally) a chance to shine, which they did.

Then it was back to a tune that Hank often used to close a set at his dances and shows, and one that could be called the highlight of the album, the traditional *Nine Pound Hammer*, written by Merle and featuring his guitar and Junior Nichols' drumming. Merle handled the intro and rose to the occasion with the first turnaround, hitting tasteful licks that are still talked about in guitar circles. As if this wasn't enough, the next turnaround featured a state-of-the-art performance by Garrett who definitely was "in the zone", with Nichols switching to the high hat for emphasis and Dubert providing tasteful fills during the final verse and chorus.

Hank then changed the pace with one of his best ballads, *She's Just A Whole Lot Like You*, with Dubert joining the fiddles for the turnaround. Then it was back to tradition for another ballad – Lulubelle and Scotty's country standard *Have I Told You Lately That I Love You*, a tune Hank had wanted to record for years and one that was well received by the crowd. Changing the pace again, Garrett was unleashed on a version of *Steel Guitar Rag*, so explosive that it threatened to get away from him as the fiddles and Dubert's trumpet vamped behind him.

"I've had an awful lot of compliments on that particular arrangement," remembered Garrett some years later, "but it was very simple. We just played a fairly standard arrangement, but everybody played it *together*. I came up with the idea for the intro and the ending, and Billy had the rest of the band complement me and add all those phrasings in the middle. I don't know how many times we did it before they got the one they wanted on tape, but I don't think it was many."

A standard arrangement of the Thompson/Gray composition *Just one Step Away* was next, followed by another highlight, the Leon Payne classic *Lost Highway*, a tune that Hank Williams had taken to number twelve in 1949, and a song very well suited to his friend with the same nickname.

For the finale, Hank went to his standard closing song for all the bartenders, *A Six Pack To Go*, which, putting it mildly, was well received by the now-euphoric crowd, most of whom had a beer in hand.

To say that The Brazos Valley Boys rose to the occasion is an understatement. Gray and Nichols established a tempo and rhythm for each song that was right on, and Nichols augmented the rhythm with a mixture of thwacking propulsion and flurries of jazzy detail. Travis didn't miss a note, despite an aggressive approach to his instrumental breaks on *John Henry* and *The Nine Pound Hammer*, and Garrett was simply out of his mind. Also, the album documents how much Hank had come to rely on Dubert's trumpet which, although not by any means dominant, makes its presence known on most of the thirteen songs, ranging from tasteful fills to taking the instrumental lead or sharing it with the fiddles. For a musician who was hired ten years back based on a resume that included loading and setting up the equipment and driving the bus, Dubert had come a long way.

But despite all these stellar performances, if there was a reward for the Most Valuable Player, a strong candidate would have been the Capitol engineer, Johnny Kraus, who, with immaculate miking and mixing, produced a sound that was not a compromise from the studio sessions yet captured the live ambience.

The best takes of the thirteen songs were easily compiled and the album, *Live at The Golden Nugget*, was released later in the year. On the cover, Hank stands smiling and prosperous, dressed in one of his Nudie suits (this one was black, trimmed in gold) outside the Nugget's garishly lit marquee, holding a handful of silver dollars. And the smile was prescient – the album was not only the first live album for a country artist on a major label in the history of country music, it was a huge artistic and commercial success.

Hank at The Golden Nugget

Today, Hank recalls the album with pride.

"Other people didn't have the band or the facility to do it. We were the only country act at the time that could play a place like the Nugget, where you could isolate the sound and actually record and make it sound good. With ten shows over the two nights, we had ten shots at it, and we kept doing them until we were sure we had the best cuts we could get."

*

The same time Hank was performing and recording at The Golden Nugget, Patsy Cline was playing at the Mint, another Las Vegas casino across the street from The Golden Nugget. In what turned out to be a rather infamous engagement, she did four shows a day for thirty-five straight days at the ungodly hours of midnight to 5 A.M., for less than the going rate. Several days into the engagement, she lost her voice, and had to lip-sync her numbers for a few days until her voice returned. During this time she went to see one of Hank's shows. Afterwards, they visited for a few minutes.

"Charlie (her husband, Charlie Dick) is leaving tomorrow," Patsy told Hank in a subdued whisper. "That means that tomorrow night, maybe I can get some strange stuff!"

*

Hank and the band were back at the MB Corral in Wichita Falls, just as *A Six Pack to Go* had ascended to number ten in the nation. Sure enough, Jerry Miller came by to say hello – the same Jerry Miller who had promised to send the song to Hank in 1959 but neglected to tell them that he didn't write it.

Hank couldn't wait to ask Jerry a question.

"Jerry, whatever happened to that song you wrote and were going to send me, called *A Six Pack to Go?*"

Chapter Forty

In mid-1961, twenty-four-year-old Bert Rivera, married and with two young children, was playing steel guitar for a local band, *The Swing Boys*, in Austin, Texas. He was also going to school at the University of Texas and working a day job. The steel guitar was his passion – he had become fascinated with it at age ten and had been playing it ever since.

The Swing Boys played Western Swing and a lot of Hank Thompson. One night Lee Brown, a rhythm guitar player for the band and a big fan of Hank, journeyed to Brenham, Texas, to see Hank and The Brazos Valley Boys perform at a roller skating rink. He knew Billy Gray and was visiting with him before the show when Gray told him that their regular steel player, Bobby Garrett, was sick with an overdose of alcohol and couldn't make the job. Gray asked Lee if he knew any good steel players in the area. Lee rushed to the phone and called Bert.

"Bert, how would you like to play steel for Hank Thompson tonight?"

"Lee, if this is one of your jokes, it isn't funny."

"I'm not kidding. I'm a friend of Billy Gray, and he's right here. Hank's regular guy is sick and they need someone. They are going on in a few minutes. Get here as fast as you can."

"Well, OK, but if you are pulling my leg, I'll kill you."

After surviving a driving rainstorm and a flat tire, Bert made it to Brenham in time to start the second set. Relying on his familiarity with Hank's style and taking on-stage cues from Billy and Hank, he made it through the set.

After the show, Billy and Bert were standing side-by-side taking a leak in the trough in the men's room, and Billy asked Bert if he would be interested in the job on a permanent basis in case Garrett couldn't come back. The reply was in the affirmative.

"I was thrilled to death with the possibility of becoming a Brazos Valley Boy," Bert recalled. "I had never been on the road with a band, but everyone knew that the Brazos Valley Boys was one of the best country bands in the business. And the pay was good."

But it turned out that Garrett was able to come back. A few months later, however, Gray called Bert and told him that Garrett was still plagued with his problems with alcohol and had to get off the road again, and Gray offered Bert the job. Bert was just finishing up the spring term at UT and had three months off in the summer before the fall term started, so he accepted with the understanding that he would probably quit in time to enroll at the university for the fall term.

The leak that Billy Gray took with Rivera was probably the most productive leak that Gray ever took. Not only did Bert excel as a steel guitarist for the Brazos Valley Boys for the next three months, he joined The Brazos Valley Boys later on a permanent basis and helped anchor the band for nine years.

*

Some of the artists that carried the real, or traditional country music flag during the fifties, including Hank, Webb Pierce, Johnny Cash, Ernest Tubb, Hank Snow, Ray Price, Faron Young, and Lefty Frizzell, continued their hit-making into the sixties. In the early sixties, Merle Haggard and Buck Owens joined them and helped keep the music high on the charts. Despite this, there was a change brewing in the recording studios in Nashville. The traditional country sound was being eschewed in favor of what can best be called "light country", to use a beer analogy, which was a watered-down version of traditional country. This type of music abandoned the grit of the steel guitar and fiddles in favor of pseudo-pop arrangements featuring choral backings, violins, and honey-drenched songs that bore little resemblance to traditional country music. But it sold.

The switch to light country by the record buyers and radio listeners also carried over to the relatively large Western Swing bands to the extent that only Hank, Bob Wills and Leon McAuliffe could afford to carry decent "big bands". Since Wills and McAuliffe seldom ventured out from their base locations, Hank and the Brazos Valley Boys, in effect, were the last act standing when it came to playing Western Swing at the large venues across the country.

One of these venues, of course, was The Golden Nugget, which also was the site of Bert Rivera's first job on his three months' tour of duty as a Brazos Valley Boy in mid-1962. It was a swing shift from 8:00 P.M. to 2:00 A.M. with each show lasting forty minutes, giving the band a twenty-minute break between shows. Bert remembered it well.

"This was the first time I had been to any place like Vegas. During the twenty-minute break between shows, all of the band members would go to the casino, get a bite to eat, chat with the fans, have a drink, and/or enjoy the other amenities of the hotel. I really wanted to join them, but Billy Gray had other plans for me.

"He and Hank wanted the arrangements in the live performances to sound just like the records; and although I was well versed in Hank's style, I didn't know the exact licks. Therefore, during each break at The Golden Nugget, Gray made me pack up my steel, carry it up a flight of stairs to a dressing room and practice Hank's songs. This was tough, because I had a huge, triple-neck Wright steel guitar at the time, and it was heavy. In the dressing room, Gray would meticulously go over each song with me and teach me the exact arrangement and when to fill in, note-by-note, for the leads. He was like a drill sergeant and made me play each song over and over until we had it down. I hated him at first but, in retrospect, he made me a better player.

In fact, after I got over the initial shock of the drills, and got to know him better, I loved him to death – he was a great guy and a hell of a bandleader."

*

After accumulating about two thousand hours flying his Apache, Hank traded it in on a Cessna 310, a twin-engine workhorse that served him well for the next twenty-two years. Also, a Dodge station wagon was purchased for transporting The Brazos Valley Boys, along with a customized trailer that housed the uniforms and the sound equipment.

*

Hank and Merle were sitting backstage with Mother Maybelle Carter and her two daughters, June (later, Mrs. Johnny Cash) and Anita, just before they all were to appear on a show in California. Hank and Merle were slightly uneasy, and no wonder. Not only had Merle adapted Mother Maybelle's guitar style, but he and Hank had made a huge success of *The Wildwood Flower*, one of the Carter family standards. They had also recorded two more guitar driven instrumentals, *Weeping Willow* and *Gathering Flowers*, which were other staples in the Carter family repertoire.

However, everything was fine backstage as everyone engaged in some small talk. But when show time drew near and there was some discussion about who would go on first, Mother Maybelle looked at Hank and Merle and said:

"If you two go on first, we won't have anything left to play."

193

Chapter Forty One

Of all the Brazos Valley Boys, Dubert had the least body fat, due in no small part to the "Dubert Dobson Three Day On – One Day Off Liquid Diet". The diet was based on some special liquids and solids, administered according to the following regime, which Dubert followed fairly regularly.

For three straight days, he would adhere strictly to a liquid-only diet, with the particular brand of liquid not being important as long as it did not lack in significant alcohol content. Quantities varied, as long as he was able to maintain a constant buzz yet not be impaired musically when performing with The Brazos Valley Boys.

On the fourth day, Dubert eschewed the above liquids and switched to solids, in the form of a whole pie that he ate in one sitting. He then washed the pie down with a quart of milk.

Then the cycle was repeated ad infinitum.

That's it.

*

A basic tenet of marketing theory is that competition among retailers and service providers is good for the customers. The heated battle on the west coast between Black Rider and Hurricane Shirley for the affections of country music musicians provided another layer of enjoyment at The Brazos Valley Boys Invitation Only Fun and Games Unwinding Parties. However, it turned out that Hurricane Shirley apparently couldn't stand the pressures of competition.

Dubert broke the news to Bert Rivera in the fall of 1962, just before Bobby Garrett replaced Bert in the band and Bert enrolled again at the University of Texas.

"Did you know that Hurricane Shirley went pop?"

"What do you mean?"

"She is no longer a full service groupie for the Brazos Valley Boys. She dropped us and is now doing the Lawrence Welk band."

During their stays in Las Vegas for The Golden Nugget engagements, Hank and the band usually stayed at the Ferguson Franklin motel in the Las Vegas downtown area. This motel was especially appealing because it was only six blocks from The Golden Nugget, and the management was fairly tolerant of the Brazos Valley Boys Invitation Only Fun and Games Unwinding Parties. The motel was a double-decker type that wrapped around a swimming pool and Hank and the band had rooms on both the first and the second floors. On one particular day there were no performances scheduled and, as late afternoon rolled around, the most popular place at the motel was the ice machine. It was a pretty evening, and several of the guests, including Hank and some of The Brazos Valley Boys, were out on their balconies on the second floor having conversation and drink.

Suddenly a ruckus was heard on the motel grounds.

Dubert and Paul McGhee were at it again. Paul had kept in contact with The Brazos Valley Boys since leaving the band, and, at this particular time, he was working with a combo in Las Vegas and also staying at the Ferguson Franklin. Earlier that evening he had hooked up with Dubert (his first mistake) to take in the Las Vegas neon (his second mistake). Afterwards, they were well fortified with a more than ample volume of drink, and had either caught a ride or walked back to the motel. (Opinions differ on how they got there, considering that they could hardly walk, much less drive.)

As they approached the area of the motel near Paul's room on the ground floor, he started swearing.

"Some asshole has parked his car in my parking spot!"

Sure enough, a Volkswagen Beetle was parked in Paul's parking spot, right in front of his room.

Dubert agreed that this indeed was a despicable crime and that the perpetrator should be swiftly brought to justice. He verbalized this to Paul even though, in the back of his fogged mind, he wondered what the big deal was, since Paul didn't have a car.

"Let's get this son-of-a-bitch out of here," said Paul as he tried the front door of the car and, surprisingly, found it open.

Paul put the gear in neutral, pointed towards the swimming pool across the parking lot and said to Dubert, "This car needs a bath, help me push it." It seemed like a good idea to Dubert at the time, and he was happy to oblige.

Slowly but surely, they shoved the Volkswagen out of the parking space and towards the pool.

The size of the cocktail crowd on the upstairs balconies increased as word of the events transpiring below quickly spread.

As the car got closer to the pool, the night clerk, an elderly lady, came running out of the office screaming and waving her arms, "Oh no, you can't do that. Stop or I'll call the police!"

Paul and Dubert continued pushing.

The lady ran back into the office, presumably to call the police.

Another lady in her fifties, also a guest of the motel and a fan of Hank, staggered out of her room on the first floor with a large iced beverage in her hand and shouted, "What the hell are you doing with my car?" It was clear to all that the beverage was not lemonade or tea, and that cocktail hour had started much earlier for her.

Paul and Dubert, concentrating on the task at hand, kept pushing while Paul shouted, "What the hell does it look like? We're going to push this fucker into the pool!"

The laughter and shouting from the balcony crowd increased.

The fan suddenly realized that the two car thieves were Brazos Valley Boys and that a role reversal was taking place – Hank Thompson and some of the other Brazos Valley Boys were watching *her* from the balcony. She rose to the occasion, immediately changed her attitude, and started playing to the crowd.

"Good riddance," she slurred after another sip. "I never liked that damn car anyway."

Now there was cheering from the balconies.

This was all the incentive that Paul and Dubert needed, and the car began its final approach to the pool. As Paul and Dubert continued pushing, it became apparent to the onlookers that the angle from which the car was approaching the pool was such that the diving board was going to block the car's entry into the water. Paul and Dubert were in no condition to determine this geometry as they made their final shove, let go, and watched as the car hit the diving board and then came to a standstill. Apparently, Paul was not sober enough to let this bother him all that much.

The only activity by the fan was another long pull on her drink.

"Nobody parks in my parking place!" Paul shouted to the balconies as he and Dubert staggered to their rooms.

Chapter Forty Two

As the sixties began, Hank was having trouble matching the songwriting pace that he had established in the fifties. In fact, in early December 1961, he was short on songs for the scheduled recording sessions later that month. In an effort to ameliorate this, he took Billy Gray and the rest of The Brazos Valley Boys to Los Angeles a few days before the scheduled sessions. Although they had a couple of jobs in California, the primary purpose of the early arrival was to concentrate on writing songs.

One or two nights before the recording session, with a couple of new songs written, Gray had an inspiration.

"I've got an idea for a song," Gray said to Hank. "It has to do with a recipe for a heartache. But it's an idea only. Let's get the guitars and a fifth of VO, stay in the motel, and write until it's finished."

"Sounds good to me," said Hank. The idea of the VO sealed the deal.

Later on, as the melody and lyrics finally were coming and the VO was going, they started writing. Literally. The problem was that there was only one small sheet of paper in the room, and they filled it with some of their scribbled lyrics. A drink or two later, as they thought of more lyrics, Gray started canvassing the room for some more paper.

"Here we are writing a song and there's no damn paper!" said Gray.

But there was plenty of ice, and they had another drink.

Gray, getting more desperate by the minute, finally ripped some paper off a shelf in the motel room, and they were back in business.

More drinking and more writing, this time on the shelf paper.

Finally, the VO was finished and so were they.

The next morning they reconvened over breakfast with plenty of orange juice and aspirin.

"I can't remember," Hank asked Billy. "Did we finish that song last night?"

"Hell if I know," said Billy. "Let's go look at the lyrics that we wrote down."

They did and found the lyrics absolutely and positively undecipherable, a clear product of the effect of the VO. Moreover, neither Hank nor Billy *remembered* what they wrote.

"Looks like we start over," said Hank. They did, and, with less distracting circumstances, finished the song, along with one or two others just before they headed for the studio.

A slightly revamped version of The Brazos Valley Boys was present for the recording sessions. Gray had hired a new fiddle player, Billy Jack Saucier, and a new drummer, Bernard Young, whom Bobby Garrett had recommended. It was a productive session, yielding, among others, *That's The Recipe For A Heartache, How Many Teardrops Will It Take* and *Drop Me Gently (So My Heart Won't Break)*.

Another cut was one of the most unusual songs that Hank had ever recorded, the bleak *I Cast A Lonesome Shadow*, a clear departure from the rollicking, beery, broken-heart, honky-tonk norm.

Hank remembered the history of the song.

"Lynn Russwurm, a Canadian boy, sent me that idea. It reminded me of Edgar Allen Poe's poem 'The Raven' that ends with the lines '*And my soul from out that shadow that lies floating on the floor /Shall be lifted never more.*' I liked the idea. It had a real subtle implication, and so I was attracted by the idea of the title and the song. A lot of it was based on Russ' idea – he had a little bit of a lyric and some melody, but I pretty much wrote the song."

The somewhat unusual lyrics of *I Cast a Lonesome Shadow* are as follows:

Every evening when the sun goes down I sit here in my room,
And the lamplight streaming over me projects my lonely gloom,
My counterpart in agony mocks each tear that falls,
And I cast a lonesome shadow on these lonely, lonely walls.

He's always by my side at night no matter where I go,
He lurks out in the darkness or in the neon's glow,
He follows me across the steps and up and down the hall,
And I cast a lonesome shadow on these lonely, lonely walls.

I sit and watch the candle and the flicker of the flame,
My writhing shadow twists and turns as though it is in pain,
I'm trying to escape the memory my mind recalls,
And I cast a lonesome shadow on these lonely, lonely walls.

The image of a love I lost and all the things I'd planned,
Are as empty as this bottle that I hold in my hand,
My soul is buried in the depths of love and life's pitfalls,
And I cast a lonesome shadow on these lonely, lonely walls.

Hank's resonate vocal nailed the mood, and the twin fiddles interspersed with subtle whining fills by the steel guitar created an constant haunting backdrop. To say that the arrangement was unusual for Hank would be putting it mildly; it was one that even caused Hank's best fans to do a double take when they first heard it.

Students of Hank's music have to be amazed that *I Cast a Lonesome Shadow, How*

Many Teardrops Will It Take, and *Drop Me Gently* – three of the best songs in Hank's entire body of work – did not get off the ground, chart wise.

*

In the early sixties, Jude and Jody, who had become mainstays on Hank's television shows and many personal appearances, went off on their own. They secured their own television show in Oklahoma City, opened a furniture store, and promoted the store highly on the show. Jody (his last name is Taylor) was married to Miss Norma Jean, an Oklahoma City girl and a mainstay in Nashville for several years as Porter Wagner's sidekick. As a result of her Nashville ties, she got Jude and Jody on *The Grand Ole Opry* and was instrumental in getting many artists who came through Oklahoma City to appear as guests on *The Jude and Jody Show*. In a role reversal, Hank would also often appear as a guest on their show, in exchange for furniture and/or appliances.

"Hey Hank, can you appear on our show on June 4th? We'll ship you a freezer."

"Sure!"

The Jude and Jody Show ran on television until the mid-eighties, and they are still in the furniture business in Oklahoma City.

*

During one of The Golden Nugget engagements at Las Vegas, Billy Gray and fellow band-mate Curtis Potter were sharing a suite at the Ferguson Franklin Motel in Las Vegas. (Yes, the motel let The Brazos Valley Boys back in, even after the Volkswagen-nearly-in-the-pool incident). Gray had a reputation for bumming incidentals from his fellow band members which included everything from cigarettes and hair spray to toothpaste and shoe polish – you name it; he needed it. As it happened, Curtis Potter was very proud of a pair of gold boots that he had recently purchased, and he kept them immaculate. One day he sprayed the boots with a can of gold lacquer in the bathroom and left the can on the sink.

Later, Gray walked in the bathroom and hollered out to Potter, "Ace, can I borrow your hair spray?"

"Sure," replied Potter who had some Gillette hair spray in the medicine cabinet.

Potter heard a spraying sound followed by Gray shouting a series of expletives as he walked out of the bathroom with his golden, freshly lacquered, hair.

Chapter Forty Three

With the success of the *Live at The Golden Nugget* album, the marketing people at Capitol Records would have been remiss had they not looked at other live album possibilities. Two other venues were naturals – Cheyenne, Wyoming, for the *Cheyenne Frontier Days*, the planet's largest outdoor rodeo; and Dallas for the *State Fair of Texas*, the largest state fair.

For the Cheyenne recordings in July 1962, The Brazos Valley Boys included regulars Gray, Travis, Garrett, Dubert, Round Boy, and Bernard Young. Gray brought in Jimmy Belken specifically for the session to play fiddle with regulars Billy Jack Saucier and Keith Coleman, who had recently re-upped. Roy Clark, who was also managed by Jim Halsey, was tapped to lend his electric guitar talents.

The bad news was that the Cheyenne facility was a large metal building, which, from an acoustic standpoint, was the diametric opposite of the acoustically-friendly casino in Las Vegas. Hank remembered it well.

"The sound quality was nowhere near as good as The Golden Nugget. We couldn't get any decent sound at night with all of the crowd noise reverberating off the metal building and into the mikes, so we tried it in the afternoons without a crowd. The music was okay, but we were all disappointed. We even considered scraping the project but went ahead with it."

Bobby Garrett agreed.

"It was a big old metal and concrete coliseum-type thing, where they had the big rodeo. I thought my sound was thin and hollow."

Most of the songs consisted of old favorites, with the exception of *Rose City Chimes* (an instrumental that Bobby Garrett wrote), the Gene Autry favorite *Darling What More Can I Say*, and a hot version of Merle's early Capitol hit *Cincinnati Lou*, sung by Hank, with Merle handling the guitar work.

In order to add to the effect of a rodeo, Ken Nelson added a lot of sound to the music including a chuck wagon race and several mooing cows.

In a touch of irony that is only possible in the music business, the album was awarded second place in the NARAS awards for technical work and originality – an award that escaped the infinitely better-recorded *Golden Nugget* album.

*

About this time, the club owners, especially those in Oklahoma and the dry counties of Texas, started playing hardball with the financial aspects of booking Hank and other acts at their clubs. When it became apparent that Hank could draw a capacity or near-capacity crowd at nearly every outing, they began to insist that the booking be for a flat rate, or guarantee, so that they did not have to pay Hank the entire door, or at least a high percentage of the door.

For example, if Hank could draw five hundred people at two dollars per person, he would get the entire one thousand dollars under a full door arrangement. The owner would have to rely on the sale of set-ups and food (and beer in some Texas counties) to make any money. Even if the deal were for a percentage of the door, such as seventy percent, Hank would get seven hundred dollars and the owner only three hundred. Some of the owners started insisting on a booking for a flat rate of, say, five hundred dollars, stressing that it was guaranteed, no matter how large or small the crowd. Since he could usually fill up the club, Hank urged Jim to resist the pressure from the owners to any guarantee deals. But it became a fact of life.

*

Back in the mid-fifties, Hank and Dorothy had purchased a house on Lake Tenkiller, nestled in the foothills of the Ozark Mountains near Tahlequah, Oklahoma, for use as a second home when Hank took a break from the road. In 1962, they sold the house in Oklahoma City, made some improvements to the lake home, and moved there permanently. However, it turned out to be less than permanent for Hank.

*

The recording of Hank's performances at the State Fair of Texas was scheduled during Hank's two-week engagement there in October 1962. The Brazos Valley Boys lineup was essentially the same as at the Cheyenne recordings, sans Roy Clark and with the addition of Roddy Brisol, a legendary hot fiddler who became an honorary Brazos Valley Boy just for the fair shows. Hank and the band did several shows a day, and the Capitol engineers came in to record the action over a three-day period.

Hank wanted to record a song Ernest Tubb had made popular, *There's a Little Bit of Everything in Texas*, but he wasn't too sure about the lyrics. Fortuitously, after Hank had started at the fair, and before the scheduled recording session, Ernest was playing at the Longhorn Ballroom one Saturday night. Since Hank's last show at the fair was around 8:00 P.M., he decided to go to the Longhorn and see Ernest. He could get the lyrics and have a drink and a visit with an old friend.

As Hank entered the Longhorn that night, Ernest, who was on a break, greeted Hank and suggested they go sit down at a table at the back of the room to the side of the bandstand. After ordering up a drink, Hank queried Ernest about the lyrics to *There's a Little Bit of Everything in Texas*. As Ernest went over the lyrics with Hank, several cowboys, obviously feeling little pain after having consumed more than their share of drink, started fighting near the front door. Since this was not exactly a rare occurrence at the Longhorn, nobody paid much attention until they knocked over a table, moved to the next table, and then to the next table. Ernest and Hank noticed that the fight was increasing in intensity and progressing towards the back of the room to their general vicinity. They ended their conversation and watched the action.

As the fight moved ever closer to Ernest and Hank's table, Hank become concerned.

"If this lasts much longer," he said to Ernest, "they're going to be on top of us!"

"Let's get the hell out of here", said Ernest, as he escorted Hank to a non-public, backstage area.

A few minutes later Dewey Groom, the owner of the Longhorn (and the featured vocalist at Hank's and Dorothy's wedding) came rushing backstage.

"Are you guys O.K?" asked Dewey. "Somebody told me that you two were fighting each other back here!"

For the recorded shows at the fair, the main emphasis was on Hank's standards, with a departure for *There's A Little Bit Of Everything In Texas* as well as two other songs dealing with Texas – *Beautiful Texas* (written and originally recorded by Hank in early 1950) and the standard, *Deep In The Heart of Texas*. Instrumentally, the old pop standards *Charmaine* and *The River Road Two Step* were dusted off.

Again, it was difficult to capture an adequate sound to send to the tape recorder.

"With all the noises at a fair, including the large crowd noise and echoes off the buildings and other structure around the stage, it just didn't work," said Hank. "We finally took it over to another location at the fairgrounds, and actually did the recording there."

As he had done in Cheyenne, Ken Nelson taped sounds around the fair site. Some time after the fair, he had Hank record some 'tour of the fair' commentary, and dubbed in the fair sounds to break up the songs on the album. Ironically, the sounds that Nelson so diligently recorded at the fair got in the way of the music in a big way.

Neither the *Cheyenne* or the *State Fair of Texas* albums sold well, possibly due to the sound issues and because they were recorded only months apart and fairly soon after The Golden Nugget recordings. Afterwards, Hank strongly suggested to Nelson that they get back to recording in the studio, and Nelson agreed.

*

The Brazos Valley Boys received a blow when Dubert decided to retire. Not only did the band lose a first-rate musician, but also his unfailing contributions to the bus chemistry and to the social atmosphere at The Brazos Valley Boys Invitation Only Fun and Games Unwinding parties had been significant. He stayed in Oklahoma City, where he worked as a fireman and played in some amateur bands.

Chapter Forty Four

Preparations for Hank's recording sessions were evolving away from the meticulous rehearsals well in advance of the studio sessions. Instead, Hank and the band adopted a more spontaneous method of using significant creativity right in the studio before starting the recording gear. This was partly because he was writing fewer songs than in the fifties, and also because he no longer had a studio at his home to pre-record some demos.

"Much of my songwriting, especially in the later years, was based not so much on inspiration as on desperation," said Hank. "We often were writing songs on the way to a recording session, or even at the studio during the session. But once we got in the groove, things would start flowing."

Bobby Garrett also remembered the sessions.

"It was my understanding that, in the previous years, when Bobbie White and Pee Wee Whitewing were playing steel with Hank, they always rehearsed about two weeks before each recording session so that everybody would have plenty of time to get familiar with the songs. But they stopped that once they reduced the size of the band. We'd come in the studio, and Billy would outline the song and give us the arrangements right there. We'd have just a few minutes to work up whatever we were going to do."

For a session in Los Angeles in December 1962, the game plan at studio B was to cut some tunes for another studio LP titled *Golden Country Hits*, Hank's first album of recordings featuring hit songs by other country artists. The first session produced *San Antonio Rose* and a version of the old Wesley Tuttle hit, *Detour*. Also recorded were covers of Hank Snow's *I Don't Hurt Anymore*, Charlie Walker's hit *Pick Me Up On Your Way Down* and an instrumental version of the standard *Beer Barrel Polka*. *Wabash Cannonball*, a song Hank had been singing since he was ten years old, was also cut, along with the Floyd Tillman favorite *Then I'll Keep On Loving You*. Recording Tennessee Ernie Ford's 1950 country/pop hit *Shot-Gun Boogie* was no problem, since Hank often sang it onstage. Two other songs completed the collection – *Back Street*

Affair, the 1952 Webb Pierce hit, and Ernest Tubb's *You Nearly Lose Your Mind*, the inspiration for the first song Hank wrote, *California Women*. *Golden Country Hits* was not released until 1964.

The next day, Merle Travis was not needed for the afternoon session but was expected for the evening session since Hank had planned to use him on *I Wasn't Even In The Running*, a song that was well-suited for a instrumental break featuring Merle's thumb picking.

But he didn't show.

Ken Nelson was infuriated, a feeling that was exacerbated by the fact that he was fully aware of Merle's genius.

"When he didn't show up, we sent someone out to his house to get him," remembered Ken. "When they got him to the studio, it was quite obvious that he was so drunk he couldn't play. So we had somebody take him back home. The next day he called me and said, 'Gee, Ken, I'm sorry I didn't make the session.' He didn't even know he had been there!"

Hank confirms the story. "Merle came in and he went to sleep, sitting there with his guitar in his lap until someone took him back to his house. He didn't even remember being there."

Bobby Garrett became a last-minute replacement to take the instrumental break on *I Wasn't Even in the Running* and, incredibly, achieved a more than reasonable facsimile of the Merle Travis effect on the steel guitar. At the instrumental break in the song, he played regular steel on the first part of the chorus, the fiddles took the bridge and Garrett played the last eight bars in a style that bore an uncanny resemblance to Merle's thumb picking style – a true testament to Bobby's enormous talent. In fact, even the more astute disciples of Hank's music probably didn't notice the difference. *I Wasn't Even In the Running* was a number twenty-three single in the fall of 1963.

The group also recorded *The Luckiest Heartache in Town*, a class-A tune, which Hank decided to save and make the title tune for a future album.

During this time, Jimmy Dean hosted the popular Washington, D.C. television program *Town and Country Time* and became a favorite in the region. He had a hit song entitled *Bumming Around* in 1953, and he helped launch the careers of both Patsy Cline and Roy Clark. Later, he hosted another TV variety show in New York for CBS and became best known for his 1961 song *Big Bad John*, which went to number 1 on the Billboard charts and won the 1962 Grammy Award for Best Country & Western Recording.

Dean also occasionally hosted NBC's *The Tonight Show* before signing with ABC in the early sixties to do a one hour, early morning, national television variety show five days a week. This program originated in Washington, D.C. before it moved to New York. Hank was asked to appear on the show for a full week.

Two one-hour shows – one for the east coast, and one for the west coast – were aired Monday through Friday and turned out to be the most grueling engagement of Hank's career.

The shows were broadcast live in the early morning about two hours apart to accommodate the difference between the eastern and western time zones. The performers were required to report at the studio at 3:30 A.M. each day for a rehearsal before the early-morning show. Then they would take a break, do the second show, and then rehearse about three hours for the next day's performances. Despite the grueling schedule, Jimmy and Hank got along famously, and the week went very well.

On the Saturday after the shows, Hank played a concert at *Constitution Hall* in D.C. to a sold out, enthusiastic audience.

"I never was so glad a week was over in my life!" said Hank.

Jimmy became a big fan of Hank, and they kept in touch through the ensuing years. In fact, in 2006, forty years after the shows, Hank got a call from Jimmy in Virginia.

"Hank, I've been listening to the radio show *Hank's Place* (now *Willie's Place*) on XM radio and they really play your songs," said Jimmy. "You ought to call them and thank them."

"I have, replied Hank. "I've also done a couple of interviews with them."

Jimmy went on. "I'd give anything to see one of your shows. Please let me know when you are appearing on the east coast, and I'll come."

*

The Brazos Valley Boys received some good news when they arrived in Los Angeles in May 1963, for some recording sessions. Hurricane Shirley was back in the fold, albeit not on an exclusive basis. She apparently had the capacity to service The Brazos Valley Boys and the Lawrence Welk Band. And others. (In fact, it was rumored that another band – The University of Southern California Marching Band – should be added to Shirley's resume, but this is unconfirmed.)

Prior to the recording sessions, Bobby Garrett had to get off the road on a permanent basis to fight his over-reliance on alcohol, which was exacerbated by the constant road trips. He returned to Texas, where he joined Dewey Groom's Texas Longhorns playing out of Groom's Longhorn Ballroom. In an interview before his death in 2000, caused by cancer, Garrett remembered his days with Hank with special pride.

"That was the highlight of my career, the time I spent with Hank Thompson. Hank is a super human being. He's great to be around, he's a lot of fun, he's witty, very intelligent, and just a great person."

A prodigal son returned to the fold – Curly Chalker, who'd been gone a decade and who, in the meantime, had become a top voice among pedal steel guitar players. Also, Curly Lewis returned to the band to anchor the fiddle section for the next eight years.

At Studio B, some more songs were recorded for the *Luckiest Heartache in Town* album, including *Twice As Much, Just To Ease The Pain, Reaching For the Moon* and *Stirring Up The Ashes*, all of which were written or co-written by Hank.

As it turned out, Chalker's second tenure with the band was short-lived. After a few months, he quit to return to a job in Las Vegas. Bert Rivera, still a student at the University of Texas, got the call. Bert went to his wife with a pitch.

"I want to join on a permanent basis," he said. "The money is good, The Brazos Valley Boys are the best that I will ever play with, and I want to work at least long enough to earn enough to buy a new steel guitar."

She graciously agreed, and Bert reported for duty. He quickly earned enough to buy the new steel guitar but, along with Curtis Potter, stayed with the band through most of the decade. Hugo Chambers did the drumming honors through the first half of the decade before R.D. Thatcher (aka "Tommy Dee") took over. When Keith Coleman joined the band in 1966 and teamed with Curly Lewis on the fiddles, they formed what was probably the best fiddle duo in the band's history. Although The Brazos Valley Boys were pared down in size in the interest of economy and efficiency, the basic Hank Thompson/Western Swing sound was not compromised.

Left to Right: Curly Lewis, Keith Coleman, Hank, Hugo Chambers, Curtis Potter, Bert Rivera

This efficiency also carried over to their sound equipment. Hank had to balance the need for a system that would produce sound pressure levels sufficient for the bigger dance halls and yet be as easy as possible to transport. To this end, he looked to the electronic experience he had gained in Waco and designed and built a PA system that consisted of a custom preamp and power amp for driving two JBL 15 inch speakers housed in two custom wooden cabinets, which he also built. The steel guitar, the electric bass, and each fiddle had its own stand-alone unit in the form of a Standall speaker with a built-in amp. (Later, Hank got an endorsement from Fender and replaced the Standalls with Fender units). Of course, the band members themselves unloaded and loaded the equipment and set it up for each job.

"It was nothing like the bands today, which literally carry a truckload of equipment and have roadies to set it up," said Bert Rivera. "But our system sounded great – even in the big places."

Although Hank, who was still flying to each job, often took at least one band member with him, things sometimes got crowded in the station wagon. Often, Bert was very uncomfortable.

"Sometimes there would be five or six of us in the station wagon, traveling for five hundred to six hundred miles," said Bert. "I was uncomfortable, to say the least. And it was *really* bad when three of us had to sit in the back seat. At first, since I was the newest member of the band, I had to sit in the middle of the back seat. When I would fall asleep and lean to my right, the guy on my right would push me to the left; and then the guy on the left would push me to the right. Therefore, I did not get a lot of sleep."

However, the band chemistry during this time was never better. Bert and Curtis, working alone, in tandem, or sometimes partnering with Curly Lewis, explored new frontiers in the art of practical jokes.

This was very apparent when a tour of the Pacific Northwest took them to Bellingham, Washington, the location of the Naval shipyard from which Hank had shipped out in his previous life. The gig at Bellingham was at the *Crystal Chandelier*, quite an elegant name for a honky-tonk; but it was a *nice* honky-tonk.

Fiddler Merle David, although not a regular member of The Brazos Valley Boys, was on board for the tour. Merle was a great fiddler, but it turned out he was a beer or two short of a six pack when it came to catching on to some of Potter's and Rivera's antics. That night at the *Crystal Chandelier* proved to be no exception.

Hank and The Brazos Valley Boys were in their dressing room between sets when the promoter, Chuck Roberts, came back to say hello. Chuck was always dressed in a dark suit, white shirt, and tie, and nobody ever offered an explanation of why one would wear an outfit like this at a country music honky-tonk. After he entered the room and everyone was introduced, one of the Brazos Valley Boys said, "Chuck, you look like a preacher!" When Curtis Potter heard this, a light went on, and it became even brighter when he noticed that Merle David, who had left the dressing room to get a drink, had not yet returned.

Curtis quickly called a meeting that included Chuck, Hank, and the other Brazos Valley Boys, and outlined a plan, or rather a script. Then he and Bert left the room, and the plan went into action.

A few minutes later, when Merle David walked into the room, Hank and a couple of the Brazos Valley Boys were standing in the middle of the room visiting with Chuck. Hank called Merle over.

"Merle", said Hank, looking over at Chuck, "I'd like to introduce you to Reverend Roberts, who is the minister at the First Baptist Church here in Bellingham. Reverend Roberts is a big fan of country music".

"Nice to know you, Reverend," said Merle, palpably humble.

"Pleased to meet you too, young man," was the reply as Chuck stepped right into his role, "and God bless you."

Hank then led the conversation in small talk until Potter and Rivera came in the door on cue and headed straight for the group. Both were revved up.

"God damn!" said Rivera, "we just met a broad out there with the nicest ass and the biggest tits I've seen in a long time."

"You got that right," said Potter, as he went on to describe, in no uncertain terms, her physical attributes and what he would like to do to her, using every four letter work he could muster, including some very descriptive adjectives.

Words cannot adequately describe the look on Merle David's face as he stepped behind Reverend Roberts, looked at Potter and Rivera, pointed at Roberts, and mouthed the word "preacher."

Reverend Roberts, whose attention was still focused on Hank, Bert and Curtis, delivered the final punch line: "You know, I think I'm going to like you fuckers after all!"

*

Billy Gray decided to leave The Brazos Valley Boys for the second time to go out on his own and headline a syndicated TV show called *Music Country Style*. Hank took over the responsibility of the band and gave Billy nothing but encouragement.

A young rhythm guitarist by the name of Billy Thompson (no relation to Hank) became the newest Brazos Valley Boy.

Chapter Forty Five

Hank has always had an ear for pop standards and was pleased that he was able to convince Ken Nelson to record some at the sessions in Los Angeles in December 1963. The game plan at Studio B was to record an album to be titled *Breaking In Another Heart*, mixing several pop standards with some of Hank's originals. Despite leaving the band a few months earlier, Billy Gray was there for the session, and guitarist Joe Maphis substituted for Merle Travis, who had a previous engagement. Standards that were recorded included the Mills Brothers' *You Always Hurt The One You Love* and *Till Then*, along with their 1942 hit *Paper Doll*. Frank Sinatra and Nat King Cole were represented by *There's No You* and *That's All There Is To That*, respectively.

Hank's songs included the title song, along with *How Do You Hold A Memory*, *Don't Take It Out On Me*, *I'd Never Have Found Somebody New*, *It's Better To Have Loved A Little*, and *Just An Old Flame*. If a recording session is measured by the quality of the songs that are recorded, this one was a winner.

*

Curly Chalker, after leaving The Brazos Valley Boys for the second time, lent his steel guitar talents to Hank Penny's band, which was based in Las Vegas. Steel players have always been noted as being anal about the tuning of their instruments, and Curly was no exception. This, plus his idiosyncratic personality, came to the forefront one time when he had an encounter with Roy Clark.

One evening in Las Vegas, Hank Penny and his band, with Curly manning the steel, were sharing a bill with Roy, who was beginning his rapid ascent to stardom. Hank Thompson was not there but heard about the incident from several sources.

Roy opened for Penny and was knocking 'em dead. He had the audience in the palm of his hand as he sang, picked an electric hollow-body guitar, and interspersed the music with some well-timed humor. As he was closing up his set, the audience was on its collective feet clapping and cheering as Roy was hammering it home.

In the meantime, Penny's band was backstage waiting to come on and Curly was standing in the wings watching Roy with a big frown on his face.

Roy finished his last encore, took his final bow, and exited the stage with the audience still in a frenzy. As Roy passed Chalker with a triumphant look on his face, Curly gave him an acerbic look and growled, "Why don't you tune that fucking guitar!"

*

A period of incompatibility was beginning to set in between Hank and Dorothy, exacerbated by Hank's heavy road schedule. This lead to a prolonged separation that lasted through most of the sixties.

"There is no way you can turn on or turn off a human emotion such as love," said Hank. "Whenever it's not there, you can't generate it. The fact of the matter was that our marriage had run its course."

*

Throughout the years, Hank has always enjoyed considerable success in Minnesota. The Flame, a famous nightclub in Minneapolis, became one of his steady venues. One winter in the early sixties, a week's engagement at The Flame started on a Monday, preceded by a job in Portland, Oregon, on the previous Saturday. Unfortunately, one of the worst blizzards in years hit Oregon, Washington, Montana, and North Dakota on Sunday, making ground travel from Portland to Minneapolis impossible.

Hank went to plan B. He and a couple of The Brazos Valley Boys took a commercial flight from Portland to Minneapolis early Sunday morning before the airport closed, and the remaining Brazos Valley Boys were to wait it out in Portland and then drive to Minneapolis as soon as they could. In the meantime, Hank would fill in the band with members of The Flame's house band.

Although the blizzard did not extend to Minnesota, the cold temperatures did and, when Hank and the boys stepped off the plane in Minneapolis, it was ten degrees below zero.

Nonetheless, very large crowds attended the shows. By the third night, everyone had gained such a significant respect for the extreme weather that they came up with their own medical remedy – the consumption of significant amounts of antifreeze for the body, the kind that comes in pints and fifths. This led to an after-performance party one night at the motel where Hank and the band members were staying.

The party was in one of the rooms on the second floor. All the rooms opened up to the outside and overlooked a parking lot and office on the ground floor. Because of the cold weather, only a relatively small, but select, group attended the party – Hank, the band members, some fans and friends, and a select group of females. Also, there was also plenty of antifreeze.

When Hank entered the room that night, the party was already in full swing. He noticed that everybody was gathered around one of the beds, gazing down intently. Thinking that it was a little early in the evening for any of the standard bed activities, he ventured closer for a look.

A very attractive lady with a full-figured body was sitting on the bed, painting a picture on a small canvas. She looked as if she had stepped out of the pages of Playboy Magazine and had a paintbrush in her hand, a smile on her face, and not a stitch of clothing on her body. Hank got a drink and joined the crowd of art critics surrounding her. Music was playing, conversation picked up, stories and lies were told, and the party went on, with everybody keeping their eyes on Notta Stitch on the bed.

Later, around daylight, the supply of antifreeze was getting low and the temperature outside was getting lower. Hank remarked that he had a fifth of VO in his room three doors down and started looking for his overcoat. But one of the art critics jerked a blanket off of a bed and wrapped it around Hank.

"You don't need an overcoat with this," the critic advised.

It seemed like a good idea at the time as the blanket was wrapped, toga style, around Hank.

As Hank headed for the door with the encouragement of all concerned, Notta Stitch jumped up from the bed, put down her paint brush and headed for Hank. The room got quiet.

"The end of your toga is dragging on the ground," she said, "so I'll carry it for you."

"But you have to go outside and three doors down to get to Hank's room, and its freezing out there," said one of the art critics, before really thinking.

"No problem," said Notta Stitch.

Apparently everyone else in the room went brain dead at the time, since no one offered to provide Notta Stitch with her own toga or any other type of wrap.

Notta Stitch grabbed the trailing end of Hank' toga, someone opened the door, and Hank dashed out in his toga, followed by Notta Stitch in nothing. (Hugh Hefner, eat your heart out.)

They made the round trip in good time, and soon the party was again in full swing.

Later on that day, one of the attendees went to the office and heard an interesting story from the front desk manager.

It seems that an elderly couple was in the office checking out of the motel early that morning. While the husband dealt with the check-out, the wife sat down in the lobby and gazed out the window at the rooms. By the time the check-out was complete, the wife had a funny look on her face.

"What's wrong?" asked her husband.

"I just saw a man wrapped up in a blanket leave one room, go outside and walk to another room three doors down, and come back."

"So?"

"A naked woman was carrying the end of the blanket."

"Are you crazy? It's ten degrees below zero!"

"Yes, I saw it!"

"Woman, I suspected you were getting senile, and now I know it."

That night, Hank was at the bar at The Flame having a drink and conversation with Notta Stitch, who was fully clothed, and another girl who also attended the party. Naturally, the conversation was centered on the party, the toga incident, and Notta Stitch's critical role as toga bearer.

"Oh, you're the one who carried the toga!" said the other girl. "I didn't recognize you with your clothes on!"

*

Hank was pleased to be invited as the featured guest artist on NBC's *The Tonight Show* from Burbank, California, hosted by Johnny Carson.

Hank did a couple of songs including *John Henry* and then went over to the guest couch with his guitar to visit with Johnny. Johnny was apparently enamored with *John Henry* and, as commercial time drew near, he asked Hank, "Take us into the commercial with a little more of that *John Henry*." Hank picked up his guitar and started in as they faded to a commercial.

"Johnny and his staff could not have been any nicer, and Johnny was very kind to me," Hank recalled.

*

One time, as Hank and The Brazos Valley Boys were heading west on a tour, they worked at The Clover Club in Amarillo, owned by Jack Jackson, a friend of Hank. After the dance, Jack came up to Hank with an offer that resulted in the most unusual performance contract Hank ever made.

"Hank, I looked at your schedule and noticed that next month you are going to be in Farmington, New Mexico, on a Saturday and then in Jackson Hole, Wyoming, the following Monday. I have an idea. I also own a club in Lake City, Colorado, near Gunnison, which is roughly half way between Farmington and Jackson Hole. It's a supper club, so why don't you fly from Farmington to Gunnison on Sunday, use our house band, and do an early evening dinner show at Lake City? You can spend the night and fly on to Jackson Hole on Monday."

"What would the financial arrangements be?" asked Hank.

"I'll make you a really good deal," was the reply. "I'll give you the entire door and I'll pick you up and take you back to the airport. I'll give you lodging, all the food you can eat, and all you want to drink – and I guarantee you a really good piece of ass!"

Hank hesitated about two seconds. "Sounds like we got a deal!"

The show went well, and Jack delivered on all counts.

*

At the end of 1964, The Brazos Valley Boys received their thirteenth straight – and final – award for the Best Country and Western Band in the nation from Billboard magazine. It was an amazing string, considering the fact that, when Hank and Billy Gray formed the band and set up their base at the Trianon in 1952, one of their main goals was to be the best band in *Oklahoma*.

Chapter Forty Six

Capitol Records was undergoing a dramatic change. It was now the home of the Beatles, as their style of rock music swept the nation. In addition, Buck Owens was now the label's top-selling country singer, with a phenomenal streak of hits done in the basic, Telecaster-heavy, A.M. radio-friendly, Bakersfield style.

This gave Hank an uneasy feeling about Capitol, especially since his contract with them was to expire in late 1964.

But all hands were on deck in June 1964, for a session at the Tower with the main focus being centered on recording a Christmas LP. The only significant personnel change for the sessions was that Joe Maphis again replaced Merle, who was vacationing in Alaska.

In addition to recording several Christmas standards, including the Louvin Brothers' *It's Christmas Time*, Hank wrote several tunes for the occasion. The highlights were *I'm Gonna Wrap My Heart In Ribbons* (co-written with Weldon Allard and Johnny Hathcock), Hank's *I'd Like To Have An Elephant For Christmas*, and *Mr. and Mrs. Snowman*, written by Hank and Lyle Gaston.

*

There was a new dance hall in Oklahoma City. Merle Lindsey, who had been one of Hank's competitors when Hank initially set up shop at the Trianon, had started phasing out of that business and into promotions. He leased a large dance hall near the Farmers Market in Oklahoma City and dubbed it Lindseyland. It was bigger and better than the Trianon, a natural venue for Hank and The Brazos Valley Boys, and became their base for the next several years.

But that didn't mean that the usual cast of characters changed. For example, one Saturday night soon after the switch, San Antonio Rose made her Lindseyland debut.

With Hank and the band holding forth to a packed house, Rose, unencumbered by sobriety and decked out in her usual attire, managed to negotiate some stairs to the side of the stage, When she reached the stage, she charged towards Hank, who was in the middle of a song and shouted out her usual demand.

You guessed it – "HANK, PLAY THE SAN ANTONIO ROSE!"

On her way to Hank, Rose had to pass by Bobbie White, who was playing the steel just to Hank's left. Bobbie managed to intercept her before she got to Hank, and they started wrestling on stage with Hank still trying to sing. As Bobbie starting pulling her offstage, but before she was pulled away from the range of Hank's mike, she screamed at Bobbie in a voice that was heard by all.

"GET OUT OF MY WAY YOU CURLY HAIRED SON-OF-A-BITCH, I WANT HANK TO PLAY THE SAN ANTONIO ROSE!"

If any of Hank's other fans from the Trianon were having difficulties adjusting to Lindseyland, this certainly should have made them feel more at home.

*

Throughout the years, Jim Halsey engineered several investments for Hank and other partners, with the partnership varying in personnel, depending on the deal and the investment. One was the acquisition of radio stations KTOW-AM and KGOW-FM in Tulsa. This lead to an affiliation with other stations in Wichita, Omaha, Lincoln, Nebraska and Kansas City and the forming of a mini network, called Proud Country Broadcasting. The group would sponsor contests and special events, key elements in promoting Hank and other clients of Jim.

*

For a show in Miami, Florida, the promoter agreed to fly Hank and the band by commercial airlines to and from Dallas. Everyone was thankful to get out of the summer heat in Dallas, and both the flight and the show went well. The next morning, everyone was in good spirits as they boarded a Convair 600 to fly back to Dallas. The weather was great in Miami, the show had gone well, and some very gregarious fans had joined them for the Brazos Valley Boys Invitation Only Fun and Games Unwinding Party at the motel after the show. The bad news was that it was around 110 degrees in Dallas.

As the plane progressed, a bored Curtis Potter, who was seated near the back of the plane, cupped his hand over his mouth so as to simulate an announcement over the plane's PA system. His announcement started, "Ladies and gentlemen this is the captain speaking."

Since the words *security* and *airplanes* were very seldom used in the same sentence in 1964, the only thing the flight attendant closest to Curtis did was look on with an amused expression as he continued.

"We are approaching Dallas' Love Field and will be landing shortly. According to the report we just received from the tower, it is approximately forty degrees with a light snow, but the conditions are such that we should be able to land without any difficulties."

An elderly lady across the aisle from Hank, who had apparently never been to Dallas in July, said to the person sitting next to her, "Forty degrees and snow! Goodness, I didn't even bring a coat!"

The drudgeries of the road were relieved somewhat when the station wagon and trailer were replaced by a Dodge Travco motor home complete with bunks. Also contributing to the comfort of The Brazos Valley Boys was a redhead from Kansas, who started showing up at every job within a three hundred mile radius of Oklahoma City. The Brazos Valley Boys nicknamed her the "Owl" since she wore huge horn-rimmed glasses. She was not particularly slim, but this did not affect either her admission into The Brazos Valley Boys Groupie Society or her popularity at the Brazos Valley Boys Invitation Only Fun and Games Unwinding Parties, where she established herself as one of the go-to groupies for the Midwest in the sixties.

*

By 1964, five years after Hank and Ann Williams had last seen each other at the Melody Club in Odessa, Ann had married and divorced and had moved to Dallas. She was working at Love Field as a flight scheduler for Trans-Texas Airlines (which later became Texas International Airlines). Her duties included scheduling flights for the pilots and the stewardesses.

One day, a stewardess called in to Ann with a request.

"Ann, am I going to be flying Saturday night?"

"I'm not sure yet. Do you have a conflict?"

"Yes, I can't work that night. I'm going to see Hank Thompson at Panther Hall in Ft. Worth. I'm a big fan and I would like to go."

Ann didn't hesitate: "Well, I guarantee that you won't be flying that day because you and I are going to that dance!"

At Panther Hall on the Saturday night in question, Ann again found herself standing in line for Hank's autograph.

When she made it to the first of the line, Hank looked at her, stood up, picked her up, hugged her and said, "Ann Williams, I always knew I would see you again."

After a brief exchange, Hank said that he was busy with the autographs but would like to come to her table when he finished. Ann told him where she and her friend were sitting.

"Ok, I'll be over there in a few minutes," said Hank. "Don't leave before I get there."

Ann still remembers her thought at the time:

"I thought to myself that a team of wild horses could not keep me away from that table."

They had a nice visit at the table and made plans to see each other again.

*

After a dance at a club in the Northwest, the band was clearing the equipment and loading it into the motor home. Curtis Potter and Keith Coleman were carrying a large speaker, each holding a handle on opposite sides of the unit. Curly Lewis, who had been sipping steadily from a paper cup for most of the night, was on the stage as the speaker was being carried on the floor adjacent the stage. Curly jumped on top of the speaker for a free ride. Curtis felt the additional weight, looked up, saw Curly on top, and simply dropped his side of the speaker, sending

Curly sprawling to the ground as the rest of the Brazos Valley Boys joined together in laughter.

Curly rushed to the nearest bottle, poured a tall one, and plotted his revenge. He noticed that there was a depression in the loading dock behind the building where the equipment was to be loaded. He found some cardboard and covered the depression, confident that Curtis and/or Keith would step on the cardboard and fall into the hole as they carried out the equipment. But a few minutes and sips later, Curly also got involved in the loading process, stepped on the cardboard himself, and fell into the depression as the rest of The Brazos Valley Boys had their second big laugh of the night.

*

In the mid-sixties, Hank was flying a friend, his wife and baby from a job in Nebraska to Oklahoma when they had a bizarre experience. They got to the airport around two in the morning, took off in the Cessna, climbed to six or seven thousand feet, and headed for Oklahoma. Hank and his friend were in the front seats of the planes and the wife and baby were asleep in the back. Around dawn, as they were flying over the Wichita, Kansas area, Hank saw an amazing sight, the details of which he remembers very well to this day.

"I saw a very bright object moving at a very fast rate as it traversed the entire horizon. I was used to seeing large jet planes take this same course and it would take them minutes to pass across the entire horizon; but this object, which looked like a flat plate, took *seconds*. The only possibility I could think of was that it might have been a satellite, but it was traveling much too fast for a satellite, and in the wrong direction."

Hank immediately called the tower at Wichita, and a sleepy voice answered.

"We just saw this object on the horizon and it sure was moving fast. Have you had any reports on any unusual aircraft in the area?"

"No" said the person on the other end, obviously irritated at being awakened from his early morning nap.

There was only one conclusion that could be made, and Hank expressed it to his friend in the plane. "A lot of people are seeing unidentified flying objects these days, and you and I just saw one!"

Also, in the mid-sixties, Hank and The Brazos Valley Boys were booked on a European tour that covered several countries. On one leg of the tour, they were based at the Intercontinental Hotel in downtown Frankfort, Germany, for a week. Each morning a bus picked them up and took them to a different military base, where they did their shows before returning to the hotel that night.

Once during this week, they had a day off and Bert suggested that everyone come to his room on the thirteenth floor of the hotel that morning to decide on something to do to relieve the boredom. The first decision they made at the meeting was that some liquid refreshment was needed to help them in the remainder of the decision-making process; and the ingredients for a large quantity of Bloody Marys quickly materialized. When Breakfast With the Brazos Valley Boys was in full swing, Curtis Potter idly picked up a sheet of paper from a stationary tablet on the desk, folded it into a paper airplane, opened a window, threw the plane out, and watched it glide down to the fairly heavy pedestrian and vehicular traffic on the street below.

"Hell, I can sail one further than that," said Bert as he took another sip, picked up a sheet of paper from the tablet, and imitated Curtis' actions. Their competition did not go unnoticed by the other guys, and soon the consumption of Bloody Marys was complemented by a constant barrage of paper airplanes gliding down from the thirteenth floor to the street.

There was knock on the door, and Hank walked in to survey the scene.

"What's going on?" asked Hank as he was handed a Bloody Mary by the time the door closed behind him. When he realized the challenge involved in the aeronautical engineering exercise that was taking place, his experience in aviation kicked in and, soon, several Thompson specials were also gliding their way to the street.

"By the time we got through and we all looked down at the street, it looked like it had been snowing," said Bert.

*

Only four songs were recorded at the Capitol Records Tower in September of 1964. The last two were *In The Back Of Your Mind* and *Then I'll Start Believing In You*. The latter was a clever class-A tune with nursery-rhyme implications that reached number forty-two in August 1965; and it was the last of Hank's nursery rhyme songs. But these two songs were notable for another reason, which was soon to be discovered by Hank and Jim Halsey.

*

By 1966, Hank and Ann were seeing each other regularly and were clearly an "item", by anybody's definition. Ann often accompanied Hank on his tours, one of which led them to La Habra, California. After the show, everyone was having an iced beverage as The Brazos Valley Boys starting finalizing their guest list for The Brazos Valley Boys Invitation Only Fun and Games Unwinding Party to be held at their motel.

Suddenly Hank called out to Ann, "Quick get the camera!"

Ann jumped to it, since she rarely had seen Hank so excited. She brought the camera to Hank and was surprised to find him with each arm around a female.

"What's this?" asked Ann

"Just take the picture!" urged Hank, with the same level of excitement.

She did.

Later, Hank explained. "You didn't realize it," he said, "but you made history with that picture."

"What do you mean?" asked Ann

"You just took a picture of me with Black Rider and Hurricane Shirley!"

It is clearly not in Hank's nature to brag; but, a few days later, he sent copies of the landmark photo to several of his friends with the following note:

"You guys think you're something, but I'm the only one to have his picture made with Black Rider and Hurricane Shirley!"

With Black Rider and Hurricane Shirley

Chapter Forty Seven

The basic issue of the royalties that Hank received in connection with his original Capitol contract had always been an issue between Capitol and Hank, but now there were other concerns, and major ones at that. By this time, in addition to the Beatles and Buck Owens, Capitol had signed, or had become the American distributors for, many other rock artists, including Badfinger, The Band, The Beach Boys, Joe Cocker, Bobby Darin, Grand Funk Railroad, Steve Miller Band, Pink Floyd, and Linda Ronstadt. Also, the label was now under British ownership, which cut off a line of communication that Hank enjoyed with the executives of the previous regime.

"It used to be that I could call (Capitol president) Glenn Wallichs on the phone, and get extra promo records or anything within reason," remembered Hank. "But later on it was clear we were getting the run-around. They let our records lie there while they promoted the rock acts."

Nonetheless, Jim Halsey and Hank put together a new proposed recording contract and presented it to Ken Nelson, who came back with the news that Capitol wouldn't buy it. Thus, the release of *Then I'll Start Believing In You* backed with *In The Back Of Your Mind* in 1965 turned out to be Hank's grand finale with Capitol, ending an eighteen-year relationship that started with the release of *Humpty Dumpty Heart* in 1947 – a relationship that that produced over three hundred and twenty recorded songs including seventy-seven charted singles and twenty-five albums.

It was time for Plan B and Jim went into action. He called an executive with Warner Brothers, a man who had been an executive with Capitol during Hank's tenure. Jim and Hank presented essentially the same proposal that Capitol had turned down. Warner Brothers wanted to establish a country artist roster and wanted Hank to be the flagship act, so they bought the proposal; and the contract was signed.

The timing could not have been worse.

Two years earlier, Warner Brothers had released an album of harmony-driven acoustic-driven folk music by *Peter, Paul and Mary*, a fairly obscure trio at the time, but the album had become an instant classic. (It stayed in the Top Ten for ten months, remained in the Top Twenty for two years, and did not drop off the Hot 100 album chart until three-and-a-half years after its release.) Follow-up albums by the group were also successful and, in the third week of November 1963, they had three albums on the Billboard Top Six. In the meantime, Nancy Sinatra had come out with her mega left-field hit, *These Boots Are Made For Walking*, also on the Warner label. Moreover, like every other U.S. record label, Warner Brothers was also trying to find its own version of the Beatles. Thus, it was safe to say that the Warner promotional people clearly had their hands full with folk and rock music, and that Hank was not a priority act. Hank and Jim were well aware of this, going in, but they felt that they could overcome it. As it turned out, they were wrong. Hank's records got little, if any, promotion; and sales were disappointing.

"We thought we had a lot of good material that went down the drain," said Hank. Indeed.

Warner Brothers was based in Los Angeles but didn't have a studio, so they made arrangements to record Hank at Studio B at the Capitol Records Tower, Hank's old stomping grounds with Capitol. Joe Allison produced the first album, *Where is the Circus?*, which was released in 1966 and included six new songs, all of which were stellar, along with six new recordings of Hank's older hits.

To confuse those who try to follow such things, in 1966, Hank had four albums released by two labels. Apparently trying to counter the Warner Brothers release of *Where is the Circus*, Capitol released three albums – *A Six Pack To Go*, *Breakin' The Rules*, and *Luckiest Heartache In Town*. Hank's second Warner Brothers album, *The Countrypolitan Sound Of Hank Thompson's Brazos Valley Boys*, was released in early 1967 and featured instrumentals that simply did not have the impact of the Capitol instrumentals. The third and final Hank Thompson/Warner Brothers collaboration, entitled *The Gold Standards Collection*, was released in late 1967, and contained an eclectic mix of hits made by everyone from Hank Williams (*Cold Cold Heart*) and Ernest Tubb (*Walking the Floor over You*) to Merle Travis (*Sixteen Tons*). This album also generated less than stellar sales. Also in 1967, Capitol released *Just An Old Flame* and *The Best of Hank Thompson, Vol. 2*, making a total of eight Hank Thompson albums released by the two labels in the two-year period.

In 1968, Hank and Jim Halsey asked, and were granted, permission to be released from the Warner Brothers contract.

"I don't blame Warner Brothers for putting their focus on the rock and folk acts on their label that were selling," said Hank, "but they left us out in the cold."

*

As the sixties progressed, Jim Halsey's steadily increased his stable of artists to include The Oak Ridge Boys, Mel Tillis, Tammy Wynette, Minnie Pearl, Freddy Fender, Donna Fargo, Don Williams, Jimmy Dean, and many others. "I started building my company by signing other acts, hiring other agents, and opening other offices," said Jim. "But Hank was always the center point of all of it."

In 1968, after Hank's severance with Warner Brothers, it was on to plan C, and Jim engineered a deal where Hank would sign with Dot Records. In the meantime Roy Clark, who had been recording for Capitol Records, had also been released by Capitol and was somewhat in limbo. Jim, who still represented Roy, tried to dovetail him in with Hank in the deal, but the Dot people were skeptical.

"We appreciated Roy's immense talent," said Jim, "but it was hard to sell him, since most people didn't know what he did at the time. Yet even though Dot Records felt the same way, we got him signed on Hank's coattails."

Hank's deal with Dot Records was somewhat different than those with Capitol and Warner Brothers. According to the Dot arrangement, Dot underwrote the recording expenses, but Hank and Halsey formed a production company, produced the records, and were to eventually own the masters.

Larry Butler, a well-respected producer in Nashville, headed most of Hank's recording sessions for Dot, but Hank was never comfortable with the production. The recordings were plagued with The Dot Records' attitude that Western Swing was out and "Light Country" or the "Nashville Sound" was in. Thus, the twin fiddles/steel guitar Thompson model was eschewed in favor of a more pop sound that was often layered with pop-infused strings and background vocals. Hank was reluctant to let this happen; but Dot insisted, and they were paying the bills.

Despite this concern, things started fairly well. In 1968, *On Tap, In The Can,* or *In The Bottle* went to number seven and *Smoky the Bar* to number three. John Rumble of the Country Music Foundation described both songs as follows:

"Both numbers demonstrate basic elements of the Thompson formula including a standard rhythm section of piano, bass, guitar, and drums, with electric guitar, twin fiddles and steel guitar taking lead and fill parts. Tinkling piano backgrounds also flesh out the honky-tonk sound, but Thompson's exuberant vocals, along with strong swing-influenced rhythmic effects on the introductions and ending, help singer and listener transcend the pain of lost love."[17]

A steady stream of singles followed, six of which hit the low end of the charts in 1969 and 1970 - *I See Them Everywhere* (No. 47), *The Pathway of My Life* (No. 46), *Oklahoma Home Brew* (No. 60), *But That's All Right* (No. 54) and *One of the Fortunate Few* (No. 69).

---

[17] From the liner notes to Hank's "Country Music Hall of Fame Series" album released on MCA (MCAD-10545).

Chapter Forty Eight

It was fortuitous that Ann's job as a flight scheduler permitted her to keep up with Hank's demanding road schedule, at least on occasion. She had to work Mondays through Fridays until 9:00 P.M., but she was off on weekends. Therefore, on a typical Friday night she would leave her office at Love Field, walk down the stairs and jump on a free Trans-Texas flight to the city where Hank was playing. Often, she would arrive in time to go to the club with him; but when she and Hank entered the club, Ann would be overwhelmed by the people who would surge towards Hank to say hello.

"I was very shy back then, and it scared me to death," she remembered. "There would be hundreds of people there, all trying to get to Hank. No one wanted to talk to me, and people would elbow me out of the way to get to him. Hank had the ability to say hello to everyone, yet keep moving through; and I finally learned to keep moving with him."

Afterwards, she and Hank would usually attend The Brazos Valley Boys Invitation Only Fun and Games Unwinding Party at the motel where they were staying. This usually meant that they didn't get to bed until dawn. Unfortunately, on these weekends, Hank's schedule was hardly compatible with Ann's work schedule in Dallas.

"Many Monday mornings, I would fly back to Dallas after a weekend with Hank, walk up the stairs, go directly to the office without any sleep, and try to stay awake the rest of the day," Ann recalled.

Also during this time, when Hank had a few days off, or when he was working in or near Dallas, he would fly to Dallas late at night after the job. After she got off work, Ann would hurry to her apartment, which was about ten minutes from Love Field, jump into bed around 9:30 P.M. and try to get some sleep until Hank touched down at Love. She would then get dressed, pick him up, and they would have a meal when they got back to her place.

Ann's roommate would sometimes join them for the meal and was delighted to have charcoaled steak, beef Wellington or shrimp Dijon for breakfast.

Finally Ann had to say it. "Hank, I can't stand this pace any longer. You have got to marry me!"

And, in 1970, he did.

*

Another tour of the Northwest included a job at a club near Seattle, Washington, and the Puget Sound. The Brazos Valley Boys spent the night in a hotel near the club, and the next day, about an hour before the show, they drove the motor home to the club. During the trip, Bert Rivera was going over a map of the area when Merle David asked a question.

"What is this 'Puget' sound I keep hearing everybody talk about?" Merle was an exceptional fiddle player but an unexceptional student of geography.

Bert was all over this immediately and quickly responded.

"You've never heard of a Puget sound?" he asked, as his mind quickly latched onto a story. "It has to do with old Indian ghosts that reportedly make this very unusual noise across this body of water between Seattle and Tacoma. It still happens often and is a famous thing."

Curtis Potter jumped right in and said, "Our job tonight is near the Puget Sound, and you may get to hear it!"

Bert pulled Curtis and Curly Lewis over before they arrived and said: "After we arrive, you stall Merle here in the motor home for a few minutes, and I'll go behind the building and make a 'Puget sound'".

As soon as the bus arrived, Bert jumped off quickly and went back to a rear corner of the building.

Curtis and Curly stalled Merle for a few minutes, exited the bus with him, and said. "Merle, let's see if we can hear that Puget sound we were talking about." Merle bought it.

As they walked along towards the club, they heard some strange noises coming from the rear of the building.

"Woooooooooo. Woooooooooo. Woooooooooo." Bert, in his Nudie suit, was bent over at a rear corner of the building, howling.

"Can you hear that?" asked Curtis, faking excitement. "That's the Puget Sound!"

"Woooooooooo. Woooooooooo."

"Yes!" exclaimed Merle, with genuine excitement.

About that time a few patrons, arriving early so they could get a good table, were walking towards the club from the rear where they saw what looked like a Brazos Valley Boy bent over and going, "Woooooooooo. Woooooooooo."

"Goodness," said one of the patrons, "The Brazos Valley Boys sure have a funny way of warming up!"

*

Hank and Dorothy had been formally separated in 1968, and divorce papers were filed. After the separation, Dorothy stayed at the Lake house in Tahlequah; and Hank, after a brief move to Dallas, bought a house in a development called Candlestick Beach in Sand Springs, Oklahoma, six miles west of Tulsa. Later, Ann quit her job in Dallas and moved in with him.

At the beginning of Hank's fourth decade of personal appearances, The Brazos Valley Boys got a new ride. Hank ordered a state-of-the-art, fully tricked-out vehicle from the Newell Coach Company of Miami, Oklahoma. Although often referred to as a bus, it was actually a cross between a coach, a motor home, and a bus. It was custom built at the very impressive Newell factory in Miami, and Hank was able to design the interior and baggage compartment to his specifications. Included were a television in front, a queen-size bed in the rear, and several other amenities. Hank took delivery a few months later, the old motor home became history, and the band was delighted.

The expense of the new bus was significant, but there was also a major development on the other side of the ledger when a long-available potential business opportunity became a reality. Ann remembered it well.

"When I first started going to the clubs and dance halls with Hank, I noticed that his product sales consisted of The Brazos Valley Boys leaving a few albums on the stage at the start of the intermission, and then running off to have a drink and hustle the girls. Then, right before they started back up again, they would spend a couple of minutes at the stage trying to sell the albums. Also, Hank would sign autographs on a wet napkin, a coaster, or whatever. However, I was too busy partying to bother, even though Hank had asked me to consider selling some of his albums."

All of this changed when a promoter booked Hank for a tour of the Northwest. He was a good promoter and an extraordinary salesman, and, before the tour, he called Hank and asked him to bring any items that had *Hank Thompson* written on them, and he would sell them. Hank and Ann put together a few tee shirts and albums and took them along.

At intermission at the first show, Ann watched in amazement.

"He was a super salesman, and he hustled those tee shirts and albums until he sold them all," said Ann. "He also had someone take a Polaroid picture of Hank with a fan and charged the fan five dollars for the picture."

A light went on. Ann had always been interested in marketing, and this provided the needed inspiration. The next time Hank went to Nashville for an appearance, Ann went with him and paid a visit to *Screenplay*, a large tee shirt manufacturer. She ordered a few white tee shirts with Hank's name in black and a few black baseball hats with Hank's name in white. She also was able to acquire some CDs at a good price from a distributor and a new business was born.

*

In 1970, Hank's divorce with Dorothy was final. Soon thereafter, in order to avoid Oklahoma's required six-month period between a divorce and a subsequent marriage, Hank and Ann were married in Siloam Springs in northwest Arkansas, about eighty-five miles from Tulsa.

A large crowd was in attendance, which became a large, uneasy, crowd when the ceremony time came and went and there was no bride and groom. However, Hank and Ann were only a few minutes late. They had become lost on their way to Siloam Springs, and finally were assisted by a kindly motorist who not only told them the proper directions but even led them to the site of the ceremony.

Hank's attorney lived just outside Siloam Springs, and his mother hosted a reception after the wedding which turned out to be one of the top social events of the year in the small town.

*

Hank and Faron Young played a package show together in the early seventies; and Hank, being very aware of Faron's well-known behavioral extremes, gave a warning to Ann before the show.

"Be careful around Faron; he can be bad news sometimes."

After the show, Ann scolded Hank.

"I don't know what you were talking about. Every time I saw Faron and talked to him, he was a perfect gentlemen."

Hank smiled but didn't reply.

A few months later, when Ann was flying in and out of Love Field in Dallas on a regular basis to and from Hank's shows, she ran into Faron at the airport, and they had a conversation. Again, Ann told Hank, "I saw Faron again today at the airport. He was so nice to me and was a perfect gentleman. You were really wrong about him."

Again, Hank smiled but didn't reply.

Later, Hank and Faron shared the same bill at a show in Poteau, Oklahoma. After the show, Ann was on The Brazos Valley Boys' bus unwinding with some friends, band members, and beverages when Faron staggered on the bus. He was aided by a couple of his band members since he was obviously too overcome by an enormous ingestion of alcohol to walk. But his mouth was running.

Ann remembered it well. "He described in a loud voice that everyone in the bus could hear, some sexual adventures he had had with some big-name female country singers. I was used to the usual four-letter words and they really didn't bother me that much. But he took crudeness to a new level as he described, very explicitly, the various sex acts that he had engaged in with those well-known partners."

Ann finally left the bus in disgust, found Hank, and told him the story.

This time, Hank smiled and replied, "Now you know the *real* Faron."

*

Beginning in 1971 and continuing for several years thereafter, Jim Halsey put together an annual "Tulsa Ranch Party", held at the twenty-five-hundred acre Circle R Ranch, located south of Tulsa and jointly owned by Jim, Hank, Roy Clark and others. Once a year, talent buyers, television producers, record company executives and radio personalities from all over the world were invited to spend a three-day weekend at the ranch as guests of the Halsey Agency.

The ranch house was located at the top of a hill overlooking thousands of acres of beautiful, rolling Oklahoma pastureland sprinkled with grazing cattle, and it looked like something out of the Bonanza television series. No one lived in the house, but it was fully furnished, with the bedrooms outfitted as offices that were used for private sales meetings. The parties were held in early autumn, not only to take advantage of the beauty of the season in Oklahoma and to celebrate the harvest, but also to thank the agency's best customers – the promoters and other talent buyers – and to make sales presentations before their annual late November meeting in Las Vegas.

There was a natural amphitheater at the ranch in which Hank and the other acts in Jim's growing stable performed before the promoters and buyers. In keeping with Jim's Cherokee heritage, tepees were scattered around the property, Native American art was on display and the entertainment included Indian dances. The guests were treated to barbecued ribs, brisket, links, turkey and chicken, and, needless to say, the beverage(s) of their choice.

Members of the press from all over the country were also invited; and Ralph Emery, the noted DJ from Nashville, broadcast live from the Ranch. Also, a taping of Ranch Party highlights was televised every year as a syndicated special.

To further gild the lily, the important sponsors of the radio shows on the two above-mentioned Tulsa radio stations were also invited, and the stations booked a lot of heavy advertising dollars for the coming months.

"It was a sales event without parallel in the industry, a private showcasing of Halsey Company artists before the most important buyers in the world," said Jim, "and it upset many of our competitors, because we had the first opportunity to book our acts with fair buyers for the coming year."

Chapter Forty Nine

In fulfillment of one of his earlier visions for promoting Hank, Jim Halsey booked jobs for Hank in many foreign venues, including the Netherlands, Belgium, the Scandinavian countries, Germany, Africa, and Asia. He also was a headliner at the first Brazilian country music festival to feature artists from the United States; and, for several years during the seventies, he headlined a huge outdoor country festival at the famous arena in Wembley, a suburb of northwest London.

The Wembley Arena was London's busiest music venue, seated a maximum of 12,300 for concerts, and was regarded as having the best sound quality and the best backstage amenities for touring music acts. One such tour included, among others, Hank, George Jones and Tammy Wynette (after their divorce) and George Richey, who played piano for Tammy and eventually married her. They were all staying in a Wembley hotel that had a large lobby complete with a piano. One afternoon before an evening show, George Richey sat down at the piano, George Jones and Hank brought their guitars, someone set up a small amplifier/speaker, and a jam session ensued. A young man drifted in with a guitar, said hello, plugged in, and joined the session. It turned out he was a big fan of Hank and an excellent guitar player, albeit from another music genre. As he and Hank traded songs and licks on the guitar, Jim Halsey looked on in amazement.

"It was very interesting to watch Hank and Eric Clapton play together," said Jim. "It turns out that Hank and Merle Travis were huge influences on Eric, something that Eric has often mentioned throughout the years."

Jim received a lot of criticism from his contemporaries in the booking business, since most of the foreign venues didn't pay as well as in the United States.

"But what these critics, and even some of the artists that we booked, didn't realize," said Jim, "was that these tours generated significant records sales in each country. Also, many of the shows were televised, which further increased the artists' exposure. Some artists balked at the low pay, but Hank was willing to sacrifice for the benefit of record sales and exposure, and it certainly paid off in the long run."

Speaking of record sales, from 1971 to 1973, Hank sent three singles to the top twenty – *Next Time I Fall in Love I Won't* (number fifteen), *The Mark Of A Heel* (number eighteen), and *I've Come Awful Close* (number eleven). In 1972, he also recorded an entire LP of Mills Brothers hits for Dot, and two singles from the album made it to the charts - *Cab Driver* (number sixteen) and *Glow Worm* (number fifty-three).

Two gems were released 1974 which made it big – *The Older The Violin, The Sweeter The Music*, and *Who Left The Door To Heaven Open*, which reached number eight and number ten, respectively.

After that, a string of Hank's releases produced ten charted songs for Dot (including its successor companies – ABC/Dot, MCA, and MCA/Dot), none of which made it to the top twenty. The string ended with the song *Tony's Tank-Up Drive-In Café* in 1980, the year Hank's contract with Dot expired.

Eighteen albums were also released during the thirteen years Hank was with Dot and its successor companies, including the above-mentioned Mills Brothers album, a tribute to Nat King Cole, an instrumental album, several albums with new versions of his hits, and several albums with original material mixed with country and Western Swing classics. One of the best of the albums in the last category was *Take Me Back To Tulsa*, which was released in 1980 and featured a photograph of Hank standing near the famous Cain's Ballroom in Tulsa. (He also recorded an album for MCA/Dot in 1986, six years after the contract expired, entitled *Hank Thompson*, which was a one-shot, stand-alone, project.)

Hank doesn't exactly have a warm and cozy feeling about his experiences with Dot. "I was never happy with those records," said Hank, "and I never thought it was my thing. Nobody wanted to do my style of music, and I never was able to get the records with Dot that I did with Capitol."

To compound the problem, Hank was very frustrated with the sound quality of the Dot recordings. "I'd play one of those Dot records and compare it to those old Capitol records, and the presence and quality of the Capitols were much better."

It didn't help that Dot was sold and bought several times during this period by the likes of ABC, MCA, Gulf & Western, and 20th Century Fox. This further distanced Hank from the executives and the personal communication he had enjoyed at Capitol.

In the meantime, Hank had sold a catalog of several of his songs to a publishing company, one of which was *I'd Like To Have An Elephant For Christmas*, from his 1964 Christmas album. Later, he got a call from a representative of the publishing company informing him that the song was going to be on a Walt Disney Christmas album featuring each of the Disney characters singing a Christmas song. The esteemed vocalist, Goofy, was going to do *I'd Like To Have An Elephant For Christmas*.

"Aw hell," thought Hank, "Walt Disney doing country music for kids? That won't do anything," and he forgot about it at approximately the same time that he hung up the phone.

Hank was wrong. Months later, he received a check based on sales of five hundred thousand albums, and later another check based on sales of about a hundred thousand albums. Still later, Disney quit pressing the album and closed it out from their catalog, and Hank received yet a third sizable check. More recently, Disney did a "sing-a-long" DVD of the old Christmas album – and still another check came in. Hank vowed that if he ever ran into Goofy, he would tell him he owed him one.

*

Since her start with Hank in 1953, and her duet with Billy Gray in 1954, Wanda Jackson made a series of records that cut a swath through a broad spectrum of genres. For example, in 1958, she recorded the rockabilly hit *Fujiyama Mama*, which was number one in Japan for six months. In 1960, her version of *Let's Have a Party*, a rock song if there ever was one, was a U.S. Top 40 hit; and a year later, she was back on the country charts with two top-ten numbers – *Right or Wrong* and *In the Middle of a Heartache*. Wanda received two Grammy nominations for the best performing female singer and developed a huge following in several foreign countries. She has recorded in the German, Dutch, and Japanese languages, and her German recording of *Santo Domingo* became a number one song in six different German-speaking countries. But she still remembers the early days with Hank.

"I learned so many things working with Hank. For example, he has always loved his fans. I remember that, between sets at the Trianon and at his other shows back then, he would walk from table to table, seeking out and greeting the fans. In fact, when my daddy saw this, he made me do it when I was on my own later.

"In all the years since I started with Hank, if any issues came up in my career, I would always ask myself 'how would Hank handle this?' Hank is really a unique individual. He is just magnificent and I still love him with all my heart! Even today, I feel blessed to be one of his and Ann's friends."

*

Despite the successful implementation of the Halsey Crossover Plan, the popularity of the large, classic ballrooms and dance halls was on the decline during the eighties, and honky-tonks were becoming more and more fashionable, especially with the younger crowd. Although a "honky-tonk" is hard to define (a dictionary definition is "a cheap, noisy, and often disreputable bar or nightclub"), a simple distinction between it and a dance hall would be that the dance halls emphasized dancing with a large dance floor and a relative small seating area; while a honky-tonk had a smaller dance floor and a larger seating area to facilitate the consumption of beverages, an advantage that was important to the owners. Thus, more and more honky-tonks were springing up where liquor and/or beer were sold. (The no-liquor laws in Oklahoma or Texas were subverted by having each patron join a "private club" at a nominal fee, which permitted them to consume liquor.) When a club owner could make his money on liquor sales, was usually more generous with the payments to the band. As a result, Jim was able to attain substantial numbers of bookings for Hank in the honky-tonks.

Good bookings were also often found at the various fairs throughout the country, usually during the summer months. One year, the promoter for the annual fair in Union City, Missouri, booked Ferlin Husky, Faron Young and Hank on consecutive days, in that order. Hank and some of The Brazos Valley Boys were in a restaurant in Union City on the day he was to perform, and a waitress told them a story about something that had happened at the fair the previous day.

It seems that a fan had come up to Faron with a complaint.

"Faron, I hope you are nicer than Ferlin Husky. I met him after his show yesterday, and he was rude to me and said some really bad things", said the fan.

"What did the fucker say?" asked Faron.

In the early days of his performing life, Hank had joined the musicians union—the American Federation of Musicians (the AFM).

"Back then, it was a big honor for a country music musician to get into the union, since they had a prejudice against 'hillbilly music,'" said Hank.

The modern day web site of the AFM lists "Twenty great reasons to join the AFM".

But as the years went on, Hank began to realize that there were just as many reasons *not* to join the AFM.

"I have nothing against organized groups of any kind, whether they be business groups, political parties, church groups, employee groups, or whatever. But when the group gets so big, and a few people are controlling a great deal of people, it leads to problems, not the least of which is graft and corruption.

"One of the reasons that the AFM became so big was that so many non-musicians, such as bandleaders, booking agents, and some entertainers, including Minnie Pearl, for example, were coerced into joining. With so many types of people in the union, there was no one to bargain with, which was the main purpose of the union in the first place. On top of this, I resented the coercion and intimidation that the AFM exerted on the musicians to join; and, after they joined, the dues, taxes, and fines that were levied against them. Another problem was that they required us to use their form contract when we contracted with a promoter, which named the purchaser of the music (the promoter) as an employer, thus setting into motion an employer-employee relation that required significant obligations on the part of the employer. Also non-union musicians were not allowed to work with union musicians, which was still another farce."

Hank withdrew from the AFM in the early sixties and asked the Brazos Valley Boys to also resign with the understanding that, if they left the band, they could be reinstated. Often after his resignation, a Union leader would approach Hank, saying that he could not play at a certain venue because they had a contract with the place.

"But I don't belong to the Union, so you have no jurisdiction over me," was Hank's standard reply. And he usually played the job.

Chapter Fifty

In 1974, DD Bray, her husband Larry, and their two young daughters moved to Candlestick Beach, two doors down from Hank and Ann. DD wasn't aware of her neighbors until Larry, a native Oklahoman, broke the news to her soon after they moved in.

"Did you know Hank Thompson and his wife live two doors down?" asked Larry.

"Hank Thompson? You mean the baseball player?" she asked.

Although Larry explained who *this* Hank Thompson was, DD didn't realize the full impact of living close to Hank until she noticed some erratic behavior on the part of Larry and his brothers. The brothers would often come to their house and play music, which was not unusual. But what *was* unusual was that the sessions started occurring at an odd place (in their garage with the door open), and at odd times (late at night). And the music was loud.

When confronted by DD, Larry confessed his motive.

"We are hoping that Hank will hear us and maybe hire us to be his opening act."

This piqued DD's interest in her new neighbors, but all she could learn over the next few years was that the Thompsons traveled a lot, and that, when Hank was home, he often worked in a wood shop he had set up in his garage. She also noticed that, during the summer months, he and Ann would often leave in the morning with their boat and return at the end of the day.

One day, UPS delivered two large boxes to the Bray house addressed to Hank. Later DD got a phone call.

"Hi! This is Hank Thompson. I live two doors down. The UPS guy left me a note saying that he delivered two packages to your house that are for me. Did you get them?"

"Sure did, and I'll be glad to bring them over."

She did and met Hank, and they had a pleasant conversation. That night Larry was furious with DD when he heard the story.

"You should have waited until I got home from work," said Larry, "and I could have taken them over!"

Later, a neighbor and friend of DD's called her and asked her to help do some odd jobs for Hank and Ann, such as wrapping and mailing Christmas gifts. This appealed to DD, since she was looking for a job she could do at or near home so that she could be there for her daughters.

Later, she got a call from another neighbor who was doing Hank's fan club newsletter, flight bookings and other general secretarial duties. The friend was going on vacation and asked DD to take over. DD did so and, after a few months, she took over the job on a permanent basis. She and Hank and Ann became friends, and she was at their house nearly every day.

In the meantime, Hank and Ann attended quite a few social events in Tulsa, including several in the Candlestick Beach neighborhood. They developed a circle of friends who consistently commented on what an easy life Hank and Ann had in show business.

"You all just go out and party and have fun and leave us working stiffs back here," was a typical line from one of the friends.

Ann finally got so tired of it that she asked one of the couples to accompany them on a two-week tour of one-nighters. The couple readily accepted.

"When we got back to Tulsa after the two weeks, the couple was so tired they could hardly move", said Ann. "From then on, if anybody mentioned our easy show-biz life, the couple was all over them."

*

Hank worked a big package show in San Antonio with Willie Nelson and Faron Young. It was a charity event held in an auditorium with no drinking or dancing, so that the fans could bring their families. The artists' buses were parked between the auditorium and a big public parking lot, and after Willie closed the show, people leaving the auditorium passed by the buses on their way to the parking lot. Hank was already in his bus and noticed something unusual going on around Faron's bus. A lot of the people who were passing by, including wives, grandmothers and children, stopped and stared into the windows of the bus. But the parents were grabbing their children and hurrying them away. No wonder. Faron and the boys were showing hard-core pornographic movies on the bus's television set, which could clearly be seen through the windows.

Speaking of buses, in 1973, Hank had sold the Newell bus to Archie Campbell of *Hee Haw* fame, and The Brazos Valley Boys reverted to a station wagon and trailer. A few years later, Hank was playing a dance at San Marcos, California, and noticed a bus in the parking lot that looked familiar. It looked like a Newell. Hank walked over to take a look.

"This bus sure looks familiar," Hank said to a guy in the bus.

"It should," was the reply. "It's your old bus. Joe Maphis bought it from Archie Campbell and redid the interior to convert it into a motor home."

*

In the mid-seventies, Claremore Junior College in Claremore, Oklahoma, was looking to expand its curriculum. Jim Halsey, who knew some of the people at the school, had an idea. Why not have a full curriculum based on music, and enlist Hank to design the curriculum and participate as a guest lecturer? Hank met with the school officials and outlined what he thought should be covered in the curriculum. In addition to radio and television, he suggested including performing, song writing, managing, promoting, and publishing.

Thus, *The Hank Thompson School of Country Music* was founded. Leon McAuliffe, who owned a radio station in nearby Rogers, Oklahoma, became more involved than Hank, and served as an administrator and teacher in addition to donating some radio and television broadcasting equipment to the school. Hank made several appearances at lectures, seminars, and question-and-answer sessions.

After the school was renamed Roberts State College, Junior Brown also became an instructor at the school and met "the lovely Miss Tanya Rae," a student who eventually joined his band as a rhythm guitarist and backing vocalist. She also joined Junior in marriage in 1988 before he ascended to stardom.

"They were quite successful with the school, and many students went through it," said Hank.

The school is now Rogers State University.

*

With the airlines continually beating up on the custom Super 400, Hank purchased a state-of-the-art protective case for the guitar to withstand the assaults. He also purchased a standard sunburst Super 400 with his name inlaid on the neck and started using it interchangeably with the custom Super 400.

*

In the early seventies, with his career as a solo act at a standstill, Billy Gray briefly served as Johnny Rodriguez's bandleader. After suffering a heart attack in 1975, he underwent triple bypass surgery. The doctors initially said that the operation was successful, but Billy died a few days later. Hank lost a colleague, a business associate, and, most of all, a close friend.

Chapter Fifty One

As Hank continued with a fairly rigorous road schedule, Ann systematically increased the inventory of products to sell at all of the dates. There were several choices of caps and tee shirts in various colors, and several selections of Hank's albums, along with belt buckles, bandanas and pictures.

"People treasured those things; and the next time we would see them, they would be proudly wearing them," said Ann.

During this time, Ann started what turned out to be one of the most important projects of Hank's career, one that still exists today. Throughout the years, she has very carefully and selectively set up a network of fans in the towns and cities where Hank often appears. The fans pick Hank and Ann up at the airport, drive them to the job, help them unload and load, assist at the autograph table, and/or drive them to the motel or back to the airport. The fans became friends and Hank and Ann have tried to show their gratitude by entertaining them as often as possible.

"We absolutely could not make all the jobs we do now if it were not for these friends," said Ann, as Hank nodded in agreement.

*

One night in the seventies, Hank Thompson and Hank Snow were on a double bill; and after the show they were at a booth signing autographs. A female came up to Snow to get his autograph. Thompson was close enough to hear the conversation.

"Mr. Snow, I remember you from 'way back, when you had all of those hits," said the fan. "You sure were a good-looking guy back then, but you look a lot older now."

Without missing a beat, Snow replied, somewhat nonchalantly, as he signed the autograph, "Honey it looks like you won't win any beauty contests yourself."

*

In the mid-seventies, Hank switched from having The Brazos Valley Boys on the payroll full-time to an arrangement in which he contracted with the band members on a job-by-job basis. This was a fairly seamless transition as far as his fans were concerned, but one that was more economical from an expense standpoint. Also, Merle had continued with his solo career but still played with Hank on occasion. A few years after Hank's divorce from Dorothy, Merle was in Texas and became ill. He called Dorothy, whom he had known quite well throughout the years of his association with Hank, and asked if she knew of a doctor in the area. Dorothy suggested that he have someone drive him to Tahlequah, where he could see her doctor, which he did. This led to a relationship between Merle and Dorothy that culminated in marriage in 1977.

Later, when they were playing together, Hank would often introduce Merle as his "husband-in-law."

Merle passed away in 1983, and Hank was deeply saddened at the loss of their long lasting friendship.

*

How many records has Hank sold?

To answer this with any accuracy, the definition of a "record" must first be established, since Hank's songs have been released on every format available in the history of the music industry, including 78s, 45s, LPs, EPs, eight tracks, cassettes, compact discs and digital downloads. The industry-accepted answer to this is that each item in each of the above formats counts as a "record". Thus, each 78 rpm and 45 rpm disc, having a song on each side, and each LP, EP, cassette, eight track, and compact disc, containing multiple songs, counts as one "record". Using this is a guide, Jim Halsey's people ran the numbers after the Dot/MCA contract expired in 1980 and came up with a figure of approximately sixty million. Hank's records have continued to sell worldwide since the Dot contract expired, but the sales figures in this period are relatively modest when compared to sales in the fifties and sixties. Still, it is safe to say that Hank has sold between sixty and sixty-five million records in his career. And counting.

*

On Christmas day in 1978, Hank and Ann were hunting at the Sloan Pool Deer Lease near San Saba, Texas, when the owner came out to them and told Hank, "Hank, I just received a phone call with some bad news. Your dad died this morning."

He was eighty-four.

*

Through the years, Hank and Ann often attended the Country Music Association's annual awards show, which had moved from the Ryman Auditorium to *The Grand Ole Opry* House at Opryland, outside of downtown Nashville, in 1974. One year in the early eighties, they attended the show and were enjoying cocktails backstage afterwards. As usual, Hank was surrounded by a group of several people and engaged in conversation, but Ann was standing by his side thinking, "I wish someone would talk to *me*." As she gazed across the room she saw another lonely looking person.

"I saw this cute cowboy standing by himself and looking miserable," said Ann. "I walked over and introduced myself and told him I was Hank's wife. He introduced himself and said, 'I don't think Hank will remember me but, years ago, he played in Honolulu and I fronted the house band that opened for him. I was very thrilled to do so, and he is one of my heroes.'

"He went on to say that he had tried to record one of Hank's songs on one of his albums," said Ann, "but never could get it to come off right, and he couldn't figure out why. I told him that I would try to get Hank to come over and maybe he could help."

Ann caught Hank's eye, motioned him over, and Ann made the introduction.

"Hank this is George Strait and he has a question," said Ann, delighted to finally being engaged in some meaningful conversation. "George, explain it to Hank."

Hank recalled the ensuing conversation he had with George.

"George said he was having trouble with the song *Green Light,* and I explained that I used a split bar to create a delay in the verse:

I turned your whole card [delay] upside down...

"I also explained that, when I first wrote the song without the split bar, it sounded bad, but the split bar put some life into the song despite the fact that it made the song off meter."

George appeared to be appreciative. He and Hank became friends and later collaborated on a duet on *A Six Pack to Go.* (More on this later.)

Chapter Fifty Two

In 1965, at age thirteen, Morey Sullivan had launched his professional musical career in Kansas City by becoming the drummer for a band fronted by his dad. They played everything from pop to country. Hank's music was often in high rotation on the family's record player, and the band often played Hank's songs. Morey remembered his dad telling him that The Brazos Valley Boys were the ultimate country and western band and should be an inspiration for any musician aspiring to make country music a career.

The seventies found Morey working days as a talk show host on a radio station in Bartlesville, Oklahoma, and nights as a musician. He started forming small bands and touring the region, following his dad's model of playing anything that could get them a good job. But of all the musical genres that he and the band played, he found himself gravitating more and more towards Western Swing. He was pleasantly surprised to discover that nearby Tulsa was a hotbed for Western Swing musicians. Morey formed a Western Swing band called the Caney River Band, consisting largely of Tulsa musicians that included two fiddles, a steel guitar, and drums along with his bass, and hit the "Holiday Inn" circuit. One of the fiddle players was Curly Lewis, a prominent member of The Brazos Valley Boys Alumni Association.

In the early eighties, Morey became a frequent visitor at the Halsey Agency's office in Tulsa, trying to get some bookings for his band. He finally got an an offer from the agency to back Hank for a job on a barge in Tariko, Missouri. Before the job, he and the band practiced Hank's songs, and the show went well. Hank was impressed with Morey and the quality of musicians in Morey's group.

Soon Morey's band became Hank's go-to band. Morey moved to Topeka, Kansas, in 1988 to take a day job with the government, but has continued to front a band that backs Hank throughout many parts of the country, especially the Midwest and West Coast.

Since Morey is a professional musician, a student and proponent of Western Swing, and has been associated with Hank for nearly twenty years, his take on Hank's music is interesting.

Just as the United States is a melting pot for all people, our music is a mixture of many kinds and types of music. This concept was made clear in the nineteen sixties when the musical term "crossover-music" was made a part of our language. This term was often used when a country song "crossed-over" to the pop or rock charts, and vice-versa.

Long before the sixties, Hank was creating crossover music and probably did not even realize that he did so. He was taking music from several different genres and melding them together to make a new type of Western Swing. John Wooley, a music critic of the Tulsa World newspaper, called Hank's style of Western Swing 'sophisticated swing'. And it was. Hank's creation had as much commonality, musically, (chord structures, instrumental harmonies, etc.) with big-band swing and be-bop jazz music as it did with country. Hank's Western Swing did differ from jazz groups in that Hank's arrangements were without improvisation and each band member had a specific part to play. In fact, the music was really "charted" and carefully rehearsed – a noticeable departure from Bob Wills' improvisational, jam sessions.

The big-band great Woody Herman, whose recording of "The Woodchopper's Ball" was a giant hit, said that Hank and the Brazos Valley Boys' rendition was better than his own. And Woody wrote the song! Hank's creativity and willingness to try new things should be as important in the annals of musical history as Hank Williams' and Bob Wills'. He was crossing over into new musical styles many years before it was a popular thing to do.

"Hank has been a big influence on my career," said Morey, "and I learned many things from him, such as how to sequence songs and some tricks in vocalizing. Also, many people don't realize how good a guitarist Hank is. To pick up that Merle Travis style was quite a feat, but he is even better as a rhythm guitarist. Some of the songs Hank does are fairly sophisticated, and yet Hank hits all the right chords, notes, and licks, no matter how complicated they are.

"But the most important thing I learned from Hank was how to treat the fans.

I have never seen him turn away a fan; and, in fact, he almost solicits the fans while many other artists turn their backs on them. He is very gracious towards each fan and tries to remember their names. No wonder that at every job, many fans come up to him and say 'Hank, do you remember me?'"

In addition to using Morey and his band as the Brazos Valley Boys, Hank has a non-exclusive contract with Morey that allows Morey to use the Brazos Valley Boys' name at jobs in which Hank does not participate.

Also in the eighties, Hank and DD set up another regional version of The Brazos Valley Boys in New England, headed by Terry Miller. This band has backed up Hank in the New England area for the last twenty years.

*

In 1983, Hank, Morey and the band were booked for three weeks at a hotel in Reno, Nevada. There were three shows a day, with the last show ending around 2:00 A.M. However, relief from the grind was found at the hotel bar each night after the last show. The band members made friends with several cocktail waitresses, most of whom were Oriental. The band members soon discovered that the waitresses' affinity for country music was exceeded only by their affinity for country music *musicians*. This led to a highly convivial atmosphere at the bar, and strong friendships were forged, most of which were nurtured later in the band members' rooms in the hotel.

The waitresses didn't speak good English, but they didn't have to.

One night, or rather morning, Morey was returning from one of the latter events and was walking across a courtyard that included a pool. He saw Hank walking across the courtyard on the other side of the pool. Hank waved, and Morey was surprised when Hank, obviously aware of the action at the bar that evening, uncharacteristically vocalized an interest in Morey's social life.

"Hey, Hoss, are you getting any?"

One evening during the same Reno engagement, Hank, Morey and a few of The Brazos Valley Boys were between shows and had adjourned to their dressing room. The distilled spirit of the day was wine, and the oenophiles were raising their glasses and enjoying good conversation.

In walked Roger Miller, who was also booked in Reno that week. He had come by just to say hello and have a drink. Actually, it was more than one. With Roger's presence, the party atmosphere went up a notch; but after several rounds of stories, laughs, and sips, Hank had to leave the dressing room. Roger watched him leave and then said to all, "That Hank Thompson bastard, he doesn't know how good he is!"

*

An interviewer once asked Hank a question about his knowledge of music theory.
Question: Hank, you must be well versed in music theory?
Answer: Maybe so, but I don't let it interfere with my playing.

Morey Sullivan, to Hank's left, with his band.

Hank and Ann

At their wedding reception

With Sapphire, Ann's mother

Chapter Fifty Three

The tendency by Nashville and the record labels to gravitate towards Light Country, and even further towards a more pop sound, hit a crescendo with the release of the movie *Urban Cowboy* in 1980. This movie is often credited with having started the eighties boom in country music appeal (that is, if you call it country music). It grossed almost fifty-four million dollars in the United States alone, and spawned a hit soundtrack album featuring such songs as Johnny Lee's *Looking for Love*, Mickey Gilley's *Stand By Me*, Anne Murray's hit *Could I Have This Dance,* and the top-five hit *Love The World Away*, by Kenny Rogers.

This music was even further removed from the grit of traditional country and paved the way for the release of album after album of what best can be described as collections of insipid, honey-drenched, pabulum-infested "country" songs done by artists that couldn't tell a steel guitar from Shinola. But it sold. In fact, the *Urban Cowboy* soundtrack album weighed in at about four million copies and converted a lot of people to what they thought was country music. As long as they were wearing Wrangler jeans that were one size too small, riding mechanical bulls in a big dance hall, and listening to Kenny Rogers on the jukebox, everything was country cool.

This, of course, led to a decline in record sales for the traditional country artists. To add insult to injury, *Urban Cowboy* started the line-dancing craze that swept the dance halls and clubs in the early eighties, contributing to a proportional decrease in the popularity of traditional country and Western Swing.

Of course, Hank and Jim Halsey were concerned but were steadfast in their agreement that the only real way to counteract the problem was to continue to present Hank's music in a quality manner at his personal appearances all over the world. Jim expressed it as follows:

"In the early eighties, country artists who had enjoyed substantial record sales in the past were not selling nearly as well. However, many artists continued to be successful, based on the fact that they had developed large fan bases and could make a lot of money on their personal appearances."

Hank is a perfect example. Despite the fact that his recording contract with a major label terminated in 1980, and his bookings in the early eighties were lower than in the glory days of the fifties and sixties, Hank stayed on the road, brought his A-game and his A-team to each and every appearance, and stuck to his musical values. As a result, his fan base remained largely intact.

One such road date led Hank to an appearance at a small town in southern Kansas. A few minutes before show time, the electronics on the Super 400 wouldn't work. A red alert went out to everybody associated with the show; but no one had, or knew of, an available electric guitar, that is until a kid who lived in the town was contacted and agreed to loan Hank his guitar – a purple Fender Stratocaster. Not only did Hank not like Fender guitars, the fact that it was purple made it even more bizarre. He had no choice but to use it, but he successfully avoided having any pictures made.

*

Roy Clark's contract with Dot (and its successor companies) was also terminated in 1980, leaving Jim Halsey with two of his artists without a record label. So he took some fairly dramatic action and founded a new record label, Churchill Records, and signed Hank and Roy. According to the agreement, Churchill fronted the recording expense, did the marketing, and Dot/MCA did the distribution. Hank recorded an album entitled *1000 and One Nighters* for Churchill as well as two singles – *Rocking in the Congo* (a re-recording) and *Once in a Blue Moon* – that landed fairly low on the charts in 1981 and 1983, respectively. Roy also hit the lower echelons of the charts with some of his singles. But neither artist was able to produce a big seller, and the enterprise was a failure.

Once in a Blue Moon became Hank's last charted song. Between 1947 and 1983, he had placed some seventy-nine songs on the charts (the top 100), with at least one each year except for 1962 and 1982.

Although *1000 and One Nighters* was not a commercial success, Hank received a windfall in connection with the album. Churchill produced an excessive number of LPs, cassettes, and eight tracks and sold them to Hank at a bargain, and Ann was able to sell them all at Hank's jobs.

After the release of *1000 and One Nighters*, ten more albums were released on various labels, including Step One, Curb, and Hightone (more on these albums later), making a total of approximately sixty albums over the course of Hank's career. With over forty-five of these album being on labels other than Capitol, that's around four hundred and fifty songs that Hank has recorded in additional to the approximately three hundred and twenty he recorded for Capitol – making a total of around seven hundred and seventy.

*

A radio station in Amarillo, Texas, sponsored a live country music show each year that featured both a traditional country artist and a "new" country artist. Hank was contacted about appearing as the traditionalist artist but was given a warning. The booking agent explained that an incident had happened the previous year that had left everyone on edge.

Hank Snow had been the traditional artist that previous year, and his show had been very well received. The next morning, the radio station got a lot of calls from fans thanking them for the show and telling them what a great job Hank Snow had done – so many calls that a DJ at the radio station got the bright idea of calling Snow up at the motel where he was staying and interviewing him.

"Hank, you got a great response to the show last night", said the DJ.

"Thanks very much," said Snow, in a subdued voice. It was fairly early in the morning. Too early.

After a couple of standard, routine questions, the DJ went on, "What is the biggest difference between county music today and what it was like back when you started out."

"Well, there's quite a bit of difference." Snow said, still subdued. "Back then, everywhere you went there were plenty of women. You never had a problem getting a good woman. But now you have to carry your own pussy around with you."

There was a slight pause as the DJ gagged.

"Hank, we are on the air!"

Snow's tone of voice changed dramatically.

"Oh,…well…HELLO THERE, FRIENDS AND NEIGHBORS!"

*

In 1983, Hank was distraught when he learned that Dubert had passed away. He had plans to attend Dubert's funeral, but he had to change the plans and fly to Waco when he got even worse news – Hank's mother had passed away in Waco at age 75. He has many fond memories of her. "She was only sixteen when I was born, and she was both a mother and a friend."

Hank's parents

After putting seven to eight thousand hours on the Cessna 310, including several engine replacements and paint jobs, Hank sold it. Since he had bought his original Cessna 180 in 1954, he had logged over twelve thousand hours of flying. But to keep the 310 just wasn't practical.

"It just got to where expenses started going up and up along with the restrictions on private planes and the requirements for more equipment," said Hank. "In the meantime, the commercial airlines had become much more reliable, and cheaper. So I sold the plane and started flying commercially."

Chapter Fifty Four

In 1984, Hank was no longer using Jim Halsey on an exclusive basis. The personal relationship between the two men remained on a very high level despite the fact that the business relationship had plateaued. The very simple reason was that the demand for Hank's personal appearances was not as high as for other artists represented by the Halsey agency.

"There wasn't any room in the agency for someone like me," said Hank. "I can't blame Jim at all. He had to go with what was bringing him the money. Just like a store, he had to push the merchandise that was selling."

So Hank decided to carry out an idea he had been entertaining for months, which led to a conversation he had with his neighbor, DD Bray, who, in the meantime, had done very well helping Hank and Ann with their various secretarial needs throughout the years.

"You know," Hank said, "I helped make Jim Halsey into a very successful booking agent. How would you like to go into business with me and do the same?" asked Hank

"But I don't have a clue about what a booking agent does," said DD.

"That's OK. I'll teach you."

"Well I don't know, my goal is to stay home with my daughters."

"It's all telephone work, and you can work from home when the girls are in school. With your personality and work ethic, you would be good at it."

In January 1985, DD became Hank's exclusive booking agent. Hank began mentoring her on the business, especially including the pitch to give to the "buyers", i.e. the club owners, fair and tour promoters, etc. At first, she made the calls and Hank would sit at a desk across from her and prompt her. The routine went something like this.

"Hello, Mr. Smith, I'm DD Bray and I'm the agent for Hank Thompson. I would like to book him with you. What does your schedule allow?"

Then she would listen to the reply. Early on, in most cases, she would then put her hand over the phone and ask Hank what the reply to the reply should be. For example, she might have asked Hank, "How much would you charge to appear with

The Brazos Valley Boys in Houston on October 23rd?"

After Hank quoted the figure to DD, she would offer it to the buyer.

"Hank was very patient with me," said DD.

Soon, as DD kept at it, things started working. DD's first booking was at the Hank Thompson School of Music, but her joy in scoring her first booking was tempered somewhat when she learned that Hank would perform for free. The second booking was from Morey Sullivan, who, in addition to fronting his version of The Brazos Valley Boys, also led a nine-piece Western Swing band called the Oklahoma Legends. (Morey used some of the Legends' band members as the Brazos Valley Boys when backing Hank.)

The bookings gradually increased as DD gained confidence in her new profession. In addition to sending the contracts to the buyers, getting the signed contracts, and collecting the down payments, she also took care of all logistics related to the job such as hiring the back-up band and making travel and hotel reservations for everyone. She also continued to produce and mail out the fan club newsletter.

Later in the year, a business opportunity came up in Dallas for her husband, Larry, and she and Hank agreed that, after the move, she could continue booking Hank from her home in Dallas.

A few months after DD and her family settled in Dallas, Hank and Ann came to the realization that Dallas would also be much better for *them* than Sand Springs. Since they were traveling to all of their distant jobs by commercial airlines, and since a great majority of their flights from Tulsa went through the Dallas-Ft. Worth International Airport, they would not only save on the flight costs from Tulsa to Dallas, but would also have access to more flights in Dallas. Hank and Ann made the move to Keller, a suburb of the Dallas/Ft. Worth metroplex, in December of 1986.

*

Hank was playing in Las Vegas and, on an off night, took Ann to see George Strait's show at one of the hotels. After the show, Hank and Ann were invited to come backstage and see George. Hank and George started talking shop.

Hank: "Great job on *Six Pack to Go*. I didn't know you did that song."

George: "Oh yes, I do it at all of my shows. It's one of my favorites."

Hank: "We should record that song as a duet sometime."

George: "Good idea. Let's do it"

"Sometime" came in 1986 when Hank was scheduled to record the MCA/Dot album entitled *Hank Thompson*. After all the legal agreements were made, the song was recorded (the first duet for both of them). It was put on both the *Hank Thompson* album and on George's box set, resulting in some nice royalty checks for Hank.

*

With DD on board and getting into the swing of things, Hank's bookings increased significantly. In addition to her job as director of product sales, Ann was given the job of collecting the balance due on each contract on the night of the job. This seemed logical since, by this time, Ann was going to all of Hank's performances, and it was agreed that Hank should not have to be the "heavy" when collection became an issue.

"That seems easy enough," thought Ann.

Not necessarily so, as she found out one night in connection with a job at a club in a suburb of Denver – a place that Hank had never before played.

Prior to the job, the club owner and his girl friend could not have been nicer. They sent the down payment on time, paid for a suite for Hank and Ann at very nice hotel in Denver, and even took them to dinner the night before the job. As a result, Ann's guard was down.

The night of the show, the place was packed to the roof, and things were very hectic at the autograph table, especially during the intermission. A cowboy-type came up to Ann, introduced himself, and told her he was a big fan of Hank. He then asked a question. "Have you collected your money yet?"

"No, I have been too busy," said Ann.

"Well, the owner is getting loaded and you had better collect soon. I'll be glad to go with you back to his office and help."

This was fine with Ann, especially since he was big enough to be a professional football player.

The cowboy escorted Ann back to the owner's office and walked in with her. The owner was sitting at his desk, looking somewhat self-medicated, and probably not with alcohol.

"I would like to collect now," said Ann.

"I don't have the cash," was the reply, "and I haven't had time to go to an ATM machine. So I'll write you a check."

"We don't take checks, only cash," said Ann. "It's in the contract."

The owner's demeanor changed from relaxed to nervous as he started pulling out cash from the drawers of his desk. But it wasn't nearly enough.

In the meantime the cowboy was leaning against the wall behind Ann taking it all in. As the owner continued to fumble for cash, the cowboy said to Ann.

"Ann, hold on. I live near here and I'm going to go home and get something."

"What else could it be but a gun?" thought Ann.

After the cowboy left, the owner became even more nervous.

"I'll just have to pay you later," he said.

"No, I think I'll just wait here until I get it," Ann replied, showing no signs of backing down.

The owner's girl friend came in with a wad of cash and gave it to the owner. But it was still well short of the amount that was owed.

Then the cowboy came back into the room.

The owner was now sweating. He whispered something to the girl friend, and she left. A few minutes later an employee entered with a big wad of cash, and Ann was paid in full.

But that's when *Ann* got nervous and she remembered it very well.

"The club was in a bad part of town, and it was dark. "I was scared that, once we left the club in our rental car carrying all that cash, we were going to get robbed. So I went back to the autograph table, bent over so no one could see me, and wrapped the money, as well as the money we received from product sales, in some tee shirts. I gave them to my friend and told her to follow us when we left the club, and, when we stopped, she could give it to us."

The plan worked, and, later, Ann learned from some other artists that they had gone through the same scenario with this owner, with the exception that they didn't get paid. She also heard that the reason for the cash shortage was that the owner and his girl friend were heavy cocaine users.

"This is the one part of the business that I hate," said Ann. "But like Hank says, if you don't deal with some unsavory people in this business, you don't work much."

*

In 1987, Morey Sullivan approached DD with a suggestion.

You need to start a campaign to get Hank in the Country Music Hall of Fame."

"How do I do that?"

"Start a movement by getting people to write to the Hall of Fame and suggest that Hank be nominated. I'll write the first letter and you can use it as a sample."

DD put a notice in Hank's fan club newsletter urging people to write in, and included Morey's letter as a sample.

Five hundred letters later, including ones from governor George Nigh and Oklahoma University football coach Barry Switzer, the executive director of the Country Music Association gave DD a call.

"We appreciate all the letters we have received from Hank's fans, but it's not going to do any good. Please ask them to quit sending them in."

DD decided not to do so, and she continued to run the notice in the newsletter.

In 1987 and 1988, Hank was nominated but not elected, but the fans kept sending letters. He was nominated again in 1989 and, before the winners were selected, DD got a call from an official of the Country Music Association.

"DD, we haven't made our selections yet, but we need to ask you a favor. We need some pictures of Hank, and we need to know who he would want to introduce him?"

"Then we knew," remembered DD.

Later that year at the nationally televised Country Music Association awards show, Roy Clark took the stage and did the honors.

"You will never know what a great pleasure it is for me personally to add one more gentleman to the Country Music Hall of Fame. Hank Thompson, come up here, Hoss!"

As Hank took the stage, Roy continued.

"For more than forty years, this man has been creating and singing some of the finest country music ever made. He's a Texan who has blended Western Swing with honky-tonk and added his own great lyrics and has given us a long string of wonderful songs. And at the same time, he was always eager to help newcomers get started. He was pretty instrumental in my beginning. So, he's not only a hero to millions of fans who love him, but just about everybody in country music loves him too. Hank buddy, you're in the Country Music Hall Of Fame."

Hank's emotional acceptance speech was as follows:

"Thank you Roy, thank you. You know, if this were the Horizon award, it would mean that I would have this exciting and rewarding career all ahead of me. But, I don't mean to say that this is the end of the line, because I intend to pursue this business I love and enjoy for a long time to come. And, therefore, I consider this award a giant milestone along that pathway. I appreciate being exalted into the realm of some very distinguished company. I appreciate that.

"I appreciate the good Lord not only giving me a little talent but giving me the desire and incentive to really do something with it. I've had a lot of help from many along the way, and I would like to acknowledge a select few – Hal Horton, Tex Ritter,

258

Ken Nelson, Billy Gray, Jim Halsey, Dorothy and Merle Travis, and a very special lady, my personal manager DD Bray, who keeps it happening. Most of all, I'm grateful to my wife Ann, whose love, encouragement, and companionship make it all worthwhile. And, along with all you fans and friends for making this one of the single greatest moments of my life, I want to thank you very, very much."

Chapter Fifty Five

In the late eighties, Hank was very pleased when he learned that he was playing on the same bill as Thom Bresh, Merle Travis' son and a performer in his own right. Merle had taught Thom the thumb picking style when Thom was quite young, and, in addition to working as an actor and stuntman in California, Thom forged his own successful career as a singer, songwriter, impressionist, and instrumentalist. He performed often in Las Vegas with Hank Penny's country/pop/jazz stage show (he replaced Roy Clark) and hosted a weekly television variety show of his own creation, *Nashville Swing*. He also was a regular on the Merv Griffin Show and the Dinah Shore Show and now, in addition to performing, he also works as a producer and a videographer in Hendersonville, Tennessee, a few miles from Nashville.

Although they had little time to visit at the job they played, Hank did tell Thom about an inside joke that he and Merle had.

It seems that Merle liked to call all of his friends by a nickname, and he called Hank "Rock". In turn, Hank gave Merle the nickname "Cecil".

Hank and Thom were able to establish a friendship that continues today. One thing Hank did have time to discover at the job, however, was that Thom was one hell of a guitar player and, since then, he has been a featured instrumentalist on Hank's last three albums. He also calls Hank "Rock" and Hank calls him "Cecil".

*

In 1989, The Gibson Guitar Company closed its factory in Kalamazoo, Michigan, and moved all production to its other plant in Nashville, Tennessee, after which the Heritage Guitar Company took over Gibson's Kalamazoo factory. Despite the fact that the new case for Hank's custom Super 400 offered better protection for the guitar, the airlines had beaten it up so badly that it was in need of repair. Hank called Heritage with the hopes that they could repair the Super 400, since many of the

Gibson employees stayed at Heritage and had probably built it. Hank received bad news and good news in reply to his inquiry.

The bad news was that the Heritage people no longer had any connection with Gibson and were not interested in repairing any Gibson guitar. The good news was that they offered to build Hank their version of the Super 400, which they called the *Heritage Hall of Fame* model. Moreover, they agree to give it to Hank at no cost as long as they could include him as one of their "artists" that used a Heritage. It was an offer that Hank could not refuse.

A few months later Hank took delivery of the Heritage guitar and was very pleased.

"To tell you the truth," Hank said, "I really like playing the Heritage better than the Super 400. It does not have quite the tone that the Super 400 does, but the difference is somewhat subtle and probably not discernable at most of my shows."

The Heritage became his regular performing guitar, but he still wanted to get the custom Super 400 repaired. Incentive for this was provided by a fan who told him that he knew the lady who had made the original headstock for Merle's original custom Super 400. The rumor was that she made an extra one (Hank's custom Super 400 was like Merle's in every respect with the exception of the headstock). Hank called her and was delighted when she informed him that she still had the other headstock. He made arrangements to buy it from her at a bargain price of $140. He then shipped it, with his Super 400, to The Apprentice Shop in Columbia, Tennessee, a guitar shop that did custom work for Gibson. A few weeks later, he had his refurbished custom Super 400 with a new neck and the headstock.

He also decided to get the Bigsby neck and headstock put back on the J-200 and to get the Stella 12-string refurbished. The Apprentice Shop did the honors, and Hank now has all three guitars at his home in Keller.

*

Hank with the J-200

In the late eighties, Hank and Ann were scheduled for an early Sunday flight out of Nashville. They got to the airport early and went to the Admiral's Club for breakfast before the flight. The dining area was empty except for one person sitting at a table, reading a newspaper. Hank and Ann took the table next to the occupied one, sat down, and Hank looked over and said, "Hello Johnny, how are you?"

"Well, I'm fine," said Johnny Cash.

After exchanging pleasantries with Hank and Ann for a few minutes, Johnny turned serious.

"Hank, I want to tell you something. When I was stationed at Landsberg Air Base in Germany in the fifties, I didn't know anybody and became very homesick. It was one of the blackest, loneliest times of my life, and the only thing that kept me from going insane was your music. I had one of your albums and listened to it all the time, and it kept me from losing my mind."

This reminded Ann of other comments she has received over the years, compliments which have helped her gain an appreciation of what Hank's music has meant to so many people. Ann gives the following examples:

"It's our favorite dance number."

"We went to one of Hank's dances on our honeymoon."

"It's *our* song."

"We fell in love to that song."

*

Hank's induction into the Hall of Fame precipitated a release of several compact discs containing compilations of his recordings. In 1989, Capitol released twenty of Hank's originally recorded hits on a compact disc entitled *Capitol Collectors Series*, and followed it up in 1996 with another compilation entitled *Vintage Collections*. These two albums are very noteworthy, since they give record buyers access to the original Capitol recordings without having to invest in the Bear Family Box Set.

Not to be outdone, in 1989, MCA released a compilation of Hank's hits entitled *The Country Music Hall of Fame Series*. In 1996, *The Best of Hank Thompson 1966-1979* was released, also containing highlights from the Dot/MCA years.

Also in 1989, Hank went to a studio in Nashville and recorded an album entitled *Hall of Fame Classics*, which were re-recordings of twenty-three of his top songs. Studio musicians were used in the original recordings; but, after the fact, Hank had Bobby Garrett and Buddy Spiker come in and overdub the steel parts and fiddle parts, respectively. As a result of a complicated set of business dealings, Hank ended up owning the masters. Therefore, in addition to receiving a percentage of the sale of each record based on his role as the recording artist, the songwriter (when applicable), and the publisher, he also gets a profit based on the sales of the album. The album is not available in record stores, but Ann sells it at Hank's appearances, and it is available on the internet.[18]

*

---

18 http://www.hankthompson.com

With the eighties drawing to a close, Hank could take comfort in the fact that he had realized his ultimate career goal – induction into the Country Music Hall of Fame. He also was very proud that he had recorded songs that made it to the charts in each of his first six decades (the forties through the nineties), one of his most impressive achievements of all.[19]

*

In 1990, Jim Halsey sold the booking-agency division of his company to the giant William Morris Agency. At the time, the Jim Halsey Company, Inc. was the number-one country music agency in the world, representing over forty country and pop acts and employing agents all over the globe. After the sale, Jim continued to represent a few acts, including the Oak Ridge Boys, and started lecturing and teaching extensively at colleges, universities, and educational seminars around the world. He also created the music and entertainment business program at Oklahoma City University, which became the first college in the world to offer a bachelor's degree in the business of entertainment. He also was a co-creator of the Billboard Song contest, held annually under the auspices of Billboard magazine, which offered aspiring songwriters a chance for their work to he heard by professionals.

Jim and Hank continue to be close personal friends and, over the past several years, have worked together on several projects.

*

Curtis Lovejoy, a country music vocalist and bass player, was playing the Texas music circuit in the late eighties and ran into Hank at a couple of Hank's appearances. In 1990, at the Burleson Jamboree in Burleson, Texas, he sat down with Hank and Ann and gave them a proposal. He offered to put together a band of musicians that he knew in the area and back Hank on some of his jobs around the Southwest.

Hank considered the proposal for quite a while before making a decision. He was more than satisfied with Morey Sullivan and Terry Miller's versions of the Brazos Valley Boys, but he realized that it would make sense for him to also have a quality Texas-based band.

In 1992, DD hired Curtis to back Hank at a festival in Alexandria, Louisiana. Curtis put together a band that included members who were familiar with Hank's music, rehearsed them, and impressed Hank at the job. Thus, another contemporary version of The Brazos Valley Boys was born. This led to more and more jobs backing Hank throughout the Southwest, as well as some special jobs including trips to foreign countries. Curtis has used some of the original Brazos Valley Boys including Jimmy Belken, Pee Wee Whitewing, and Bobby Garrett, for some of the assignments. As a result of these associations and talks with other ex-Brazos Valley Boys, Curtis has gained a unique and very simple perspective on what it was like to work with Hank.

"I never met a musician that worked with Hank who didn't enjoy their time with him," said Curtis.

---

[19] In an interview with The Fort Worth Star-Telegram in 1997, Hank was asked how he felt about charting his songs in six consecutive decades. His reply was:
> "Well, it was a hell of a lot easier than doing it in six *nonconsecutive* decades."

With Curtis Lovejoy (to Hank's left) and his version of
The Brazos Valley Boys band on Hank's 81ˢᵗ birthday

Later on that year Hank was saddened when he heard that Dorothy had passed away.

"I always appreciated that Dorothy was a very high quality person and that, during our marriage, she was always on my side in connection with any issues that came up in my career," said Hank.

*

In 1994, Jim Halsey was involved in a project that resulted in Hank's receiving a unique award. Jim described the details as follows:

"In 1926 General Sarnoff, the head of NBC, was making plans to do the first coast-to-coast live network radio broadcast, and he was rounding up talent for the show," said Jim. "At the head of the list was Will Rogers; but, on the night in question, Will was performing in Independence Kansas, my home town. Will told Sarnoff that he would be pleased to perform on the NBC broadcast as long as it was done from Independence.

"You can imagine the kind of electronic equipment it took in those days to make a remote broadcast. But General Sarnoff got NBC hooked up to Independence and broadcast fifteen or twenty minutes of Rogers' show coast-to-coast.

"In 1994, I thought it would be a good idea to commemorate the anniversary of the broadcast in Independence each year with a banquet and the presentation of a Will Rogers Commemorative Award to a celebrity. We could even broadcast it nationally. It was a big success and Hank and Roy Clark shared the first award. The program was broadcast on KFDI in Wichita, and I was told it reached an audience of five million that evening, which was probably more people than General Sarnoff had reached with his broadcast sixty-eight years earlier!"

*

After being elected to the CMA Hall of Fame in 1989, Hank made a point of attending every subsequent CMA awards show in Opryland in Nashville. He especially enjoyed visiting with all of his peers in the very large backstage area at *The*

Grand Ole Opry House after the show. One year in the mid-nineties, Hank, Ann and three friends from Dallas went to Nashville to enjoy the festivities. After the show they went backstage and began mingling. But soon a young female wearing a "Staff" tag accosted Hank. He doesn't remember her name so we'll call her Brain Dead.

"Do you have a backstage pass?" asked Brain Dead.

"No, I didn't know they were required," replied Hank,

"Sorry, but you'll have to leave," said Brain Dead.

"But my name is Hank Thompson. I'm a charter member of the Country Music Association and I'm *in* the Country Music Hall of Fame," said Hank, thinking that this must be a practical joke.

"I'm sorry, sir, but you'll have to leave," repeated Brain Dead. She was serious.

Ann's and the friends' jaws dropped as they looked on in disbelief.

"You must be kidding," said Hank. "I've been coming to this event for the past several years, I've always been welcomed here, and I've never needed a pass."

"Sir, you have to leave," repeated Brain Dead, as she motioned to a security type who came over and assisted her in escorting Hank, Ann, and their friends out of the room.

Hank never returned to this event.

Chapter Fifty Six

In 1996, after an eight-year hiatus, Hank recorded a new album in Nashville for the Curb label entitled *Hank Thompson and Friends* featuring duets with several notable guest artists. Hank's idea of recording an album of duets had been around for a long time.

"We never could seem to get anybody interested in it," said Hank. "We just ran into one stumbling block after another. But finally it all came together."

As the guest artists for the *Friends* album were being recruited, Vince Gill was the first to come on board and lend his high lonesome sound to *A Six Pack to Go*.

"Vince and his brother used to sing the song together when they were kids," said Hank. "So, he came in and said, 'I want to do *A Six Pack to Go*.' That kind of kicked open the door. Then people knew that we were for real and that this wasn't still just an idea. After Vince's appearance, everything else fell into place."

Ronnie Dunn had been a local musician in Tulsa when Hank and Ann lived in nearby Sand Springs. He was a big fan of Hank before he joined up with Kix Brooks to form Brooks and Dunn and begin their ascension to the upper echelon of country music. When asked to play on the duets album, they readily accepted. It was decided that they record a song that had been recently given to Hank entitled *Hooked on Honky-tonk*. The day of the scheduled recording, Ronnie and Kix came into the studio somewhat weary, having just returned from a road trip. Ann greeted them at the door of the studio.

Ronnie, who had assumed that they were to record their part of the duet without Hank, was shocked when Ann told him that Hank was in the next room waiting to sing with them.

"He's *here?*" exclaimed Ronnie. "Oh my God! I don't know if I can sing in front of him!"

Hooked on Honky-tonk was one of the highlights of the *Friends* album.

Hank's resonate voice wove in and out with the velvet throated Lyle Lovett on the song *Total Strangers*. Hank wasn't in the studio when Lyle did his part, but he did call the studio while Lyle was there. Someone handed the phone to Lyle.

Lyle grabbed the phone and said "Hank, thank you so much for letting me be on your album."

Bekka Bramlett, a Nashville resident at the time, and an accomplished singer, lent her booming voice for the song *I Picked a San Antonio Rose,* and she recommended her parents, rock superstars Delaney and Bonnie, to sing with Hank on a rendition of *Dry Bread.* Junior Brown contributed both his resonate voice and his famous "guit-steel" to *Sell Them Chickens,* and George Jones checked in with a song Hank wrote especially for them, *Hey George, Hey Hank* based on the jam session at the hotel lobby in Wembley.

Hank also did two songs solo on the album – *I'll Still Be Here Tomorrow,* written by his friend, Bill Mack, the noted DJ who is now on XM radio; and *Sobering Up,* a song Hank wrote for the album. *Sobering Up* is about friends drinking at a bar, and two lines from the song clearly show that Hank had not lost his mastery in the art of lyric writing:

It would be a shame to lose this buzz when our bell has not been rung,
There's lots of lies we haven't told and songs we haven't sung.

But the coup de grace on this album has to be Hank performing his classic *Wild Side of Life,* only to be answered, *in the same song* (as he was fifty years earlier in a separate song), by Kitty Wells' rendition of *It Wasn't God Who Made Honky-tonk Angels.* This time Kitty was assisted by Tanya Tucker on the verse and chorus of the song that had made Wells a household name.

Hank still speaks in glowing terms of the artists who donated their time and considerable talent to the *Friends* project.

He also was impressed by the sound quality of the album.

"I wanted to capture the sound and presence of the old Capitol recordings, and Mike Curb (the owner of Curb Records) agreed," said Hank. "The obvious thing to do was to use those old tube amplifiers instead of the hi-tech transistor stuff, and we found a studio (Sound Emporium in Nashville), that had tube equipment. We were able to get the analog and tube sound that is unlike anything they are recording in Nashville now. If you like a warm, analog sound, that's it; and it's the same type of sound we got at Capitol."

The musicians backing Hank and his friends on the album were studio types, with two exceptions.

"Before I accepted Curb's offer to record the album, I said that there were two people that I definitely wanted on this recording," said Hank. "One was Bobby Garrett on steel guitar, because he played my style as well as anybody I know. And I also wanted Thom Bresh because he plays like Merle Travis, which is what you'd expect since Merle was his dad. I'd worked a few shows with Thom in the past, but I'd never really gotten an opportunity to get that acquainted. It was really a pleasure to work with him. He was so good, and we enjoyed going back to a lot of those old stories about Merle and me."

Later, Hank also made a comment about Thom that must have resonated through the guitar players' community:

"The Merle Travis guitar style has been a part of my sound throughout my career. No one can do it any better than Merle's son, Thom."

People Magazine included the following quickie review of the album:

This felicitous tribute album celebrates the long career of the folksy Nashville singer-songwriter with the help of an impressive array of guest stars.... But the real highlights involve older stars.... The package generates two immediate reactions: "They don't make 'em like Hank any more" and "Too bad."

"Folksy?"
"Nashville?"

*

In 1997, Hank was inducted into the Songwriters Hall of Fame in Nashville. Hank attended the banquet-styled awards show in which songs from each inductee was sung by a musician. Curtis Potter did the honors for Hank, singing *The Green Light* and *Most of All*.

Later that year, Hank had a dream in which he and Ann went to a club one afternoon to check out the stage and equipment and set up the autograph table for a show that night. As the dream continued, Paul McGhee walked in. (Hank had seen Paul on a few occasions since Paul left The Brazos Valley Boys in the late fifties).

"We're playing here tonight," said Hank in his dream. "Are you going to come see us?"

"No I can't," replied Paul. "I've got to move on, but I wanted to come by and say hello."

They had a short visit, and Paul left.

End of dream.

The next day Ann was visiting with some friends and heard some news which she conveyed to Hank. Paul had died the previous day.

*

In the fifties, Hank had recorded many of his songs for The World Transcription Service, a service that supplied the songs to radio stations throughout the country based on two needs of industry at the time. One was that there was a dearth of country music recordings available. Also, the radio stations were insisting on shorter versions of the songs so that they could air more commercials. Thus, Hank had simply recorded shorter versions of many of his songs by leaving out the instrumental breaks, certain verses, etc.

Bloodshot Records obtained rights to twenty-three of Hank's old Transcription Service songs and re-mastered them for their release in 1999 under the title *Hank World*. They billed it as "the third CD in the Bloodshot Revival/Soundies series of never-before-released transcription recordings from the 1940's to the 1960's."

The following is a marketing pitch from Bloodshot's web site.

These 23 tracks (hand-picked by Thompson) feature hits like "Rub-a-Dub-Dub" and "Humpty Dumpty Heart," and sharp-as-a-tack covers of Bob Wills and Benny Goodman tunes that stand tall alongside undiscovered gems like the lead-off track "New Deal of Love." There are clever lyrical twists and spotless musicianship for the country purist, and enough spit for you country punks. This is the man responsible for "Cocaine Blues," after all – and at 73, he's still playing honky-tonks. And still kicking ass and taking names. It's Hank's World, people. We just live in it.

This was a very flattering and well-written spiel, but there was one statement that bears discussion.

"The man responsible for *Cocaine Blues*"? Well, not quite. T.J. Arnall had written the song; and, although Hank certainly sang a definitive version of it on the *Songs for Rounders Album*, Roy Hogsed had also recorded it, and Johnny Cash also had a popular version of it when he sang it at his Folsom Prison concert. Other artists who had recorded it include Merle Travis, George Thorogood, The Rev. Gary Davis, Nick Drake, Bob Dylan, and Townes Van Zandt.

*

In 1999, Hank received an invitation to be inducted into the Texas Country Music Hall of fame in Carthage, Texas. He selected Jim Halsey to present him.

"I was honored to be able to present Hank as an inductee in the Texas Country Music Hall of Fame," remembered Jim. "I will always be grateful to Hank as a mentor and he continues to be an inspiration to me up to the present day. We have remained business associates and friends for over fifty years."

Chapter Fifty Seven

In 2000, Hank made an album for Hightone records entitled *Seven Decades*, alluding to the longevity of his career. Produced by Lloyd Maines, the album was recorded in Dallas with a band that included Thom Bresh and steel guitarist Gary Hogue, who died shortly after the recording was completed.

Hank found Maines very accommodating, and he was especially pleased that the label didn't interfere with the recording.

"This was the first time since the Capitol years that I did not have to compromise the sound or style due to 'market demands'", said Hank. "I was very pleased with what we did and the way we did it, and the sound we got. Everybody had a good time doing it, and I think it is reflected in the music."

One of the highlights of the album is the light-hearted *Sting In This Ole Bee*, which takes a humorous look at the aging process.

"A old boy in Missouri sent me that," said Hank of co-writer Joe Nelson. "I liked the appeal of it because of my age and the fact that I'd had very good success with a song called *The Older The Violin, The Sweeter The Music*. I rewrote the song and kind of adapted it to what my thoughts were on things, and it turned out to be a cute little ditty."

Another tune with an age-related theme is *New Wine In Old Bottles*.

"That was a very unusual idea," said Hank. "A lady named Ann Tygart, who had sent me several songs through the years, sent me that one a while back. I pretty much rewrote the entire song, but I used her idea, and she had a pretty good melody line. I thought that fit along with *Sting In This Ole Bee*, and a lot of people could listen and identify with it."

Condo in Hondo is the tale of what Hank describes as an "old cowboy that's become disillusioned with riding the range" who decides to settle down.

"That would be the reason he would get the condo," explained Hank. "When I was writing the song, I was down in Mexico. The condo that we had was in an area where a lot of mariachi bands would play in the evenings. So, I'd sit out there and hear that music and wrote it with that in mind. We used an accordion to get a Texas music sound to it, and it worked."

Lobo the Hobo was originally going to be a song about Waco.

"I always wanted to write a song about Waco," said Hank. "I never did get around to it; and then, of course, the Branch Davidians thing came up. So in the song I mentioned Waco only as a jumping off point for the title character. Also, we needed just an old blues boogie song for this album so the musicians could have some fun picking choruses on it. It flowed real well, we had a lot of fun with it, and a lot of folks say it's their favorite song on the album."

Several cover tunes are also on the album, including a tribute to Hank's favorite singer, the Jimmie Rodgers' classic *In The Jailhouse Now*.

Cindy Walker's *Triflin' Gal*, a number-one song for Al Dexter six decades ago, also got the Thompson treatment, along with a very unusual ballad *Dinner For One, Please, James*, a song that Hank first heard on a recording by Nat King Cole.

"I heard it on the radio one morning when I was in a motel room," Hank recalled, "and thought that it was a pretty song. So I went down and bought the album."

The most unusual song on the album was one entitled *Abdul Abulbul Amir*.

"I remember hearing that song when I was a kid, and it was a traditional number then," said Hank. "Obviously, it must go back a long way because they're talking about the Czar. So, this song had to be of a vintage of around the turn of the century."

Another clever tune is *The Night Miss Nancy Ann's Hotel For Single Girls Burned Down*, a hit for his friend Tex Williams in the early seventies.

"Back then, for some reason or another, people got confused and thought it was my record," said Hank. "I don't think that Tex Williams and I sounded a lot alike, other than the fact that we both did Western Swing music with a beat and maybe our voice enunciations were similar. But I used to have people come up and say, 'Did you do that *Nancy Ann's Hotel* song?' After the album I was able to tell them that 'Yes, I did record that song.'"

Hank with the customized Super 400

In an interview with a writer for a country music magazine in connection with the release of *Seven Decades*, the writer suggested that Hank could be considered "alternative country".

"Everybody always wants to put a label on the music," replied Hank. "What they call country music today is a far cry from the country music that I play. So, 'alternative' would be a good label if my music is compared to country music today. In this way, at least there is a distinction, since there are many people, including me, that like the older country music and do not like what Nashville is putting out and calling country music. I never listen to the modern Nashville music because I don't care for it. Actually, if you have to give me a label, in my view, my music is traditional country."

*

In September 2000, Hank played at the Red Dirt Café on the campus corner at the University of Oklahoma in Norman with Curtis and his version of The Brazos Valley Boys backing him. After Hank sang a couple of songs, the mike started sliding down the stand. Hank pulled it up, tried to tighten it, let go, and it slid down again. He repeated the drill and it continued to slide down.

"This mike keeps going down," Hank announced to the crowd. "Does anyone out there have any Viagra?"

*

Let's do the math regarding Hank's history on the road. He started making personal appearances in 1946 at the schoolhouses in and around Waco and, during that time, probably averaged approximately two appearances a week. In the fifties, with his popularity at a zenith, he made as many as five or six appearances a week; and it's fairly safe to say that he averaged around five a week for the whole decade. In the sixties, the average was approximately three or four performances per week, so we'll call it three-and-a-half; and, in the seventies, the average probably dropped off to about three per week. To keep it simple, let's say he averaged two appearances per week in the eighties and nineties, and one a week from 2000 through 2006. Taking off for vacation time and activities that did not involve personal appearances, let's assume that he was on the road about forty-five weeks a year.

Thus the totals for each decade would look something like this:

1946-1949 –	2 appearances a week for 45 weeks for 4 years	=	360
1950-1959 –	5 appearances a week for 45 weeks for 10 years	=	2250
1960-1969 –	3.5 appearances a week for 45 weeks for 10 years	=	1575
1970-1979 –	3 appearances a week for 45 weeks for 10 years	=	1350
1980-1989 –	2 appearances a week for 45 weeks for 10 years	=	900
1990-1999 –	2 appearances a week for 45 weeks for 10 years	=	900
2000-2006 –	1 appearance a week for 45 weeks for 7 years	=	315
	Grand Total	Approximately	7500

Based on the above, it can be said that Hank has made more personal appearances over the course of his career than any other country artist. In fact, he has made more personal appearances than many of the traditional artists who emerged in the forties and the fifties, such as Hank Williams, Lefty Frizzell, Webb Pierce, Eddy Arnold, and Carl Smith – *combined*.

Taking this one step further, a good argument exists that there is no one in show business – musical or otherwise – who has made as many personal appearances as Hank Thompson. Period.

(Earnest Tubb, who passed away in 1984, is probably the only other person in show business that could rival Hank in the number of personal appearances since he also kept a grueling performance schedule in his prime.)

Hank's fans can add this amazing record to his list of achievements; and, to some, this may be the most impressive of all.

*

In 2002, at the Lakeside Casino and Resort in Osceola, Iowa, Tommy Overstreet was performing one night on the same bill as Hank. As Tommy left the stage after his performance, a woman came up and said to him, "I thought you had retired, or died!" Hank was close enough to overhear and later commented to Tommy, "It's amazing; we're doing the same thing we've always done, the only difference is we're not on Billboard's Hot 100!"

Hank with Leon McAuliffe

Hank with Jimmy Dickens and Cowboy Copas

Hank with Johnny Wright
and Jack Anglin.

Hank with Minnie Pearl
and Jim Halsey

Left to right: T. Texas Tyler, Ferlin Husky,
John Kelly, Jean Sheppard, Hank

Hank with Tex Ritter and Johnny Cash

Hank with Joey Bishop on his
television show.

Hank with Dizzy Dean

Hank with Ferlin Huskey

Hank with Bobby Bare

Hank with Ann and Robert Stack

Hank and Roy Acuff

First row: Johnny Wright and Kitty Wells
Second row: Tracy Pitcock, Ferlin Huskey,
Leona William, Hank and Bobby Wright

Chapter Fifty Eight

When *The Grand Ole Opry* had first come to New York to play two nights at Carnegie Hall in September 1947, the producers and the legendary cast, featuring Ernest Tubb and Minnie Pearl, were nervous. There had been little advertising or advance press, and everyone wondered how the New Yorkers would respond.

On the first moment of the first show, Tubb won over the audience with an aw-shucks country greeting.

"Boy," he said from the stage, "this place sure could hold a lot of hay!"

The next night it was standing room only.

Fifty-eight years later, Hank got a call from New York City. The person on the other end of the line identified herself and asked if Hank would be interested in performing at the Lincoln Center for the Performing Arts in New York City. Hank thought the invitation could be a joke, since the Lincoln Center was a nationally renowned venue for the Metropolitan Opera, the New York City Ballet, the New York Philharmonic and several other resident performing arts companies. He also knew that the words "Lincoln Center" and "country music" were not often used in the same sentence. But as he continued listening, he became more convinced that this might be the real thing. He was told that the city was sponsoring a *Midsummer Night Swing Series* – a series of outdoor concerts featuring several music genres, and one was Western Swing.

Thus, on a beautiful June evening in 2004, Hank Thompson and the Brazos Valley Boys held forth on a huge soundstage in the plaza in the center of Lincoln Center's campus. The production and facilities were state-of-the-art, the people gracious, and the response overwhelming. Part of the area in front of the bandstand was roped off, and wooden floors were installed over the concrete to create a dance floor that accommodated hundreds of dancers while two or three thousand other people were standing around the area watching. What was just as interesting is that the Opera House, Theaters, and Hall mentioned above all had balconies overlooking the plaza, and people entering and leaving these venues, all dressed in formal attire, stopped and listened to the different type of music that was being presented below.

New Yorkers dance to the music of Hank Thompson and
The Brazos Valley Boys on the Plaza at Lincoln Center.

Ernest would have been proud.

The Lincoln Center appearance was not Hank's only special performance in New York City. In 1977, he, along with Don Williams, Freddy Fender, and Roy Clark, played Carnegie Hall for three nights, with the performances forming the basis of a two-LP live album. It was the very first country music show to be recorded live at Carnegie Hall for an album and to be simultaneously broadcast over a network of 50,000-watt stations.

Hank loved the place.

"We had a terrific turnout," he remembered. "That was kind of the highlight of everybody's career. Carnegie Hall is probably the world's most famous concert hall, and it's a marvelous place to perform."

Characteristically, he was well aware of the acoustics in the hall.

"The acoustics in it are just terrific, and the design of the hall is such that the audience is all around the performers and nobody has a bad seat or is very far away. It's an old building, but the old ones are the best ones." [21]

*

Speaking of interesting venues, a new musical theater in Kansas City was opened in 2005 by Rick West, age sixtyish, and his mother, Bertie, age eightyish. Rick used to operate a theater in Branson, Missouri; and, according to reports, he spent in the mid-six-fig-

---

[21] Speaking of New York, Bob Dylan once commented to Newsweek magazine that he had never felt all that at home with the New York folk-music crowd because one of his own major influences had been Hank Thompson.

ures on renovations to an old building in Kansas City to create the 450-seat theater with stage lights and curtains, offices and a ballroom. Branson comes to Kansas City.

Hank was booked in soon after the opening, and the contract called for an afternoon show followed by an evening show. Hank was to use the house band as backup.

Hank and Ann were uneasy about the job from the get-go, since there were several negative red flags that went up fairly quickly after the booking:

Flag No. 1: Rick and Bertie didn't send in the deposit until two days before the job, although it had been promised weeks before. In the meantime the air fare (which they had to pay) went up by six hundred dollars.

Flag No. 2: When Hank and Ann arrived to set up before the afternoon show, they met Rick and Bertie. Rick came across as an Elvis wannabe wannabe, with layers of makeup and dyed black hair that looked like a lacquered helmet. Not to be outdone, Bertie had on the ugliest wig Ann had ever seen. They did not give the impression of being astute business people. In fact, they did not give the impression of being business people.

Flag No. 3: During the afternoon show, every time Ann tried to engage Rick or Bertie in a conversation about the balance due on the contract, they would turn around and head in the other direction.

Flag No. 4: Before the evening show started, Ann finally corralled Bertie and told her that they needed to settle up. Bertie told Ann that she would be with her in a minute and went into an office, locked the door, and stayed.

As time for the evening show drew near, Ann kept her eye on the office door, and when Bertie came out and headed into another office, Ann followed her into the second office with contract in hand.

"I don't have all of your money, but I have part of it," said Bertie, "and I'll write you a check for the balance."

Ann replied with her standard line, "We don't take checks, only cash. It's in the contract."

"OK, I'll give you the balance after the second show," said Bertie.

"No, we can't do that either," said Ann, knowing full well that all leverage would be lost after the second show.

"I can't believe you don't trust me," said Bertie.

"I have no reason to trust you," replied Ann. "You sent in your deposit late, you have been avoiding me all night, and now you say you can't pay me. We're not talking trust here, we're talking contract. And the contract says you or your son have to pay me now."

"My son is the most honest person in the world. He doesn't drink, smoke or chase women, and I'm insulted that you don't trust him," said Bertie.

"We're not talking morals here, we're talking contract," replied Ann. "We need to get this resolved. You bring your son in here, I'll bring my husband, and we will hash this out."

Ann brought Hank into the office, one of the very few times she had to bring him in on a problem of this nature. A four-way discussion ensued along with a lot of two-way dancing on the part of Rick and Bertie, and there was no resolution.

Hank and Ann left the office, and Hank came up with a final plan to get their payment. The evening show was sold out and he suggested that they wait until the theater was full just before show time and try to collect again. If not, they would pack up and leave.

About five minutes before show time, the theater was full and the crowd was ready for the show. Ann went to Bertie and told her that Hank was canceling the show unless she was paid immediately.

She was paid immediately.

The show started; and Hank, as usual, was located front and center with the band a few feet behind him. Although Hank didn't know it at the time, Rick, with a fresh layer of Elvis makeup and hair lacquer, got on stage, slipped in behind Hank and between Hank and the band, and started directing the band, Lawrence Welk style, while half-way facing the audience to make sure that they could take in his Elvis look. During the songs, he would execute a couple of Elvis gyrations, and at the end of each song he would take a bow.

Afterwards, a friend, who knew that Hank had played the date, sent Ann an article[22] from a Kansas City publication, *The Pitch*, reporting some criminal conduct, in the form of sexual abuse of a woman, on the part of Rick in connection with his previous gig at the theater in Branson.

After reading the article, Ann smiled when she recalled Bertie's statement that Rick didn't smoke, drink, or chase women.

*

In July 2005, Hank joined Morey Sullivan and several of his musicians in a studio in Tulsa and recorded a new album entitled My *Personal Favorites*. The title of the album could have been, *Songs I Have Always Wanted to Record, But, For Whatever Reason, I Didn't*. The following is an excerpt from the liner notes that Hank wrote for the album:

"I am often asked, 'Hank, what's your favorite song?' I'm at a loss for what to say, because I don't have one favorite song. I do songs for my fans. So it would figure the songs the fans like would be the ones I like. The songs in this CD played an important part in my early career. They have sentimental value, and it's great music! That's why I say these are My Personal Favorites.

We're glad to have the opportunity to record again. After my last album, Seven Decades, I did not think I would make another one. However, Morey Sullivan, of the Brazos Valley Boys had a workable solution to make it happen.

Morey and I go back over 25 years. We have a [non-exclusive] agreement that he and the group are the Brazos Valley Boys (BVB) whether they are working with me or on their own. Two of the BVB have their own respective professional recording studios in the Tulsa area. We utilized both of these studios for this project.

I formed the BVB in 1946. At first we played schools in central Texas. We kept expanding, playing clubs, honky-tonks and dancehalls. In the 50s and 60s we were a dominant force in music, and were voted the No. 1 country/western touring band for 14 consecutive years.

Since I created the Brazos Valley Boys, I have always been proud the name is synonymous with quality Western Swing music. That legacy is perpetuated today and into the future by Morey and all the fine musicians you hear on this album. What a privilege to still be working along side the Brazos Valley Boys.

*

---

[22] http://www.pitch.com/2006-02-16/news/horn-dog/print

Soon after the *Personal Favorites* recording session, Hank performed at a private party. The host of the party assured Hank that he would furnish a good back-up band.

Right.

Other than the fact the drummer couldn't keep a beat, the steel and fiddle players had trouble finding the right notes, and the bass player didn't have a clue, everything was fine.

Later a friend asked Hank how the job went.

"Best band I ever worked against!" was the reply.

*

Hank's seven decades in the music business have earned him numerous awards and honors from various associations and organizations associated with country music. In addition to those already mentioned, Hank has a place in The Oklahoma Music Hall of Fame (2002), The Thumb Pickers Hall of Fame (2006), The Texas Trail of Fame (2006), The Southwestern Swing Society Hall of Fame (2004), and the Heart of Texas Country Music Association Hall of Fame (2004). He was also named the Oklahoma Goodwill Ambassador (1978) and has received the Will Rogers Lifetime Achievement Award (2006).

Hank and Ann with officials upon Hank's induction into the Texas Trail of Fame

*

A bar that has a picture of Hank Williams on one of its walls can't be all that bad. That is the case at *Swing Station*, a country bar located at the intersection of Overland Trail and Old Highway 287, in LaPorte, Colorado, just north of Fort Collins.

The owners, Brad Folk and Kristy Burnett, are two entrepreneurs in their twenties with a vision of bringing country music to northern Colorado. They bought the bar in the mid-two thousands and converted it from a biker bar to a country bar with a musical menu that featured traditional country, rockabilly and a splash of bluegrass. It wasn't easy. When they took over, they had to clean the place up and make major renovations. In addition to adding the Hank Williams picture, they replaced the music on the jukebox with records by all three Hanks, Lefty Frizzell, Ray Price, Webb Pierce and all the other traditionalists. They set up a performing stage on a large patio to the side of the building, hired a friendly staff, and started the process of attracting a new customer base.

One day, Brad was surfing the Internet and noticed on Hank's web site that he was booked in Colorado Springs on a particular Sunday in the near future. A light came on, and Brad immediately got on the phone and called the number on the web site. Ann Thompson answered.

"Hello, this is Brad Folk. I'm an owner of a bar in Colorado and would like to talk to someone about booking Hank Thompson when he is in Colorado."

"Hold on," said Ann.

A few seconds later, a resonate voice on Ann's end of the line said, "Hello, can I help you."

"Yes. This is Brad Folk. I'm an owner of a bar in Colorado and would like to talk to someone about booking Hank Thompson when he is in Colorado."

"This is Hank Thompson."

Brad nearly fell off his chair and started stammering.

"Is it really you? I can't believe it! I'm a huge fan! You're a God here at Laporte!"

A few minutes later, Brad had regained his composure and, for a flat fee of $5,000, Hank was booked at Swing Station on the Saturday night before his Sunday job. This was a win-win situation, since it gave Hank two bookings for the price of one trip and enabled Brad and his partner to bring Hank to the patio as Swing Station's first big-name traditional country act.

Brad agreed to furnish the back line (musicspeak for drums and amplifiers) and Morey and the rest of his version of the Brazos Valley Boys drove over in Morey's RV from Topeka.

Everything worked. The week of the show, a local radio station, KRFC, gave Swing Station some free advertising, and the local paper did an article on the bar. The show sold out quickly.

The crowd was one of the most diverse that Hank had seen: senior citizens, jeans, long hair, peasant dresses, college students, western boots, tattoos, no hair, tie-dye, tennis shoes, polo shirts, yuppies, tank tops, and motorcycle boots. And all were Hank Thompson fans.

The day had turned into a beautiful evening as Hank hit the stage to a standing ovation, and he was impressed.

"I was glad to see so many young faces in the crowd," he said. "This gives hope that traditional country music will be kept alive and well."

*

Hank's friend, George Jones, was often called "No-show Jones" for obvious reasons. In this context, Hank should be called "Do-show Thompson". Hank and Ann estimate that, throughout his career, Hank has made over ninety-nine percent of his jobs – a phenomenal figure. The reasons for his few absences were weather, mechanical failure of the airplane or bus, and illness.

Ann only remembered one missed job since the late sixties due to illness.[23]

"The only time I can remember Hank missing a job due to illness was one day in

Las Vegas when he had a flaming temperature and couldn't get out of bed," said Ann. "In fact, one time he attended a recording session in the afternoon after having a tooth pulled in the morning."

*

In the early two thousands, Hank and Ann visited some friends at a hunting lodge in the hill country of Texas. Hank and a friend were sipping wine out on the deck.

"Hank, do you ever feel that you would like to quit performing and recording and put it all behind you?" asked the friend.

"Oh no." was the reply. "In fact, when I die, I hope it's on the stage."

*

Hank and Ann hosted Hank's eightieth birthday party in September 2005, at their house in Keller. Approximately twenty-five of their dearest friends came in from all over the country. The phone had been ringing all day with congratulatory messages from well wishers, and, as usual, Hank and Ann were in high spirits.

Hank stationed himself at the end of the bar in his family room with a glass of wine in hand and carried the conversation over a variety of subjects. He then went over and pushed a button on his CD player and the room was enveloped in a rough mix of the *My Personal Favorites* album.

As the album played on, Hank's eyes began to glaze over slightly, while his left foot started tapping to the rhythm of the songs. Perhaps he was reflecting on one or more of the many wonderful things that had happened to him over the past eight decades.

Such as the profound impact that music made on his life, and how thankful he was for the God-given talent that enabled his to pursue his passion.

Such as the sheer enjoyment he gains from performing his music, and for the energy and strength to enable him to do so.

Such as the ability to create so many songs that meant so much to so many people.

Such as the unadulterated admiration and respect he still enjoys from his fans from all over the world.

Such as all of the friendships he's forged with the multitude of people who came into his life. True friendships not based on superficial admiration from glorified fans and hangers-on, but friendships based on mutual respect and feelings that flow two ways.

Such as how fortunate he was to have Ann – his wife, lover, partner, companion, and soul mate – and her undying love for him.

And such as the time when he, as a five-year-old boy, after being inspired by a Jimmie Rodgers song he had just heard on a neighbor's Victoria, ran and skipped down 17th street in Waco, Texas, singing:

T for Texas and T for Tennessee...

And T for Thompson.

---

[23] This does not count a horrific battle Hank had in connection with replacement hip surgery that initially occurred in 2006 and required three operations that extended into 2007.

Hank at his last concert in Waco

Epilogue

After this book was completed but before it went to the printer, Hank played at *The Heart of Texas Fair* in Waco on October 8, 2007. The occasion was special. Texas Governor Rick Perry issued a Message of Commendation, which states in part:

Hank Thompson of Waco has contributed to the Texas music scene for almost seven decades. Through his unique and varied style, he put his own stamp on country's honky-tonk tradition and western swing by racking up twenty-nine top ten hits, including his first single "Whoa Sailor" that he wrote following his service in the U.S. Navy during World War II.

Hank Thompson has built a legacy of accomplishment, profoundly influencing the musical heritage of the state and the nation.

Also, Mayor Virginia DuPuy declared the day "Hank Thompson Day" in the City of Waco, and made the presentation to Hank on stage at the fair.

The crowd included an extra large number of Hank's closest fans and friends who were there to celebrate Hank's big day, but who did not know at the time that they were seeing history in the making. For this was Hank's final concert, capping a career that started in 1935 on the stage at the Brook Avenue Grade School in Waco. It is only fitting that it ended seventy-two years later only a few miles away.

Soon after the Waco concert, Hank was at his home in Keller battling cancer, but with the same positive attitude and sprit that characterized the times chronicled in this book.

When Hank told me about his struggle, he asked that I get this book to the printer as soon as possible. He gave a reason that will not be surprising to all the people who knew him.

"I want to be able to autograph the book for my fans."

He lost the battle on November 6.

We were not able to get it printed in time, but I am hopeful that the book will bring pleasure and enjoyment to his fans. This is what he would have wanted.

Warren Kice
November, 2007

Acknowledgements

I could not have had a better subject for the biography and a better narrator of one's life history, than Hank. I will never forget the many times during the interviews when he would get a twinkle in his eye and launch in to one of the more "humorous" stories he mentioned in his Preface. As many of you know, he was a masterful story-teller, with a razor sharp memory, a keen sense of humor, and perfect inflections and timing. I can only hope that I was able to capture at least the essence of these stories in this book.

I would like to acknowledge, with heartfelt appreciation, the following people who took their valuable time to relate their special times with Hank to me. I should add that there was a very clear, common, thread that ran through all the interviews – each and every person had a deep appreciation and respect for Hank, and that made my job much easier.

DD Bray	J.D. (Jude) Northcutt
Thom Bresh	Curtis Potter
Jim Halsey	Bert Rivera
Wanda Jackson	Morey Sullivan
Curly Lewis	Ann (Williams) Thompson
Curtis Lovejoy	Pee Wee Whitewing
Jim Newton	

Also, I would like to thank Jonette Almon, a world-class proof reader.

A special thanks to Ann, who was never failing in her encouragement to me, and who made my in-person interviews with Hank so pleasurable. In additional to making valuable contributions to the book, Ann also heads the "A team" – a group of special people, some of whom helped me with the book, and all of whom helped Hank in manners too numerous to mention during the last few years of his career. The A team members are as follows:

Marrianne and Al Burton
Gerry and Deb Caraway
Connie Davis
Margaret Evans
Peggy Poovey
Eddie and Linda Wheeler
Jim Womack

Warren Kice
November, 2007

The Charted Singles

Debut Date	Weeks Charted	Peak Position	Title	Label
1/31/48	38	2	Humpty Dumpty Heart	Capitol
9/04/48	2	12	Yesterday's Mail	Capitol
2/05/49	1	10	What Are We Gonna Do About the Moonlight	Capitol
10/16/48	10	7	Green Light	Capitol
2/05/49	1	14	I Find You Cheatin' On Me	Capitol
2/12/49	1	15	You Broke My Heart	Capitol
10/01/49	7	6	Whoa Sailor	Capitol
10/01/49	1	10	Soft Lips	Capitol
11/05/49	1	15	The Grass Looks Greener Over Yonder	Capitol
3/15/52	30	1	The Wild Side of Life	Capitol
6/28/52	15	3	Waiting In The Lobby Of Your Heart	Capitol
12/13/52	1	10	The New Wears Off Too Fast	Capitol
3/28/53	2	9	No Help Wanted	Capitol
5/23/53	20	1	Rub-A-Dub-Dub	Capitol
9/19/53	4	8	Yesterday's Girl	Capitol
12/12/53	19	1	Wake Up, Irene	Capitol
5/08/54	2	10	Breakin' The Rules	Capitol
6/26/54	1	9	A Fooler, A Faker	Capitol
7/03/54	12	9	Honky-Tonk Girl	Capitol
7/17/54	4	10	We've Gone Too Far	Capitol
10/16/54	20	3	The New Green Light	Capitol
2/26/55	4	12	If Lovin' You Is Wrong	Capitol
3/12/55	2	13	Annie Over	Capitol
6/04/55	9	5	Wildwood Flower	Capitol
6/04/55	8	7	Breakin' In Another Heart	Capitol
8/20/55	11	6	Most Of All	Capitol
12/10/55	7	5	Don't Take It Out On Me	Capitol
12/10/55	5	5	Honey, Honey Bee Ball	Capitol
3/24/56	22	4	The Blackboard Of My Heart	Capitol
3/24/56	5	14	I'm Not Mad, Just Hurt	Capitol
2/23/57	4	13	Rockin' In The Congo	Capitol
2/23/57	2	13	I Was The First One	Capitol
10/14/57	2	14	Tears Are Only Rain	Capitol
6/09/58	3	11	How Do You Hold A Memory	Capitol
8/18/58	22	2	Squaws Along The Yukon	Capitol
12/01/58	23	7	I've Run Out Of Tomorrows	Capitol
2/02/59	3	26	You're Going Back To Your Old Ways Again	Capitol

5/11/59	10	13	Anybody's Girl	Capitol
6/29/59	1	25	Total Strangers	Capitol
11/09/59	10	22	I Didn't Mean To Fall In Love	Capitol
3/21/60	15	10	A Six Pack To Go	Capitol
8/01/60	14	14	She's Just A Whole Lot Like You	Capitol
5/29/61	11	7	Oklahoma Hills	Capitol
5/29/61	2	25	Teach Me How To Lie	Capitol
9/18/61	10	12	Hangover Tavern	Capitol
9/27/63	1	23	I Wasn't Even in The Running	Capitol
9/28/63	5	22	Too In Love	Capitol
1/11/64	2	45	Twice As Much	Capitol
8/14/65	2	42	Then I'll Start Believing In You	Capitol
10/22/66	14	15	Where Is The Circus	Warner
2/04/67	13	16	He's Got A Way With Women	Warner
7/13/68	15	7	On Tap, In The Can, Or In The Bottle	Dot
10/26/68	15	5	Smoky The Bar	Dot
3/08/69	9	47	I See Them Everywhere	Dot
7/12/69	9	46	The Pathway Of My Life	Dot
10/18/69	6	60	Oklahoma Home Brew	Dot
5/09/70	5	54	But That's All Right	Dot
10/10/70	4	69	One Of The Fortunate Few	Dot
3/06/71	14	15	Next Time I Fall In Love (I Won't)	Dot
7/17/71	16	18	The Mark Of A Heel	Dot
12/04/71	14	11	I've Come Awful Close	Dot
4/29/72	12	16	Cab Driver	Dot
9/23/72	8	53	Glow Worm	Dot
3/17/73	2	70	Roses In The Wine	Dot
9/01/73	9	48	Kindly Keep It Country	Dot
2/02/74	15	8	The Older the Violin	Dot
7/13/74	16	10	Who Left The Door To Heaven Open	Dot
1/25/75	10	29	Mama Don't 'Low	ABC/Dot
6/28/75	8	70	That's Just My Truckin' Luck	ABC/Dot
3/06/76	6	72	Asphalt Cowboy	ABC/Dot
9/04/76	3	86	Big Band Days	ABC/Dot
1/15/77	4	91	Honky-Tonk Girl	ABC/Dot
5/21/77	2	92	Just An Old Flame	ABC/Dot
10/21/78	3	92	I'm Just Gettin' By	ABC
3/03/79	3	88	Dance With Me Molly	ABC
8/25/79	12	29	I Hear The South Callin' Me	MCA
2/02/80	9	32	Tony's Tank-Up, Drive-In Café	MCA
12/19/81	5	82	Rockin' In The Congo	Churchill
7/23/83	5	82	Once In A Blue Moon	Churchill

The Albums

1952	Favorites	Capitol Hank-9111
1955	Songs Of The Brazos Valley	Capitol T-418
1956	New Recordings Of All Time Hits	Capitol T-729
1956	North Of The Rio Grande	Capitol T-618
1957	Hank	Capitol T-826
1958	Dance Ranch	Capitol T-975
1958	Favorite Waltzes	Capitol T-1111
1959	Songs For Rounders	Capitol T-1246
1960	Most Of All	Capitol T-1360
1960	This Broken Heart Of Mine	Capitol ST-1469
1961	An Old Love Affair	Capitol T-1544
1961	At The Golden Nugget	Capitol ST-1632
1962	Cheyenne Frontier Days	Capitol ST-1775
1962	#1 Country/Western	Capitol DT-1741
1963	State Fair Of Texas	Capitol T-1955
1963	The Best Of Hank Thompson	Capitol SM-1878
1964	Especially For You	Capitol Custom
1964	Golden Country Hits	Capitol ST-2089
1964	It's Christmas Time With Hank	Capitol ST-2154
1965	Breakin' In Another Heart	Capitol T-2274
1966	A Six Pack To Go	Capitol DT-2460
1966	Breakin' The Rules	Capitol T-2575
1966	Luckiest Heartache In Town	Capitol T-2342
1966	Where Is The Circus	Warner Bros 1664
1967	Just An Old Flame	Capitol ST-2826
1967	The Best Of Hank Thompson Vol. 2	Capitol DT-2661
1967	The Countrypolitan Sound	Warner Bros 1679
1967	The Gold Standard Collection	Warner Bros 1689
1968	Country Blues	Capitol Tower DT-5120
1968	New Roving Gambler	Hilltop JS-6057
1968	Hank Thompson Sings The Gold Standards	Dot DLP 25864
1968	On Tap, In The Can, Or In The Bottle	Dot DLP 25894
1969	Salutes Oklahoma	Dot DLP 25971
1969	Smokey The Bar	Dot DLP 25932
1969	Simple Simon, Simple Heart	Hilltop JS-6065
1970	You Always Hurt the One You Love	Hilltop JS-6085
1970	The Instrumental Sounds	Dot DOS 25978
1971	Next Time I Fall In Love (I Won't)	Dot DOS 25991
1972	Cab Driver–A Salute To The Mills Brothers	Dot DOS 25996
1972	Greatest Hits	Dot DOS 26004
1973	Kindly Keep It Country	Dot DOS 26015
1974	A Six Pack To Go (Twin Set)	Dot PAS 2-1041
1974	Movin' On	Dot DOSD 2003
1974	25th Anniversary Album	Dot DOS 2-2000
1975	Sings Nat King Cole	Dot DOS 2032

1976	Back In The Swing Of Things	Dot DOSD 2060
1977	Doin' My Thing	Dot DO 2091
1977	The Thompson Touch	Dot DO 2069
1977	Country Comes To Carnegie Hall	Dot DO 2087/2
1978	Brand New Hank	ABC AV 1095
1980	The Best Of The Best Of Hank Thompson	Gusto GT 0060
1980	Take Me Back To Tulsa	MCA 3250
1983	1000 And One Nighters	Churchill CR 9420
1984	20 Golden Pieces	Bulldog BDL 2042
1986	Hank Thompson	MCA Dot 39089
1988	Here's To Country Music	Step One SOR 0027
1989	Capitol Collectors Series	Capitol CDP 7921242
1990	All-Time Greatest Hits	Curb D2-77329
1991	Country Collection	Knight KNCD 13059
1992	Country Music Hall of Fame Series	MCA MCAD-10545
1995	Greatest Hits Vols. I and II	Step One SOR 0025 and 0026
1995	Greatest Songs, Vol. I and II	Curb D2-77734 and 77735
1996	Vintage Collection	Capitol 7243-8-36901-2
1996	The Best of Hank Thompson 1966-1979	Varese Sarabande VSD 5747
1996	Hank Thompson and Friends	Curb D2-77925
1997	Sounds of the Brazos Valley	RFD CD19
1997	Radio Broadcasts 1953	Fly CD 948
1999	Hank World	Bloodshot Records BS803CD
2000	Seven Decades	Hightone Records HCD3121
2001	Humpty Dumpty Heart	CTS 55471
2000	In the Mood for Hank	Jasmine JASMCD 3509
2006	My Personal Favorites	Private Label

Note: The above album list does not include numerous compilation albums, greatest hits albums, etc., that have been released on record labels throughout the world, some of which were authorized and some of which were not.